MENTAL FLOSS

The

CURIOUS COMPENDIUM

of

WONDERFUL WORDS

MENTAL FLOSS

The

CURIOUS
COMPENDIUM

of

WONDERFUL
WORDS

A MISCELLANY OF

Obscure Terms, Bizarre Phrases,

&

SURPRISING
Etymologies

BY **ERIN McCARTHY** AND THE TEAM AT MENTAL FLOSS

weldon**owen**

CEO Raoul Goff
VP PUBLISHER Roger Shaw
EDITORIAL DIRECTOR Katie Killebrew
SENIOR EDITOR Karyn Gerhard
VP CREATIVE Chrissy Kwasnik
ART DIRECTOR Allister Fein
VP MANUFACTURING Alix Nicholaeff
SENIOR PRODUCTION MANAGER Joshua Smith

weldon**owen**

an imprint of Insight Editions
P.O. Box 3088
San Rafael, CA 94912
www.weldonowen.com

INDELIBLE
EDITIONS
Printed in China
2026 2025 2024 2023 • 10 9 8 7 6 5 4 3 2 1

Contents

Intr

I f you're at all familiar with Mental Floss through our website or one of our books or calendars, you know that we're passionate about many things, from weird history and miscellany about our favorite books to the blink-and-you'll-miss-them moments from films and TV. But as writers and editors, one topic we especially love to geek out about is words and language.

The Mental Floss team is full of logophiles. Get us together, and it's not long before we start throwing out our favorite slang terms, giggling about alternative ways to say so-called "gross" words, or asking questions like, "Why do we say [insert common phrase here]?" or "What's the difference between [word] and [word]?" It's also not long before we're heading straight down the rabbit hole (a phrase we owe to author Lewis Carroll in *Alice's Adventures in Wonderland*, incidentally) into old books and dictionaries and scouring the corners of the internet to find the answer and bring it to our audience. And if the world's

obsession with games like Scrabble, Wordle, and crosswords is any indication, we're not alone.

In our *Curious Compendium of Wonderful Words*, you'll find some of the best word- and language-related content from Mental Floss, including deep dives into how to win word games, alternative ways to say common words, delightful old-timey jargon, and the strange etymologies behind common words. We're focusing mostly on the English language, but we have detours into untranslatable words from other languages and non-English roots of common English words as well.

We also know that language is powerful— it has the ability to awe and inspire, alienate and humiliate. So we're not just sticking to the nice stuff, but also bringing you stories from the darker side of the English language, like the racist origins of common phrases. And we wouldn't be Mental Floss if we didn't sprinkle in a whole bunch of fascinating facts along the way.

We had a blast putting *The Curious Compendium* together, and it's our hope that it will not only demystify why we use the words and say the things we do, but also inspire you to bust out the dictionary and expand your vocabulary in ways you never could have imagined.

o-
duc-
tion

An ALPHABET OF RARE AND OBSCURE WORDS

English dictionaries are littered with words that we said for a while, then set aside as times changed and language evolved. The words on this list were discovered through the Mental Floss team's many journeys through the dictionary— and while you're not likely to hear them used in conversation these days, given how delightful (and, sometimes, surprisingly useful) they are, we're hoping to bring them back.

A

After-wit
When *after-wit* showed up in the written record in the early 1500s, it referred not just to acknowledging a previous mistake but also changing because of it. By the mid-1500s, it came to mean knowledge that arrived after it would have been useful. The end of the century brought a new meaning: knowledge gained later in life. As the seventeenth-century poet Samuel Butler wrote, "Your after-wit is like to be your best."

B

Besmottered
Another way to describe something spattered with mud. The *Oxford English Dictionary* traces its first use back to Chaucer's *Canterbury Tales*, published between 1387 and 1400.

C

Cagment
A sixteenth-century word for an insult. Its ultimate etymology is unknown, but it may have come from the verb *cag*, meaning "to insult."

D

Dilatable
One definition of *dilatable* is the earlier word *delightable*, which appeared around 1300. Both words are now considered rare, but the *OED* found a use of *delightable* in a publication as recently as 1980.

E

Elozable
A mid-eighteenth-century adjective for someone who is easily flattered.

F

Fimble
To *fimble* is to frequently touch things with your fingers. According to the *OED*, it's probably a sound-alike version of the word *famble* (a hand) or perhaps *fumble* (which in the sixteenth century meant "using the hands or fingers in an awkward fashion").

(Honorable mention to *fairney-cloots*, a Scottish word that has both an uncertain etymology *and* definition—the *OED* even prefaces its definition with "apparently"—but was so delightful we had to include it: It's thought to refer to the area of a sheep's or goat's leg over the hoof.)

G

Gloar

Don't get caught *gloaring*, or staring steadily, at a person—it's rude. (This meaning, which dates back to the 1400s, is the same as *glower*, but the words don't seem to be related.) In the fourteenth century, however, the word was used to refer to something glittering or shiny.

J

Jiggumbob

Can't think of the name of an object you're talking or writing about? Instead of calling it a *thingamabob*, go with the earlier *jiggumbob*, which was coined sometime in the 1620s and is apparently derived from the word *jig*. (One caveat, though: Whereas *thingamabob* sometimes is used to refer to a person, *jiggumbob* rarely is.)

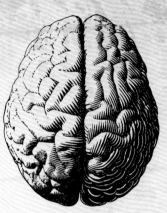

H

Hoddy

According to the *English Dialect Dictionary*, this word is another way to describe someone who is in a generally good mood and/or good health; it dates back to the mid-1600s. (Conversely, if you're *humstrum*, you're in a bad, sulky mood, per the *Scottish National Dictionary*.)

K

Kicksey-winsey

Kicksey-winsey is the word that does it all: As a noun, it refers to a flight of fancy; as an adjective, "bizarre or erratic;" and as an adverb, it means "topsy-turvy." Etymologically, it may be connected to *kickshaw*, a seventeenth-century word that initially meant "a fancy dish" (though not necessarily in a positive way).

M

Madpash

The *OED* dates this word for someone who is either foolish or mentally ill to 1611, when it appeared in lexicographer Randle Cotgrave's *A Dictionarie of the French and English Tongues*. It was created by mashing together the word *mad* with the word *pash*, referring to the head or the brain.

N

Neatifying

Don't call it *tidying up*—call it *neatifying*. This word dates to the 1820s and is derived from the English verb *neatify*, which pops up in the written record in 1581.

I

Infaustous

Infaustous or *infaust* is derived from the Latin *infaustus*, meaning "unlucky."

L

Longinquity

This word can refer to an actual long distance (the act of being far away from something), a long discourse, or a distance in time (Theophilus Gale wrote in the seventeenth century's *The Court of the Gentiles* that the Athenian historian Thucydides "could know nothing certainly of things before the Peloponnesian war by reason of the Longinquitie of Time").

O

Ointuose

Another way to describe something greasy, this rare fifteenth-century word was likely derived from the word *unctuous* (which dates back to the 1380s).

P

Prattle-basket

Before we called a person who just won't stop talking a *chatterbox*, we used *prattle-basket* (1602), followed by *prattle-box* (1671). *Chatterbox* didn't arrive on the scene until 1774.

Q

Quagswagging

If you're shaking back and forth, you're *quagswagging*. The word was derived from the verbs *quag* ("to quake") and *swag* ("to sway uncontrollably").

R

Regibbe

To *regibbe* is to kick something.

S

Scanderbegging

A sixteenth-century word meaning "rascally" or "roguish," *scanderbegging* was derived from Scanderbeg, the English nickname given to the fifteenth-century Albanian nobleman and hero Gjergj Kastrioti, who successfully resisted the Ottomans between 1444 and 1468. (As for *why* he was called *Scanderbeg*? Kastrioti's prowess on the battlefield earned him comparisons to Alexander—Iskander in Albanian—the Great, so he was called *Iskander bey*, which became *Scanderbeg*.)

T

Tussicate

A verb meaning "to cough," this word—which popped up in the late 1500s—comes from the Latin *tussicus* ("stricken with a cough").

U

Umbracle

Umbracle, an obsolete word meaning "shade" or "a spot in the shade," dates back to the 1500s.

V

Volo-nola

Use this 1672 phrase for someone who flip-flops or has trouble making a decision. It was created by combining the Latin terms *volo*, meaning "I am willing," and *nolo*, meaning "I am unwilling."

W

Wancraunt

An adjective dating back to 1422 for a person who's prone to wandering.

Xenodochy
A word derived from Greek for hospitality to strangers.

Yexer
Yex or *yesk* dates all the way back to the 1300s and could mean a gasp or gulp of air, a belch, or a hiccup. A *yexer*, therefore, is a person *with* the hiccups.

Zimme
A word for a jewel that, according to the *OED*, seems only to be found in the writing of Edward Bulwer-Lytton, the author who popularized what is widely considered to be the worst opening sentence in English literature: "It was a dark and stormy night ..." (see page 103). The *OED* posits that Bulwer-Lytton thought it was probably an Old English word, since it appears in his book *Harold, The Last of the Saxon Kings,* which is set in the 1000s.

The ONE LETTER
IN THE
ALPHABET
THAT CAN'T BE
SILENT

T he English language can be baffling at times— just look to words like *phlegm*, *receipt*, and *chthonic* for proof. Silent letters are unavoidable. Almost every word in the alphabet is occasionally guilty of taking up space without contributing anything, but there is one exception. According to Merriam-Webster, *v* is the only letter in English that consistently makes itself heard.

No matter where it appears, whether it's in *love*, *voice*, or *divisive*, *v* plays a vital role. Most letters are phonetic chameleons: That's why the *c* sounds different in *cat* and *city*, and why the *g* sounds like nothing at all in *gnash*. V is unique in that it never goes through an identity crisis. (There is an asterisk here; some nineteenth-century books say the word *sevennight*—essentially meaning a week— has a silent *v*. And it did, but in modern dictionaries the word is spelled *sennight*. The silent *v* has dropped out so completely even the spelling has changed to eliminate it.)

There are a few letters that rival *v*'s special status. Though this might vary depending on your accent, *z* is chiefly silent in words we borrowed from the French, like *chez*, *laissez-faire*, and *rendezvous*. The one silent *j* in the entire English language appears in *marijuana*, a borrowing from Spanish. But even accounting for words we've adopted from other tongues, there's not one example of a silent *v* in the English dictionary.

A *Brief History* OF THE WORD

Hello

**The word *hello* isn't as old as you might think—
and we have a famous inventor to thank for its popularity.**

M ake up a word that starts with an *h* and contains a handful of *l*s and vowels, and there's a good chance it already exists. One of the oldest in recorded history is *holla*, an early-sixteenth-century interjection meaning "Stop!" that came from an even older French word: *holà*. Variants proliferated over the next few centuries, almost all of them used to get someone's attention. *Hillo* (or *hilloa*), according to the *Oxford English Dictionary*, could get the attention of a person who was far away or preoccupied with something else. *Hollo*— or *halloo, hallow, holloa, ho-lo,* and many other spellings—was a precursor to *holler* that often involved shouting at hunting dogs.

It was only a matter of time before inventive spellers landed on *hello*, which is first cited in print in an 1826 issue of Connecticut's *Norwich Courier*: "Hello, Jim! I'll tell you what: I've a sharp knife and feel as if I'd like to cut up something or other." In that and other instances from the era, *hello* was either used to flag someone down—much like you might yell "Hey!" today—or to convey surprise. It wasn't until a few decades later that people began to utter it (and its British versions, *hullo* and *hulloa*) in greeting.

By the late nineteenth century, the word was experiencing a boom in popularity that might never have happened without one Thomas Edison, who is credited with encouraging *hello* as the go-to greeting for anyone answering a telephone call. He recommended it for callers, too.

"I do not think we shall need a call bell as Hello! can be heard 10 to 20 feet away. What do you think?" he wrote to Thomas B.A. David, president of Pittsburgh's Central District and Printing Telegraph Co., in August 1877.

In other words, Edison didn't initially think a telephone needed to ring—he thought the caller could simply shout "Hello!" to the person on the other end. So, in a way, the inventor was actually invoking the oldest usage of the word: to get someone's attention.

As the technology evolved beyond one always-open direct line between two people, it made more sense for the receiver to be the first to speak. And thanks in part to Edison's influence on the burgeoning telephone industry, operating manuals often advised that users say "Hello." The very first phone book, published in New Haven, Connecticut, in 1878, suggested "a firm and cheery 'hulloa.'" (Instead of *goodbye*, the book listed "That is all" as a suitable sign-off.)

10 WAYS *to* SAY HELLO

Hello is the go-to greeting among English speakers, but it doesn't have to be. Set a more exciting tone for your next conversation with these alternate words of welcome.

1. Ahoy
Alexander Graham Bell petitioned to make this nautical greeting the standard way to answer the phone, but his campaign never caught on.

2. As-Salamu Alaikum
A traditional Muslim greeting, *as-salamu alaikum* means "peace to you" in Arabic.

3. Ciao
This Italian word can be used to say *goodbye* as well as *hello*. Unlike *hello*, *ciao* isn't appropriate for formal meetings and is reserved for conversations with close friends and family members.

4. Coucou
Coucou—which roughly translates to "hey there!"— may be the most informal way to greet someone in France. Be mindful of who you use it with; some French speakers think the greeting is overly cutesy and should only be directed at children.

5. Howdy
Though it's associated with American cowboys, *howdy* originated in sixteenth-century England. There, people greeted each other with the phrase *how do ye* or *how do you*, which eventually transformed into the word we know today.

6. Kia Ora
This Māori greeting used throughout New Zealand literally translates to "be well."

7. M'athchomaroon
You may have heard Daenerys use this word in *Game of Thrones*. *M'ath-chomaroon* (*m'ach* or *m'ath* for short) is the Dothraki greeting linguist David J. Peterson coined when developing the language for the HBO series.

8. Moshi Moshi
Some languages do have a different way of saying *hello* on the phone versus in person. In Japan, callers greet each other by saying *moshi moshi*. (In person, they'd likely say something like *konnichiwa* or *ohayou*.)

9. Salutations
A *salutation* describes any expression of welcome. The word itself is often used as the name for the greeting in a letter.

10. What's the Craic?
In Ireland, asking *what's the craic?* is a common way to solicit news, gossip, and all-around entertaining conversation.

OBSCURE
WORDS *and* PHRASES
TO DESCRIBE
HAPPINESS

The word *happy* (derived from the thirteenth-century word *hap*, meaning "good luck") dates all the back to the fourteenth century, and sure, it sounds nice enough—but there are plenty of other words and phrases from history that describe the feeling pretty well, too (maybe even better). Here are a few of our favorites.

Abloy

This adjective likely came into English from French, and is used to refer to someone who is so joyous they can't contain themselves. You can find it in *Sir Gawain and the Green Knight* (1400): In Middle English, the passage reads, in part, "Þe lorde, for blys abloy, Ful oft con launce and ly3t," which translates to "The lord, transported by bliss, Very often did shoot and dismount."

Blithemod

An obsolete term from Old English for a friendly, happy mood.

Chicket

Chicket is a seventeenth-century way to describe being cheerful.

Clover

According to 1872's *The Slang Dictionary*, *clover* is a term for "happiness, luck, a delightful position" taken from the joy that "attends cattle when they suddenly find their quarters changed from a barren field to a meadow of clover."

Cock-a-hoop

A British term dating back to 1564 for a triumphantly happy feeling. It can also be used to describe someone who is bragging or boastful—in fact, *crowing* is a synonym, along with *prideful*, *rejoicing*, and *triumphant*.

Eucatastrophe

The Lord of the Rings author J.R.R. Tolkien coined this term, which he wrote in a 1944 letter, saying it describes "the sudden happy turn in a story which pierces you with a joy that brings tears."

Faustity

A term taken from the Latin *faustus* that, according to Thomas Blount's
1656 book *Glossographia*, means "good-luck, happiness."

Froligozene

According to 1914's *A glossary of Tudor and Stuart words, especially from the dramatists*,
froligozene was a term meaning "be happy" derived from the Dutch *vrolijk zijn* ("to be cheerful").

Leeze me

If you wanted to express how happy you are with something, use the Scottish phrase
leeze me (short for *lief is me*). Robert Burns featured it in his poem "Bessy and Her
Spinning Wheel": "O Leeze me on my spinnin-wheel, And leeze me on my rock and reel."

Moths in a best blanket

The caterpillars of certain moth species devour wool, and you might imagine
that they would be ecstatic to find themselves in a place of such ample sustenance—
hence this late-nineteenth-century slang phrase to describe being quite happy.

Suffisance

Geoffrey Chaucer used this term in his writings to describe feeling satisfied and content;
he also used it to refer to someone or something that brought satisfaction.
"She was, that swete wife, My suffisaunce, my luste, my lyfe," he wrote circa 1369.

How Many Words Are There in the English Language?

It's impossible to account for every word in the English language, but the lexicographers at the *Oxford English Dictionary* have come close: According to the second edition of the reference book, published in 1989, they have full entries for 171,476 words in addition to 47,156 terms that are obsolete. (That tally, however, doesn't take into account words that have multiple meanings, in which case we're looking at nearly 750,000 words, of which more than 100,000 are obsolete.)

> **750,000**

11

EPONYMS YOU SHOULD KNOW

Eponyms—words that are derived from the name of a particular person—are found throughout history, in the worlds of math and science, in art and in music. Here are just a few eponyms you should know. (And yes, it's true that an eponym is technically the person who has given their name to a word—but in this case, we've chosen to define the word as it's commonly used in everyday speech.)

1. Algorithm
In Latin, the mathematician, astronomer, and writer Muhammad al-Khwārizmī was known as Algoritmi—and that's where we got the word *algorithm,* rules that computers (and people) follow to solve calculations.

2. Boycott
You can *boycott* a company whose principles you disagree with by refusing to offer them your business, but the original boycott may have been a bit more like a boycott-strike hybrid. When retired British army officer Captain Charles Boycott was managing the property of an absentee landlord in late-nineteenth-century Ireland, a rent dispute between Boycott and the farmers tending to the land led the tenants to stop working the fields and to shun the Englishman en masse. Local businesses followed suit, and Boycott—rich in status but poor in access to useful resources, like food—was driven out of town.

3. Braille
In 1824, Frenchman Louis Braille—then just a teenager—took a pre-existing code and used it to develop the original braille system for reading and writing, inspired by his own needs as a Blind person. (He lost his vision in an accident in his father's tool shop when he was three years old.) Braille, a talented musician, later adapted the system so it could be used for musical notation as well.

4. Dunce
Dunce was once a descriptor for an acolyte of the Scottish theologian John Duns Scotus. As Scotus's ideas fell out of favor, the word came to its present-day meaning as a pejorative term for a stupid person.

5. Gerrymandering
Gerrymandering is the practice of drawing political districts in an attempt to advantage a certain political party or constituency. The word comes to us from Governor Elbridge Gerry and a salamander. Or, more accurately, from the misshapen district that appeared in Massachusetts while Gerry was governor, which some claimed *looked* like a salamander. One origin story for the word says that poet Richard Alsop coined it at a dinner party in 1812. That's hard to confirm, but there is a record of Alsop's sometime-collaborator Elkanah Tisdale drawing "The Gerry-Mander" as a satirical comic in an 1812 issue of the *Boston Gazette*.

6. Guillotine
Joseph-Ignace Guillotin was a French physician, and though the guillotine is named after him, he didn't invent it—in fact, similar devices had been used around the world for centuries. Guillotin didn't even design the ones used during the French Revolution. All he really did was suggest that France standardize executions.

At the time, high-class folks were usually beheaded, while most other criminals were hanged. Beheading was viewed as the more "honorable" method of execution, and was quicker and less painful (that is, if your executioner did a good job).

Guillotin was against the death penalty altogether, but apparently he realized that France was nowhere near being ready to give it up. So, in 1789, he proposed that France use an official decapitation contraption to make all executions as humane as possible. He didn't offer up any diagrams and the National Assembly wasn't exactly clamoring for details—Guillotin wasn't a very well-respected physician. One contemporary described him as "a nobody who made himself a busybody."

By the fall of 1791, however, decapitation was the official method of execution and the number of death sentences was rapidly climbing. Guillotin's call for an equitable, efficient means of execution suddenly seemed like a worthy idea. An engineer named Antoine Louis designed the machine, and another guy named Tobias Schmidt constructed it. And much to the horror of Guillotin, everyone started calling the machine *the guillotine*. After he died in 1814, his family members formally petitioned the government to pick a different name for it. When they didn't, the Guillotins picked a different last name for themselves.

7. Nicotine
Nicotine, the addictive poison in tobacco, owes its name to the French diplomat, Jean Nicot, who is traditionally credited with bringing tobacco plants to France.

8. Salmonella
Daniel Elmer Salmon was a veterinary pathologist who ran the Bureau of Animal Industry during the late nineteenth century. Although Salmon didn't actually discover salmonella—epidemiologist Theobald Smith isolated a species of it while working at the bureau in 1885—he ran the research program in which the discovery occurred and appeared as the first author on the paper about the bacteria, which was ultimately named after him.

9. Saxophone
The saxophone takes its name from its inventor, Adolphe Sax—but it isn't the only musical instrument he put his name to: He also created the saxotromba, saxhorn, and saxtuba.

10. Silhouette
It's generally agreed that the word *silhouette* comes from the French author and politician Étienne de Silhouette, but how that man lent his name to a particular style of image is a bit hard to say. On his website, Word Histories, the French teacher and linguistics enthusiast Pascal Tréguer lays out a number of theories and is most convinced by the version offered by an 1869 edition of the *Journal Officiel de l'Empire Français*: that Étienne de Silhouette himself pioneered—or at least popularized—the technique of drawing portraits in the silhouette style. This account claims that de Silhouette covered rooms of his castle with silhouette drawings, but because the castle was destroyed by a fire in 1871, unfortunately, it's unverifiable today.

11. Uzi
The Uzi submachine gun, which debuted in 1954, takes its name from its inventor, Israeli officer Uziel Gal.

SAY WHAT?

For Pete's Sake— Who Was Pete?

When it comes to devising ways to convey outrage or frustration without offending any delicate or pious ears, human creativity knows no bounds. And compared to colorful examples from history and pop culture, *for Pete's sake*—a milder version of *for God's sake* or *for Christ's sake* that doesn't violate any of the Ten Commandments— sounds a little dull. But it does carry a certain element of mystery: Who the heck is Pete?

The *Oxford English Dictionary* dates the first written instance of *for Pete's sake* to 1903 (though others have found it a bit earlier), with *for the love of Pete* appearing around the same time. By that point, *for the love of Mike* had already been in the English lexicon for quite some time. Since *Mike* is thought to have been a nod to St. Michael—and the phrases clearly have a religious connection—some have suggested that the mononymous Pete is really St. Peter.

But without any actual evidence to support that conclusion, it's also possible that Pete wasn't a person at all. *For pity's sake* has been around since the seventeenth century; its predecessor, *for pity*, dates all the way back to the fifteenth century. As Michael Quinion pointed out on his World Wide Words blog, clever cursers may have been influenced by *Pete* because it sounds like *pity*. *Pete's sake* sounds even more like *peace sake*—a phrase that popped up at various times over the centuries.

In short, we can't be sure who Pete was, if he was anyone. So feel free to pick your favorite Pete and dedicate your curse to him.

THOMAS HOPKINS GALLAUDET

AND THE BIRTH OF AMERICAN SIGN LANGUAGE

In the early 1800s, Thomas Hopkins Gallaudet was visiting his family in Hartford, Connecticut, when he met Alice Cogswell, a nine-year-old Deaf girl. Gallaudet became determined to open up her world, and in doing so transformed the Deaf community.

In the 1800s, to have a physical affliction meant there was a strong possibility one would not only be dismissed but also ostracized. Some harbored the belief that the Deaf were mentally impaired or otherwise beyond reach. To structure formal education for those who had lost hearing at birth or through illness was rare, especially in the United States.

The lack of alternatives for nonverbal individuals was socially isolating; Gallaudet could see this manifest in Alice, who appeared disengaged from other children in the neighborhood. Gallaudet became acquainted with Alice's father, Mason Cogswell, an educated surgeon of good social standing. With Mason's assistance, Gallaudet traveled to Europe to investigate something he had only read about: a burgeoning educational system for the Deaf.

Gallaudet's journey ultimately took him to France at the invitation of the abbot Roch-Ambroise Cucurron Sicard of what's now the Institut National de Jeunes Sourds de Paris. Sicard, who had been lecturing in England, told Gallaudet of a school that taught a form of sign language.

Sicard was fluent in sign language but was in no way its innovator or inventor; pocket communities had existed for hundreds of years that adopted hand signs to communicate. But Sicard's school was one of the few places where hand gestures indicating words and concepts were formally taught.

Learning sign language was an intensive process, however, and even with the Cogswells' backing, Gallaudet didn't have the money to remain in France long enough to learn everything he needed to. So Gallaudet asked Laurent Clerc, Sicard's chief assistant, who was himself Deaf, to come back to America.

Clerc was experienced in manual sign language, which dispensed with incorporating oral language and relied solely on hand cues that were assigned to words. While traveling, Gallaudet taught the Frenchman English; Clerc taught him Sicard's version of sign language. And when the pair arrived in Connecticut, Clerc began tutoring Alice Cogswell in sign language, too.

Gallaudet and Clerc also traveled the East Coast, imploring legislators and parents for a better educational system. They opened the Connecticut Asylum for the Education and Instruction of Deaf and Dumb Persons (later the American School for the Deaf), the first permanent learning facility for the Deaf in the country, in Hartford in 1817. Gallaudet was principal, Clerc was the head teacher, and Alice was among the school's first students. Naturally, the sign language Clerc taught was heavily influenced by the French language, though students helped it evolve into what would become American Sign Language (ASL).

Throughout Gallaudet's and Clerc's tenures, Deaf schools were seeded, either by graduating students who opened them or educators who learned from their example. Gallaudet's son, Edward, eventually helped create what is now Washington, D.C.'s Gallaudet University in 1864, thirteen years after his father's death.

But ASL still had obstacles to overcome: Competing theories about the best way to teach communication skills to the Deaf were routinely debated. For example, inventor and influential intellectual Alexander Graham Bell—whose mother and wife were both Deaf—favored the "oralist," or speaking/lip-reading, approach, and his strict oralist views stifled ASL for a time.

In the 1960s, a National Science Foundation grant allowed Gallaudet University English professor William Stokoe to author *A Dictionary of American Sign Language on Linguistic Principles* (1965), which argued that ASL had its own grammar and syntax. The book helped ASL become accepted, and it eventually became the dominant teaching language in the Deaf community in the United States. Gallaudet's kind gesture—to help a little girl abandoned by her peers—led to billions of gestures that have helped millions of people.

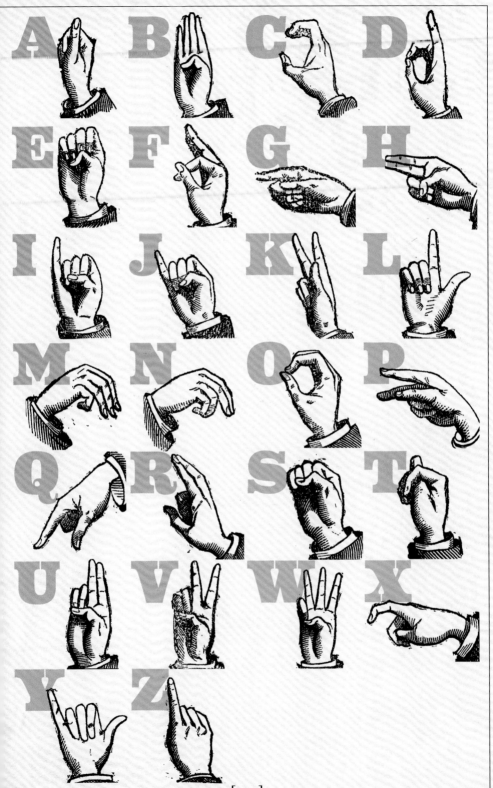

ELEMENT NAMES
INSPIRED BY
FOLKLORE
and
MYTHOLOGY

Some elements, like californium and moscovium, are named after places. Others pay tribute to important scientists, from Albert Einstein (einsteinium) to Pierre and Marie Curie (curium). And then there are those whose monikers reference—some more obviously and directly than others—famous gods and other mythological characters. Read on for eleven interesting examples.

| 58 |
| Ce |
| Cerium |
| 140.116 |

Cerium

After discovering the gray rare earth metal in 1803, Swedish chemist Jöns Jacob Berzelius and his colleague Wilhelm Hisinger christened it *cerium* after the asteroid (now considered a dwarf planet) Ceres, which had been spotted just two years prior. Ceres got its name from the Roman goddess associated with agriculture and bountiful harvests. (So did the word *cereal*.)

| 27 |
| Co |
| Cobalt |
| 58.993 |

Cobalt

Cobalt was named after tricksters from German folklore: kobolds, which were sprites or goblins believed to haunt mines (or help around the house). Cobalt, like nickel, often pairs with arsenic to create mineral compounds; when German miners tried to extract the metal from its ore—not an easy task in the first place—poisonous arsenic oxide often came with it. They reportedly blamed kobolds for these difficulties, and started calling the troublesome substance *kobold*. By the time Swedish chemist Georg Brandt successfully isolated the element in the 1730s, the name had already been spelled in various ways in other languages—including *cobalt* in English.

| 77 |
| Ir |
| Iridium |
| 192.217 |

Iridium

Iridium was named for its ability to produce colorful compounds. "I should incline to call this metal *iridium*, from the striking variety of colours which it gives, while dissolving in marine acid," British chemist Smithson Tennant wrote after discovering the element circa 1803. Tennant didn't specify exactly how he came up with the word *iridium*, but it's often said that it was inspired by Iris, Greek goddess of the rainbow (the word *iris* is also Greek for "rainbow").

| 28 |
| Ni |
| Nickel |
| 58.693 |

Nickel

As the story goes, when German miners unearthed a reddish mineral that looked like it contained copper—but didn't actually contain copper—they called it *kupfernickel*. *Kupfer* means "copper," and *nickel* refers to a mischievous, mythological demon (or sometimes the devil himself). In 1751, Swedish chemist Axel Fredrik Cronstedt figured out what was really in this devil's copper: a lustrous new metal that he named *nickel*. (The other ingredient in *kupfernickel*, which we know as *niccolite* or *nickeline*, is arsenic.)

41
Nb
Niobium
92.906

Niobium

Before it became *niobium*, element 41 was known as *columbium*. The name was a nod to the New World; British chemist Charles Hatchett had first identified the shiny metal in a mineral sample unearthed decades earlier in New England. Hatchett's discovery happened just a year before Swedish chemist Anders Gustaf Ekeberg isolated tantalum (named after the Greek mythological figure Tantalus), and some scientists concluded that the two very similar metals were actually just the same element. In the 1840s, German chemist Heinrich Rose determined that they weren't. He called columbium *niobium* after Tantalus's daughter, Niobe, and that name was eventually adopted internationally (though *columbium* remained popular in the United States for years).

46
Pd
Palladium
106.42

Palladium

In 1802, the year after Ceres was discovered, a smaller asteroid was spotted and named *Pallas*—another name for Athena, the Greek goddess of wisdom and war. Since British chemist William Hyde Wollaston had succeeded in isolating a new element around that same time, he paid homage to the asteroid by calling the metal *palladium*. Before deciding on that moniker, however, he'd briefly considered naming it *ceresium* (a plan thwarted when Berzelius and Hisinger published their discovery before his).

61
Pm
Promethium
144.913

Promethium

While developing an atomic bomb as part of the Manhattan Project during World War II, chemist Charles Coryell and his subordinates Larry Glendenin and Jacob Marinsky worked to identify elements produced during the nuclear fission of uranium. One of them turned out to be element 61—an as-yet-undiscovered rare earth metal long suspected to sit between neodymium and samarium on the periodic table.

It was Coryell's wife, Grace Mary, who suggested naming the radioactive element after Prometheus, the Greek Titan who stole fire from the Olympians and gave it to humans. The deed didn't go unpunished: Zeus had Prometheus bound to a mountain, where an eagle would come to peck out his regenerated liver on a daily basis. As Glendenin explained in 1976, the name *promethium* "not only symbolizes the dramatic way in which the element is produced as a result of the harnessing of the energy of nuclear fission, but also warns of the danger of punishment by the vulture of war."

90
Th
Thorium
232.038

Thorium

In 1815, Berzelius believed he had discovered something new in mineral samples collected in Sweden. He named the substance *Thorjord*, or "Thor's earth," after the hammer-wielding Norse god of thunder. *Thorjord* turned out to just be yttrium phosphate, but Berzelius got to honor the deity again when he identified what *was* a new element—thorium— in the late 1820s.

<table>
<tr><td>

73
Ta
Tanatlum
180.948

</td><td>

22
Ti
Titanium
47.867

</td><td>

23
V
Vanadium
50.906

</td></tr>
</table>

Tantalum

In Greek mythology, Tantalus was a son of Zeus, whom the gods doomed to spend eternity standing in a pool of water he couldn't drink, with fruit just out of reach. (His offense varies by account, but one story claims that he killed and served his own son to the gods at a feast just to see if they'd notice.)

When Ekeberg identified a new hard, gray metal in 1802, he found it was almost impossible to get it to dissolve in acid. So he called it *tantalum* "partly to follow the custom of adopting names from mythology, and partly to allude to the fact that the oxide of this metal is incapable of feeding itself even in the middle of a surplus of acid."

Titanium

The credit for discovering titanium goes to British mineralogist William Gregor, who detected a mystery metal in a sandy black mineral he called *menachanite* in 1791. The metal didn't get a name until four years later, when German chemist Martin Heinrich Klaproth identified the same metal in a different mineral: rutile. Klaproth soon heard about Gregor's finding and realized the two metals were the same unknown element, which he named *titanium* after the Titans— a group of Greek deities associated with strength and power. Though the name itself is arbitrary, titanium lives up to its moniker: It doesn't corrode easily and boasts a high tensile strength, particularly with respect to its relatively low density.

Vanadium

Though Spanish mineralogist Andrés Manuel del Río had technically already discovered vanadium—which he called *erythronium*— circa 1801, he had concluded that it was actually just a form of chromium. So it didn't get recognized as a new element until Sweden's Nils Gabriel Sefström identified it as such in 1830. Sefström renamed it *vanadium* in honor of Vanadis, a name for Freyja, an Old Norse goddess known for her beauty. Vanadium upholds that legacy by turning different colors depending on its oxidation state.

Dord

The Ghost Word That Ended Up in the Dictionary

Did you know that *dord* is a synonym for *density*? Probably not, because it isn't. *Dord* is a ghost word—a nonexistent word that slipped into the dictionary. In the case of *dord*, it stayed there for about thirteen years.

This particular flub occurred in the early 1930s, after an editor typed an entry that read "D or d," meaning that density can be abbreviated with an uppercase *D* or a lowercase *d*. During the editorial process, all dictionary entries were supposed to have a space between each letter so any pronunciation marks could be added later. The next editor simply thought a space was missing between *o* and *r*, and the word *dord* ended up in the 1934 second edition of *Webster's New International Dictionary*.

In 1939, a Merriam-Webster editor spotted *dord* and scrawled "A ghost word!" in red on a note card asking for its removal. Somehow, it managed to stay in the dictionary for another eight years. When a different editor submitted yet another note card pointing out the error in 1947, *dord* was finally deleted.

Why Do We Say "Close, But No Cigar"?

P icture yourself at eight years old, just having crossed the finish line of an egg-and-spoon race one step behind the winner. A spectator pats you on the shoulder and, shaking her head, says, "Close, but no cigar." Never having heard the phrase before, you assume the first-place finisher will soon be off somewhere smoking their hard-earned stogie.

Since cigars aren't customarily given to children as rewards (or for any other reason), the spectator in this imaginary situation was surely using the phrase as a way to convey that you came really close to success but didn't quite get there. In the early twentieth century, however, the cigar in question was a literal one.

Before stuffed animals became the gold standard for carnival prizes, people often competed to win cigars at shooting ranges and for other target-related games. As Barry Popik explains on his blog The Big Apple, carnival barkers would shout "Close, but no cigar!" to anyone who fell just short of clinching the coveted reward.

By the late 1920s, *Close, but no cigar* had started showing up outside fairs and carnivals. A *Long Island Daily Press* article from May 1929 titled "Close; But No Cigar" described an unlucky New Yorker named Hugo Straub, who was "believed to have set a world's record in the business of getting-defeated-for-the-presidency" because he "finished second in no less than two presidential races within one week . . . for the leadership of the Springfield Gardens Civic association and for the presidency of the Springfield Gardens Republican club."

Maybe Straub treated himself to a high-quality cigar (or two—one for each loss) as a consolation prize.

WORDS *that* USED TO MEAN SOMETHING NEGATIVE

Sometimes words move up in the world. Their meanings change with time, becoming more positive—a process linguists call *amelioration*. Here are some ameliorated words that were a pinch more negative back in the day.

Amaze

In the sixteenth century, *amaze* was a verb defined as "to bewilder"; it could also mean "to terrify." (It's formed using the word *maze*, which dates back to the fourteenth century and meant "confusion.") Not long after, though, *amaze* also came to mean "to surprise" or "to astound," the meaning it still holds today.

Amuse

From the 1400s up through the eighteenth century, *amuse* meant "to cheat." One citation of the word's current meaning can be found in a 1796 book by Mary Wollstonecraft: "Marguerite . . . was much amused by the costume of the [Danish] women."

Awe and Awesome

The first meaning of *awe* was "fear," and eventually, the word came to define that feeling mixed with religious reverence—so when the suffix *-some* was added in the 1570s to give us *awesome*, it wasn't used to refer to things that are super cool, as it is today. Instead, it meant "inspiring fear."

Boy

As far back as the 1200s, *boy* was used to refer to a male servant or enslaved person. The word's origins, and how it developed this meaning, are a mystery. (Fun fact: *Girl*, when it first appeared in the 1300s, was a genderless term for a child.)

Careful

In the 1200s, *careful,* from the Old English word *carful*, was an adjective used to express sadness and sorrow.

Dizzy

Today, when you're dizzy, you're giddy or literally off-balance—but as far back as the 800s, the word was used to refer to people who were foolish.

Eager

In the 1300s, one possible meaning of the word *eager* was "to feel or act angry." It came into English from the French *aigre*, which since the twelfth century has meant "sour."

Fond

These days, if you're *fond* of something, you like it. But to be fond in the late 1300s meant something very different—you were foolish. The etymology of the word is unclear, but it may have its origins in the word *fon*, a noun for a foolish person as well as a verb that meant "to fool."

Fun

Fun—which might also have its origins in the verb *fon*—originally meant "to cheat or trick." Now it's all about having a good time or indulging in a joke, occasionally at someone else's expense.

Glorious

If someone called you *glorious* in the late 1300s, it wasn't a compliment: The word was used in reference to someone who was prone to boasting or otherwise being kind of a jerk. In the 1700s and 1800s it could also be used to refer to a happy drunk.

Knight

Way back in the late 800s, *knight*—which comes from the Old English word *cniht*—was another word for a boy, and around 950, it began to be used to refer to any male servant. It came to the military meaning we know today in the 1100s.

Meticulous

Meticulous, which comes to us via Latin and French, originally meant "fearful" or "timid" when it was coined in the 1540s. In the 1820s, it came to mean being a little *too* careful regarding details, in a bad way. Eventually, however, being meticulous became a positive thing.

Mischievous

Originally, in the late 1300s, this word (from the French *meschevous*) was used in reference to disastrous events or people who were miserable. It wouldn't come to be used for someone who was charmingly naughty until the mid-1700s (and it meant actual, not-at-all-charming bad behavior earlier than that—from around 1438 onward).

Nice

In the 1300s, calling someone *nice* meant you were saying they were foolish or simple. The word came into English from the Old French *nice,* or "ignorant," from the Latin *nescius*. Over the centuries, *nice* went through a dizzying array of meanings, with stops at "timid or faint-hearted," "fussy or fastidious," and "dainty or delicate," before arriving at "pleasant or agreeable" by the nineteenth century.

Pragmatic

Pragmatic comes to English from Latin and French, and way back in the 1600s, it was a word that meant "meddling." As William Strachey noted in 1612's *The historie of travell into Virginia Britania,* "Ignorance . . . cannot . . . excuse a factious and pragmatique Tonge."

Pretty

These days, we use *pretty* to talk about something that's attractive, but in the 1450s, to be pretty was to be cunning. It was formed by combining the very old word *prat* (a joke or trick) with the suffix *-y*.

Sophisticated

The verb *sophisticate* means "to adulterate one substance with another," so in the 1600s, something sophisticated was likewise unpure—it was often used to refer to foods or booze that had been tampered with. Its current meaning dates back to 1895.

Sustainable

Today, the word *sustainable* is often used in terms of how to maintain things like natural resources (energy, for example) or activities (such as farming practices), a meaning that dates back to the mid-1970s. But long before that, in the 1610s, *sustainable* was used to refer to something that was, in the words of Randle Cotgrave in 1611's *A dictionarie of the French and English tongues*, "abideable."

No Sh*t:

PEOPLE WHO SWEAR MORE MAY ALSO BE MORE HONEST, STUDY SAYS

There are two types of people in this world: those who abhor potty mouths, and those who have turned the use of four-letter words into an art form. If you lean toward the latter, you're probably not afraid to admit it—and now, thanks to a little help from science, we know why. A study conducted by a team of international researchers from Stanford University, the University of Cambridge, Maastricht University, and Hong Kong University of Science and Technology in 2017 suggests that people who can easily let loose with a string of obscenities are likely more honest as well.

For the first part of the study, the team conducted interviews with 276 subjects to get to the bottom of both their swearing habits and just how honest they are by asking them questions like "Have you ever cheated at a game?" and "Have you ever blamed someone for doing something you knew was really your fault?" to determine their trustworthiness. (If someone answered all of the questions in the way that society deems is socially acceptable, researchers could essentially determine that the person was lying, because no one is all good all the time.)

Next, the team analyzed the status updates of nearly 74,000 Facebook users, looking for linguistic indicators of deception, such as the use of fewer third-person pronouns and more negative words, as determined by a 2003 report published in the *Personality and Social Psychology Bulletin*.

"The consistent findings across the studies suggest that the positive relation between profanity and honesty is robust and that the relationship found at the individual level indeed translates to the society level," the study concluded.

While swearing may sound uncouth to some, the researchers see it more as an honest form of expression—not one of anger or malice—and determined that the more curse words come out of a person's mouth, the more truthful they are likely to be, as swearing itself is a form of candid talk.

What's the OLDEST CURSE WORD in English?

For as long as there have been words, there have been impolite words. The first recorded use of the word *fart*, for example, possibly dates back to the eleventh century, making it the oldest known rude word. As for those four-letter words that still have the power to offend? They took a more circuitous route to find their way out of our mouths and into our language.

According to the *Oxford English Dictionary*, many of the swear words we still use today have been with us for centuries. In 2015, British historian Paul Booth discovered what is believed to be the first use of the word *fuck* in a sexual/sweary context when he found a court document from 1310 that contained the name "Roger Fuckebythenavele," which is believed to be a coded insult. *Shit*, meanwhile, started to be used derogatorily in the sixteenth century (it derives from Old English and German words meaning "dung").

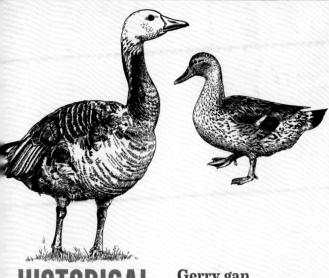

HISTORICAL CURSES

TO WORK INTO
CURRENT
CONVERSATION

Sometimes, a conversation or situation calls for a bit of colorful language. Whether you're looking to disguise your profanities or simply want to spice up your vocabulary, here are ten historical curse words and phrases to consider.

Gerry gan
Gerry gan means "shit in your mouth" (*gerry* is a sixteenth-century term for "poop"; *gan* is an old word for "mouth"). It's a way to tell someone to shut up, such as, "Gerry gan, Gerald! No one wants to hear about your new investment scheme."

Cotso!
Probably derived at least in part from a euphemism for God's Oath, *cotso* is an eighteenth-century word for annoyance or surprise.

Go and eat coke
If someone says this, they aren't telling you to drink a sweet soda or nosh on some cocaine. *Go and eat coke* is a rude nineteenth-century dismissal. The coke here refers to a fuel created from coal. For an even more spirited insult, some would say, "Go and eat coke and you can shit cinders!"

Go milk a duck
U.S. college students in the 1930s said this as a way of telling people to go away or mind their own business. If a nosy peer inquired about a test grade, *go milk a duck!* would be a rude way (but still more polite than the alternative *go fuck a duck!*) to end the conversation.

Goose and duck
Coy, nineteenth-century Australian rhyming slang for a certain four-letter f-word that means "to copulate," as in "Matt and Mary left the party early to go *goose and duck*."

Pho
Now, it's a tasty Vietnamese noodle soup. But for English speakers in the late fifteenth century and beyond, *pho* (and related words like *faugh*, *fogh*, and *pooh*) was an exclamation of anger or surprise, as in, "*Pho!* They served me the wrong meal!"

Pissed on a nettle
A sixteenth-century way of saying someone is annoyed, or in modern terms, "pissed off." As in, "Someone ate the sandwich he packed and now he's *pissed on a nettle*."

Sneck up
The next time your annoying neighbor bothers you, simply tell him to "*sneck up!*" It's a sixteenth- and seventeenth-century phrase for telling a person to buzz off, as in, "Sneck up, Steve! We're busy."

Sparrowfart
Sparrow's fart is an old term for the early morning; in Ireland, *sparrowfart* is a twentieth-century word sometimes used for an unimportant, annoying person. One character in James Joyce's *Ulysses* refers to "sparrowfarts skitting around talking about politics they know as much about as my backside."

Thunder!
Your friend who gets overly excited about the weather may yell out, "*Thunder!*" during a storm, but in the eighteenth century, people used this as an equivalent of *hell* or *damn*, as in "*Thunder!* It's raining and I forgot an umbrella!" If one word isn't enough, variations also include *blood and thunder!* and *thunder and turf!*

The Science Behind Why People Hate the Word *Moist*

People really do not like discussing moisture. A 2012 BuzzFeed post called "Why Moist is the Worst Word Ever" received more than four million views; when the *New Yorker* asked readers to nominate a word to scrub from the English language that same year, the overwhelming consensus was to ditch *moist*. The seemingly ordinary adjective inspires an excessive outpouring of ire. Why?

In 2014, a group of psychologists decided to find out. Researchers from Oberlin College in Ohio and Trinity University in San Antonio ran three different experiments to figure out how many people really find the word *moist* disdainful, and why. They found that around 20 percent of the population studied was averse to the word, but that it didn't have anything to do with the way it sounds. Rather, it's the association with bodily functions that seems to turn most people off, whether they realize it or not.

Most of the participants who told the researchers they hated the word chalked it up to phonics. "It just has an ugly sound that makes whatever you're talking about sound gross," one participant argued. However, people did not show similar aversion to words that include the same sounds, such as *foist* or *rejoiced*. People found the word *moist* most disgusting when it was accompanied by unrelated, positive words like *paradise*, or when it was accompanied by sexual words. By contrast, when it accompanied food words (like *cake*), people weren't as bothered by it.

The younger and more neurotic the study participants were, the more likely they were to dislike the word. Additionally, the more disgust they associated with bodily functions, the less they liked *moist*. The researchers postulated that people who found themselves particularly grossed out by thinking of things as moist may just be more likely to associate the word with sex. As one participant explained, "It reminds people of sex and vaginas." No disrespect to either, of course, but we're pretty sure no one wants to think about those things when they're browsing the baked goods aisle.

Words
PEOPLE
REALLY
HATE
(AND WHAT TO SAY INSTEAD)

Moist isn't the only word that people would rather avoid. Not all irksome terms on this list engender the same kind of disgust . . . but some of them do.

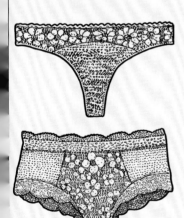

Amazing

Amazing has become an adjective of ill-repute due to overuse: If you call everything amazing, nothing seems amazing. Describing delicious food? Go for *golopshus, lummy lick,* or *tizzy-wizzy*. Complimenting someone's appearance? Try *kippy, formose,* or *pulchritudinous*. Need an all-purpose alternative to *amazing*? *Boskidillums* and "fine as a cow turd stuck with primroses" have both been used to amazing effect in the past.

Blog

Some people dislike the word *blog*—short for *weblog*—simply because it sounds ugly. Food blogger Tessa Arias once reimagined it as something you might sling as an insult: "He's such a *blog*!" Bloggers themselves often balk at *blog* because they feel it trivializes all the skills and responsibilities required to run one. *Website* always works as a substitute, or, for a more formal option, try *independent digital publication*.

Boyfriend and Girlfriend

People find the terms *boyfriend* and *girlfriend* bothersome for a number of reasons: They reinforce the gender binary. They carry stereotypical connotations. They just sound childish. *Partner* works as a one-size-fits-all replacement—but for something a bit more colorful, go for the Middle English *leman* or the eighteenth-century *sprunny*.

Panties

People seem to agree that *panties* exists at an uncomfortable lexical intersection of juvenile and sexual. Fortunately, there are plenty of old-timey options that sound far less dull than *underwear*. There's rhyming slang, like *do and dare* (meant to sound like *underwear*) and *early doors* (a loose rhyme for *drawers*). An English speaker circa 1900 might refer to them as *dessous*, meaning "underneath" in French. A 1970s college student, meanwhile, might call them *UBs*—short for *underbodies*—or *snuggies* . . . though the latter term is more for overgarments than undergarments these days.

Phlegm

The word *phlegm* is gross primarily because phlegm itself is gross. Its well-known synonyms—like *mucus, sputum,* and the more informal *loogie*—have the same issue, but old-timey terms like *blathery* and *gleim* can help you avoid the ick factor.

Pus

Phlegm took second place in a 2022 poll of English's grossest words, conducted by language-learning platform Preply. The first-place finisher? *Pus*, with about 9,800 votes. (*Moist* and *mucus* made the top ten, too, as did *seepage, fester,* and *ooze*. In general, words involving bodily secretions are gag-inducing.) You can always swap *pus* for the much less evocative *purulence* or the Old English *youster*.

The INTERESTING ETYMOLOGIES of EVERYDAY WORDS

Etymologies can be hard to establish beyond a doubt—academic disagreements often exist, misinformation is rampant, and sometimes, legends are important data points, even if they don't tell the actual story. Rather than tracing every word in this list back to its ultimate origin point, here's one cool way station each one made on its journey to the present day. That could be an analysis of the Latin roots, an interesting hypothesis about a proto-Indo-European origin, or a discussion of a pivotal change in a word's meaning.

Bouquet
Bouquet was probably introduced to English by writer Lady Mary Wortley Montagu from the French word of the same spelling. Montague, by the way, also familiarized English readers with the "language of flowers" based on her experiences abroad—the idea that a lily symbolizes purity, for example. *Bouquet* can be traced back to the Medieval Latin *boscus*, or "grove," as in a group of trees. The word *bouquet* originally meant something like "little wood."

Butcher
The word *butcher* seems to trace its origins through words like the Old French *bochier*, literally meaning "slaughterer of goats." It seems an easy enough transition from there to any person who prepares and sells meat—goat or otherwise.

Chronology
Chronology comes to us from the Greek *khronos*, or "time"; Chronus was the Greek personification of time.

Cigar and Stogie
Sometimes a cigar is just a cigar, but sometimes it's a cicada—at least according to one of the more popular theories about *cigar*'s etymology. The Spanish word for cigar, *cigarro*, is a lot like the Spanish word for cicada: *cigarra*. This has led some to speculate that cigars were named for their rough resemblance to the cylindrical bug. Another explanation is that *cigar* comes from the Mayan word *sikar*, meaning "to smoke."

And if you call your cigar a *stogie*, you have the township of Conestoga, Pennsylvania, to thank. Some say that's because an early cigar factory was built in the area, but more sources seem to think it has to do with the smoking habits of the men who drove so-called Conestoga wagons.

Clue

The word *clue* is a variant of *clew*, a word for a ball of yarn or thread. It comes to us from Middle and Old English; the ball of yarn in question is a handy method for finding your way out of a labyrinth, as Greek mythology's Theseus did after killing the Minotaur.

Companion

If you trade sandwiches with your classmate at lunchtime, you can call them your *companion*. The word comes from the Latin *com*, or "together with," and *panis*, for "bread or food." That makes the word's original meaning something like "one who you break bread with."

Crimson and Chartreuse

Crimson can possibly be traced to the proto-Indo-European *kʷrmis*, or worm, reflecting the fact that the color was once produced by crushing a specific type of worm.

Chartreuse, meanwhile, owes its existence as a color to a liqueur of the same name, made by Carthusian monks.

Fact

If you're interested in just the facts, you may want to know that the word *fact* comes to us from a verb meaning "to do." The past participle of the Latin verb *facere* is *factus*, meaning "done." As a noun that becomes *factum*, or "an event, occurrence, deed, achievement." The modern meaning of *fact*, something known to be true, implicitly contrasts things that are only claimed to have happened with something that has actually occurred.

Gossip

A *gossip* was originally a *godsibb* in Old English, and it was basically a godparent— someone who acted as a sponsor at a baptism. By the fourteenth century, the word could encompass any familiar acquaintance, especially women who were invited to a friend's birth. Through a long line of loose talkers or perhaps some old-fashioned sexism, the word evolved to mean anyone engaged in idle talk, and eventually *gossip* took on its modern meaning as baseless rumor or trifling talk.

Juggernaut

Juggernaut derives from Hindi: *jagat* for "world" plus *nātha* for "lord or protector" gave us *jagannāth*, roughly "lord of the world," a Hindu deity. One story for how that specific use led to our current understanding of the word involves the annual Chariot Festival that took place at the Jagannāth Temple in Puri, India. Reports of pilgrims being crushed under the procession of chariots may have given rise to *juggernaut*'s meaning as "a massive inexorable force," though those reports may have been the product of a biased perspective from Western sources, rather than an accurate accounting of events.

Jumbo

In the latter half of the nineteenth century, an African elephant named Jumbo was being exhibited around the world. And though Jumbo's tumultuous life as a celebrity pachyderm may well have popularized the word *jumbo* to mean anything very large, it's not necessarily where the word originally comes from: It was used to describe someone or something clumsy as early as 1823, and its use as slang likely predates that written record.

Mortgage

Mortgage comes from the Old French *morgage*, the roots of which, in literal translation, mean something like a "dead pledge." But despite what you might have read online, that's probably not because you'll be paying off your mortgage the rest of your life.

Sir Edward Coke may have gotten closer to the mark in his *Institutes of the Lawes of England* back in 1628. Coke understood a mortgage as a sort of standoff, destined to end either when the borrower failed to pay, thus rendering the property "dead to him," or when payment is delivered in full, in which case the agreement is dead to the lender.

Nimrod

In the United States, at least, few people want to be called a *nimrod*. But once upon a time, it meant you were a hunter in the vein of the Old Testament's Nimrod. Even today, Nimrod is a fairly common name in Israel.

How it came to be a synonym for *doofus* in English is unclear; it could be because the biblical figure Nimrod is sometimes (though not in Genesis) said to be associated with the ill-fated attempt to build the Tower of Babel.

Whatever the origin, it's often stated that Bugs Bunny helped popularize the derogatory meaning of the word when he lobbed it at everyone's favorite hapless hunter, Elmer Fudd. But no one ever actually mentions which toon that was in—and as it turns out, it was actually Daffy who called Elmer *nimrod* in 1948's "What Makes Daffy Duck." Bugs used it in reference to Yosemite Sam three years later in "Rabbit Every Monday."

Orchid

Orchids may be beautiful, but their etymology isn't quite so poetic. The word comes from the Greek *orkhis*, for "testicle," thought to reflect the shape of the plant's underground storage organs. In Middle English, in fact, the plant was known as *ballockwort*.

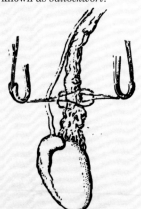

Plumber

The periodic table of the elements contains a hint about the origins of the word *plumber*. That *Pb* comes from the Latin for lead, *plumbum*, which also eventually gave us *plumber*. It originally referred to someone working with lead in a number of contexts, without its modern focus on the pipes that move water in and out of buildings. But since pipes were long made of lead, plumbers eventually became known as the people to call when your sink or toilet needs professional expertise.

Pundit

Pundit comes to us from a Sanskrit word that has been transliterated as *pundit, pandit*, or *pandita*. It originally referred to someone who had committed to memory a significant amount of the Hindu religious texts known as the Vedas. It came to refer more generally to something like "a learned man" or "philosopher" by the nineteenth century, and today that meaning has expanded to include people who like to yell at one another on cable news.

Quarantine

When ships arrived in Venice during the fourteenth century, they were sometimes required to spend forty days in port to suss out any possible cases of plague. In Italian, forty days is *quaranta giorni*, requiring just a short linguistic hop to the English *quarantine*.

Shampoo

If you've ever gotten the tingles while your hair was being washed at a salon, the origin of the word *shampoo* will make sense to you. It comes from a conjugation of the Hindi verb *campna* or *champna*, meaning "to press or knead muscles." A 1762 account from an officer of the East India Company abroad describes the process of being shampooed, which was a vigorous full-body massage done along with hair-washing. The word, if not the full custom, was exported to England, where its hair-specific meaning coalesced.

Sinister

Sinister comes from a Latin word that means "on the left side," a remnant of an outdated association between left-handed people and wickedness or other unsavory traits. That somewhat confusing anti-lefty bias may have roots in pure percentages—most of the population was, then as now, right-handed. Christianity might have also played a role: The Book of Matthew says that Jesus will divide the nations like a shepherd divides his sheep from his goats, with the (presumably pious) sheep sent to the Kingdom of Heaven on the right, and the cursed goats to the left.

Tycoon

Tycoon comes to the United States via the Japanese *taikun*, a word whose Chinese roots mean "great ruler." When Commodore Matthew Perry arrived in Japan in the 1850s, he wanted to meet with "a dignitary of the highest rank in the empire." Perry seemed to think that meant the emperor, but in fact the shogun wielded more power in Japan at the time. Japanese officials used the title *taikun* to reflect the primacy of the shogun's power.

The word caught on stateside and began to expand in meaning with usages like the one found in the *New Orleans Daily Crescent* on May 28, 1860. Critiquing then-Senator William Henry Seward's approach to anti-slavery efforts, the paper claimed he "appropriated to himself . . . the position of master and 'Tycoon' of the Black Republicans." (Black Republicans was a pejorative for white politicians who wanted to do things like abolish slavery.) The word even found fans among Abraham Lincoln's aides during his presidency—they took to calling him "the Tycoon" in letters and diary entries.

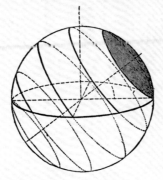

Universe

What's the origin of the universe? Linguistically speaking, that is. According to the *OED*, the word can be traced back to both the French *univers*—which referred to the entirety of everything—and the Latin word *ūniversum*, which John D. Barrow writes in his *Book of Universes* is composed of the roots *unus*, or "one," and *versus*, a form of a verb meaning "to turn" or "to change," which results in a literal meaning of something like "rolled into one." That could just reflect that the universe is everything kind of rolled up into one all-encompassing thing, or it could reflect a specific cosmological belief from antiquity, when it was thought that the sphere containing the heavens turned, thereby creating change in the planets inside.

Vaccine

The word *vaccine* derives indirectly from the Latin for cow, *vacca*. The story goes that, at the turn of the nineteenth century, a British doctor named Edward Jenner observed that milkmaids who had contracted cowpox, or *Variolae vaccinae*, were much less likely to contract smallpox, which could otherwise devastate entire communities. Jenner decided to introduce the pus from a woman's cowpox lesion into a cut he made on an eight-year-old boy's arm.

Luckily for Jenner, the boy, and the human race at large, the cowpox pus provided a strong degree of smallpox protection, and the concept of a vaccine was born. Two centuries and change later, vaccines have eradicated smallpox from the planet, and we continue to take inspiration from Jenner's coinage when discussing vaccines—even ones that don't come from cowpox pus.

Later genetic testing, by the way, actually revealed that those first vaccines may have been using a virus closely related to horsepox, not cowpox. Maybe we should be referring to "equination" campaigns today, but when it comes to the sprawling way that language develops, it can be hard to get the horse-slash-cow back in the barn.

Whiskey

Whiskey, the cause of (and solution to) at least some of life's problems, comes from the Gaelic *uisge* (or *uisce*) *beatha,* or "water of life."

Window

Window comes from the Old Norse *vindauga*, or "wind eye." It originally referred to a hole in the roof, but over the years made the jump down to glazed holes usually found on a wall.

Where Did the Term **Up to Snuff** Originate?

By the 1800s, snuff—powdered, usually snortable tobacco—had become such a long-standing societal fixture in the U.K. and U.S. that phrases started popping up around the word itself. *To beat to snuff*, for instance, meant to best your opponent so thoroughly that you figuratively reduced them to powder. *In high snuff*, meanwhile, described someone in high spirits (maybe a nod to the buzz you'd get after using tobacco).

But the most prevailing example is probably *up to snuff*, which the *Oxford English Dictionary* defines as "up to the required or usual standard." Unlike the aforementioned phrases, the connection between pulverized tobacco and being savvy or meeting requirements isn't quite clear. On his World Wide Words blog, Michael Quinion suggests that it may have had to do with snuff's largest user demographic: wealthy men who knew and could distinguish the difference between the good stuff and the not-so-good stuff.

What we do know is that *up to snuff* had entered the British lexicon by 1807, when it appeared in a London newspaper—the earliest known written mention of the phrase, according to Merriam-Webster. It came up again in *Hamlet Travestie: In Three Acts*, an 1810 parody of Shakespeare's *Hamlet* by British playwright John Poole. Rosencrantz and Guildenstern are explaining to the king that Hamlet won't reveal why he's been strangely disconsolate, and Guildenstern says, "He'll not be sounded; he knows well enough / The game we're after: Zooks, he's up to snuff."

After the play's conclusion, Poole added annotations/commentary that he himself wrote in the voices of literary luminaries and Shakespearean scholars of eras past, including Alexander Pope, Samuel Johnson, George Steevens, and William Warburton. Though Poole-as-Warburton argues that *up to snuff* was referring to Hamlet's ability to literally sniff out Rosencrantz and Guildenstern's ulterior motive, Poole-as-Johnson asserts that it was likely being used in its "common acceptation" as a reference to Hamlet being "a knowing one." *Grose's Classical Dictionary of the Vulgar Tongue* echoed Poole-as-Johnson's understanding of the phrase in its 1823 edition, and so did Merriam-Webster in its 1864 dictionary.

As for how the idiom evolved to describe someone or something that meets standards, there's no clear path—though it makes sense that someone considered knowing and astute would also be generally regarded as a person of merit.

ARE THERE ANY
SYNONYMS
for
THE WORD
SYNONYM
?

Some of the most frequently used words in the English language must have been created by someone with a devilish sense of humor. The word *monosyllabic* isn't one syllable, *long* is only four letters, *lisp* is difficult to pronounce if you have a lisp, and *synonym* doesn't have any synonyms. Or does it?

The answer to that last question is a bit complicated. Thesaurus.com lists *metonym* as a synonym of *synonym*, but their meanings aren't exactly the same. The *Oxford Dictionary of English Grammar* defines *synonym* as "a word or phrase that means the same, or almost the same, as another in the same language." *Metonym*, on the other hand, is defined as "a word or expression which is used as a substitute for another word or expression with which it is in a close semantic relationship." For example, *the crown* can be used to refer to the king, and *Washington* sometimes refers to the U.S. government.

There is another possibility, though: *poecilonym*. This is probably the closest synonym of *synonym*, although it's antiquated and rarely used. David Grambs, a lexicographer for American Heritage and Random House, included it in his 1997 book, *The Endangered English Dictionary: Bodacious Words Your Dictionary Forgot*. The word is pronounced "PEE-si-lo-nim," according to Grambs. *Allen's Synonyms and Antonyms* from 1920 also lists *poecilonym* and another word— *polyonym*—as synonyms of *synonym*. However, it says both of these terms are rare. So technically, there are two other words that have the same meaning as *synonym*, but it's a tough position to argue when those words are no longer in modern use.

To add another dimension to this question, some have argued that there are no true synonyms at all, as every single word carries a different shade of meaning. So if you want to start using *poecilonym* or *polyonym* in place of *synonym*, you'd be technically correct—but don't expect anyone else to know what you're talking about.

10 COMMONLY MISUSED WORDS

Language isn't static. It evolves over time, with words taking on new meanings based on common usage (whether correct or not). If you want to impress a grammar purist, check out the proper definitions for these commonly misused words.

1 Bemused

Bemused does not mean "wryly amused." *Bemused* is a synonym for *puzzled* or *bewildered*, while *amused* means "entertained" (though not always—see page 30). Pretending to throw a ball may bemuse your dog; if you find that funny, then you're amused by your pup's bemusement.

2 Climatic

If you want to describe a movie that ended with more of a whisper than a bang, don't call it *anti-climatic*—unless it's also a movie that really hates the weather. The word you're looking for here is *anticlimactic*. *Climatic* relates to the climate or weather, whereas *climactic* refers to something's climax.

3 Electrocuted

If you get mildly zapped while brushing up against an electric fence, you've been shocked, not electrocuted. The latter is much more serious: It's a portmanteau of *electric* and *execution*, so if someone has been electrocuted, that means they were killed or seriously injured by electricity.

4 Fortuitous

It's easy to see why some people use the word *fortuitous* to describe a stroke of good luck—it does, after all, look a lot like *fortune*. But *fortuitous* strictly describes anything that happens by chance, good or bad. Winning a million dollars in the lottery would be fortuitous, as would losing your family's valuable heirlooms in a random burglary.

5

Inflammable

Many believe *inflammable* means "not flammable," but the opposite is actually true: *Inflammable* means "flammable," or "something that can quickly catch fire." The confusion is due to the prefix *in-*; it can have multiple meanings. "Not" is a popular one, but it can also mean "into" or "on," like in *insert* or *install*. *Inflammable* comes from the second meaning. If you want to describe something that *can't* catch fire, use *nonflammable* instead.

6

Ironic

Sorry, Alanis Morissette—rain on a wedding day isn't ironic: it's more unlucky. As Merriam-Webster defines it, *irony* expresses "something other than and especially the opposite of the literal meaning." If the bride in Morissette's song remarked that rain was the perfect weather for her outdoor wedding, then that might be ironic (or sarcastic).

Nauseous

If your stomach starts churning after eating some funky food, you may be tempted to tell your dinner date you have to rush home because you feel *nauseous*. But *nauseous* strictly describes the object that makes a person have nausea, which in this case would be the questionable meal. *Nauseated* is the word you should use to describe your upset stomach.

7

Since

People often use *since* as a synonym for *because*. For grammar purists, that's improper. *Since* refers to the passage of time, as in "I haven't seen him since Sunday," whereas *because* refers to causation, as in "I haven't seen him since Sunday because I've been out of town."

8

9

Systematic

You'll often hear people calling for systematic change when they want to disrupt the status quo. But what they really want is systemic change. *Systematic* is something done according to a set, organized method, like arranging your bookshelf by color. *Systemic*, meanwhile, describes something ingrained within a system.

10

Wave

People don't *wave* their rights to a housing inspection—they *waive* them. The latter means "to give up," whereas the former is a type of motion. But no one's stopping you from giving you from giving a little goodbye wave as you sign a waiver waiving your rights to something.

A Brief History OF THE SINGULAR

The singular form of the word *they* has been endorsed by everyone from Jane Austen to William Shakespeare.

For evidence that language is constantly evolving, look at the history of *they*. The singular form of the pronoun, which has become mainstream in recent years, can describe individuals whose gender isn't specified—replacing the clunky *he or she*—and is used by nonbinary people who identify with the pronoun. The *AP Stylebook* has accepted such functions of *they*, *them*, and *their* since 2017, and Merriam-Webster announced the singular *they* was its word of the year in 2019.

The reinvention of the traditionally plural pronoun may seem sudden, but its second meaning isn't as modern as you may assume: The word has appeared as a singular, gender-neutral pronoun in English literature for centuries.

The plural *they* popped up in English around the thirteenth century, and it didn't take long for its singular form to emerge. As professor and linguist Dennis Baron writes in a post on the *Oxford English Dictionary*'s website, the earliest known instance of the singular *they* can be found in the medieval poem *William and the Werewolf* from 1375. A section translated from the Middle English to modern English reads, "Each man hurried [. . .] till they drew near [. . .] where William and his darling were lying together." Because most language changes develop orally before they're written down, this form of *they* likely had been in use for years by this point.

You don't have to dig through obscure texts to find examples of this version of the word—it's been employed by some of the greatest writers of the English language for centuries. A decade or so after the singular *they* made its debut in print, Geoffrey Chaucer used it in *The Canterbury Tales*. William Shakespeare was a fan of the usage, writing it into several of his plays, including *A Comedy of Errors* and *Hamlet*. Two centuries later, Jane Austen used *they* to replace *he or she* in *Mansfield Park*. She wrote in her 1814 novel, "I would have every body marry if they could do it properly." For centuries, this function of *they* was grammatically accepted. It could transition from plural to singular depending on the situation, similar to the pronoun *you*.

They

Only in the eighteenth century did grammarians declare that the singular *they* was invalid, their reasoning being that a plural pronoun can't take a singular antecedent. Never mind that *you*, which used to be exclusively plural, had undergone this exact change. According to these sticklers, it made more sense to use *he* as a "gender-neutral" pronoun when describing one person.

The antecedent rule is true in a semantic sense, but it ignores the conceptual meaning of the word *they* that wordsmiths have been employing for centuries. "There's a difference between conceptual singularness and grammatical singularness," Kirby Conrod, a lecturer in linguistics at the University of Washington, tells Mental Floss. "A thing is singular if it takes a singular verb agreement. So if it takes *is* in English, that makes it [grammatically] singular."

According to this convention, *you* can never be singular in some versions of English, though anyone who's ever addressed an individual directly knows this isn't the case. "Many varieties of English do not say *they is*," Conrod says. "Similarly, some varieties of English don't say *you is*—some varieties do—so by this measure, *they* and *you* aren't grammatically singular. Conceptually it's a different story."

Jane Austen, Charles Dickens, W. H. Auden, and other writers from the nineteenth century and beyond weren't the only ones who flouted this rule. Most people continued to use the singular *they* in their speech and writing, often without realizing it. This is still true today. Sentences like "everyone should bring their

towel to the beach" or "they always forget their wallet" are technically incorrect according to the rule invented a few hundred years ago, but they sound natural in every day conversation. Replacing *they* in those examples with *he / his* or *she / her*, on the other hand, would feel forced.

Though both usages are conceptually singular, the *they* that has gained prominence in recent years is distinct from the version of the word used in medieval literature. "The very old kind of singular *they*, the one that is used by Chaucer and Shakespeare and all these examples we love to pull out, if you look at all these examples of these hundreds-of-years-old singular *theys*, they are with *each man* or *every person*," Conrod says. "None of them are with *Bob* or *that guy*. The new singular *they* is when we can use *they* with a single, specific person."

The singular *they*, whether it's referring to a specific individual or the general members of a group, is accepted by many major publications today. It also attracts more hate than ever. Because the term is used by many nonbinary people, it's the target of transphobia-fueled attacks. But a word's "proper" usage isn't decided by its most vocal advocates or opponents.

The conventions of a language are shaped by the general population that uses it daily. Based on the singular *they*'s prominence in books, poems, and casual conversation since the fourteenth century, it's earned its spot in the English dictionary.

WHAT'S *the* DIFFERENCE?

Navigating English is tricky, even for people who have spoken the language their whole lives. There are many pairs of words that sound the same, or have very close and sometimes interchangeable meanings. Here are just a few examples— with some tips for how to correctly use each one.

British vs. English

English and *British* don't mean the same thing, because England and Britain aren't the same place. To make a centuries-long story short, England is one of three countries located on the island of Great Britain, along with Wales and Scotland. The United Kingdom's full title is the United Kingdom of Great Britain and Northern Ireland, meaning that England, Wales, Scotland, and Northern Ireland fall under the U.K. umbrella. The island of Ireland (sans Northern Ireland) is its own nation— the Republic of Ireland.

Because England is part of Great Britain, everything English is technically also British, but not everything British is also English.

You shouldn't, for example, refer to the Loch Ness Monster as an English cryptid. It (purportedly) lives in Scotland, so you can call it *Scottish* or *British*. In other words, only things from England are English; anything from England, Scotland, or Wales is British. Ireland is slightly more complicated. If someone hails from the Republic of Ireland, they're simply Irish. Because Northern Irish people qualify for both British and Irish citizenship, however, they might consider themselves British as well as Irish. Plus, since the United Kingdom doesn't have its own adjective, *British* can also be understood to mean "of the United Kingdom"—and Northern Ireland is of the United Kingdom.

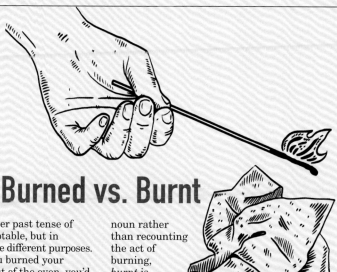

Burned vs. Burnt

Is *burnt* or *burned* the proper past tense of *burn*? Both words are acceptable, but in American English, they serve different purposes. If your instinct is to say you burned your lasagna when you pull it out of the oven, you'd be grammatically correct. When describing the act of burning in the past tense—such as "I burned my finger," or "he burned the firewood"—adding *-ed* to the end of *burn* is the right way to go. Applying *burnt* to these situations, on the other hand, feels awkward when spoken aloud or written on the page.

There is one scenario that calls for *burnt*, though: when the past participle of *burn* is used as an adjective. If you're describing a noun rather than recounting the act of burning, *burnt* is the more appropriate option. Food names like *burnt cream* are good examples of this.

Here's a handy rule of thumb to help you remember: *Burned* is the past tense of the verb *burn*, and *burnt* is a past participle used as an adjective. Both usages are proper words, though, so there's no reason to feel embarrassed about mixing up one with the other.

Can vs. May

In a 1921 entry for his newspaper column "How Do You Say It?: Common Errors in English and How to Avoid Them," Charles N. Lurie laid out the difference between the auxiliary verbs *can* and *may*. The former, he explained, "means to be able to do or to have the power of doing something," while the latter "expresses permission or probability." Many people still think that *can* specifically refers to ability and *may* refers to authorization. Based on twentieth-century etiquette, that's not wrong. But if you assumed there's some etymological history that proves the point, we have some surprising news for you.

According to Merriam-Webster, the first written mentions of *may*, dating back to the eighth century, actually had to do with power or ability; *may* meaning "permission" or "probability" came slightly later. And when *can* arrived around the eleventh century, it didn't refer to permission or ability—it meant "to know." By the fourteenth century, when that definition had evolved into "to be able to," people had already been using *may* in that sense for hundreds of years. The words later became synonyms in situations relating to probability, too; and people finally began co-opting *may*'s "to be allowed to" definition for *can* in the late nineteenth century.

Since *can*-as-permission was still relatively new in the early twentieth century—and *may*-as-permission wasn't—it's not surprising that the era's grammar sticklers felt that "Can I speak to my seatmate?" and similar statements were just wrong. But if correct word usage were always dictated by whatever definition was oldest, we should only be using *may* to talk about power and *can* to talk about knowledge.

These days, it's more common to use *may* for probability and *can* for ability. When it comes to asking permission, however, people will likely understand your meaning either way.

Disinformation vs. Misinformation

On the surface, *disinformation* and *misinformation* have a lot in common: They're both types of false information. In fact, misinformation can sometimes be disinformation, and disinformation can give way to misinformation. But despite their similarities, the two terms aren't exactly interchangeable. Here's a handy mnemonic device to help you keep the two straight: *Mis*information is often a *mis*take—in other words, the person transmitting the intel isn't necessarily trying to make anyone believe something erroneous; in many cases, they don't even know it's erroneous in the first place—while *dis*information is intentionally *dis*honest.

Misinformation is a much older term, first showing up in print during the sixteenth century. The earliest known written instance of *disinformation*, by contrast, is from 1955—possibly derived from the Russian word *dezinformátsiya*. Unsurprisingly, *disinformation* appeared a lot in reference to all the espionage and propaganda that happened on both sides of the Cold War.

Disinterested vs. Uninterested

Disinterested doesn't just mean "uninterested." The latter describes someone who is quite literally not interested in a given thing. (If *Friends* fan theories bore you to tears, you're likely uninterested in hearing why some people believe Rachel dreamed the entire series.) *Disinterested*, meanwhile, usually describes someone who has no vested interest in something, or no particular interest in one side over another; i.e., impartial or unbiased. A judge, for example, shouldn't be uninterested in hearing both sides of a case—but they should be disinterested.

Or, at least, that's what the consensus is among language prescriptivists today. According to Merriam-Webster, the blurry line between these two words has existed for centuries, and when they first arrived on the scene in the early seventeenth century, their definitions were actually reversed. These days, even Merriam-Webster recognizes that *disinterested* can mean "not interested." But if your priority is appeasing the grammar sticklers in your life, you might not want to.

Each vs. Every

If you're a native English speaker, you probably follow certain grammar conventions in speaking and writing without even realizing it. Knowing when to choose *each* over *every* (and vice versa) is one of them: *Every* can be used only if you're talking about more than two items, while *each* works for two or more items. Also, *every* can link up with certain adverbs—like *almost, nearly, virtually,* and *practically*—in a way that *each* can't, which has to do with a subtle distinction between the terms' connotations: *Each* emphasizes individuality, while *every* underscores collectivity.

Equality vs. Equity

Even if you take the time to search for the words *equity* and *equality* in the dictionary, you might walk away thinking they mean the same thing—but the two words (and their derivatives) can't be used interchangeably: *Equality* has to do with giving everyone the exact same resources, whereas *equity* involves distributing resources based on the needs of the recipients.

Consider this example: Three identical boxes are given to three people of different heights to see over a fence—it's an equal distribution of resources, but it fails to consider that the tallest person doesn't need a box to see over the fence, while the shortest person could clearly use an extra one. When the boxes are redistributed equitably, however, all three spectators can watch the game. Equality is about dividing resources in matching amounts, and equity focuses more on dividing resources proportionally to achieve a fair outcome for those involved. Recognizing the difference between equality and equity is important in just about every sphere of life: public health, politics, education, racial justice, and more.

Historic vs. Historical

When it comes to choosing whether to end an adjective with *-ic* or *-ical*, there aren't really any overarching rules to help you. With some words, both suffixes are correct and can be used interchangeably, though one might be more common than the other—like *metaphorical* over *metaphoric*. One could even be so obsolete that it seems wrong: *Scientifical*, for example, is a real word, but people almost invariably opt for *scientific* these days.

In other cases, *-ic* and *-ical* are both correct, but the words they create have separate meanings. *Historic* vs. *historical* is a special situation, because it technically falls into both of the aforementioned categories. According to the *Oxford English Dictionary*, the two terms both mean "relating to history; concerned with past events." They *also* both mean "having or likely to have great historical importance or fame." In short, anything you describe as *historic* can be described as *historical*, too.

That said, *historical* and *historic* aren't necessarily considered synonyms in modern usage. *Historical* is most often used in the "relating to history" sense; *historic* in the "great historical importance" sense. If, for example, you mention a "historic moment," people will likely understand that you're talking about a moment that made history because it was so important or noteworthy. If you mention a "historical moment," on the other hand, people might just assume you're referring to a moment that happened a long time ago.

Insure vs. Ensure

Though both *insure* and *ensure* relate to providing reassurance or security, they aren't exactly synonyms. According to Merriam-Webster, the verb *ensure* means "to make sure, certain, or safe." This definition is the looser of the two words, and it applies to scenarios where the thing being made certain is more abstract. Swimming guidelines at a public pool can ensure the safety of the guests.

Merriam-Webster gives a similar definition for *insure*. The verb is defined as "to make certain especially by taking necessary measures and precautions." That means *insure* can be used in many of the same sentences where *ensure* appears, but it's especially applicable to situations where concrete actions are being taken to guarantee something.

The dictionary also lists another, more specific entry for *insure*: "to provide or obtain insurance on or for." This is the main area where the two words differ. While both terms describe making something certain, only *insure* should be used for legal and financial matters dealing with actual insurance.

There's a reason why these words are so easily confused. Centuries ago, *ensure* and *insure* were just alternate spellings of the same term. It wasn't until the mid-nineteenth century that people started to differentiate them—but many English speakers still use them interchangeably today.

Mistrust vs. Distrust

You can technically use *mistrust* and *distrust* interchangeably without fear of being corrected. As verbs, they both basically mean "to be suspicious of" or "to lack trust in," and their noun forms similarly mean "suspicion" or "a lack of trust." Even the most well-respected dictionaries use the terms to define each other. If you'd prefer to favor the older option, *mistrust* wins by several decades: According to the *OED*, it appeared in print as early as the 1380s. The earliest known reference to *distrust* didn't come until 1430.

Although *mistrust* and *distrust* are essentially lexical twins, they've evolved with their own separate connotations. These days, *distrust* often implies a lack of trust predicated on previous experience or knowledge. *Mistrust*, meanwhile, implies a broader absence of confidence that doesn't necessarily stem from something specific. If your fourth-grade teacher had a tendency to misspell words and mix up facts, you might start to distrust whatever they taught you. But if you, as a kid, had a general sense of suspicion toward all teachers, coaches, and other adults in your life, you could say that you mistrusted authority figures.

You could even make the argument that *distrust* better applies to situations where something caused you to lose trust, while *mistrust* refers to a lack of trust where there never really was any to begin with. It's more a product of the atmosphere than of the past. But, again, these distinctions are based on general trends in modern usage, rather than any hard-and-fast rules.

Titular vs. Eponymous

According to the *OED*, the sense of *titular* as "from whom or which a title or name is taken" has been around for quite a while. In Alban Butler's eighteenth-century work *The Lives of the Fathers, Martyrs, and Principal Saints*, he repeatedly refers to "titular" saints and patrons after which certain churches were named. *Titular* has also been used to describe the thing itself. "Wee reach Medina, the titular towne of the great Duke of Medina," British Jesuit William Atkins wrote in the mid-1600s. In other words, Medina is the titular town of the duke—and the Duke of Medina is the titular duke of the town.

These days, the situation with *eponymous* is similar. The noun *eponym* historically referred to a person (or character) who lent their name to something. The eponym of Ford Motor Company, for example, is Henry Ford. Lady Bird is the eponymous teenager of the film *Lady Bird*. But over time, *eponymous*, too,

has gone the way of *titular*. You might call Ford Motor Company "Henry Ford's eponymous business," or mention that Lady Bird is a hilariously relatable character in her eponymous movie.

If you've been led to believe that *titular* isn't a synonym for *eponymous*, it's probably because *titular* has more than one meaning. Merriam-Webster's first definition of the term refers to having the title and privileges afforded to a particular position without actually having to do the day-to-day work. For example, a CEO who always dines out on the company's dime but rarely shows up to company meetings might be considered a titular CEO; basically, a CEO only in title. But since *titular* has been used so often (and for so long) in the sense we discussed earlier, using it whenever your best friend gets cast as the eponymous character in the school play is totally fine.

Worse vs. Worst

If you're talking about a first date so horrible that no other date could ever come close to being as bad, you could call it the *worst* first date of your life. That's because *worst* is the superlative form of the adjective *bad*—it's the most bad. If you're comparing two dates, you might decide that one was worse than the other. *Worse* is *bad*'s comparative adjective form: You use it when you're comparing two (or more) things. In other words, *worse* is to *better* what *worst* is to *best*.

In situations where it's obvious that you're either comparing things or talking about the most extreme version of something, experienced

English speakers usually use *worse* and *worst* correctly without even thinking about it. *Worse* often precedes *than* (i.e., something is worse than something else) or describes a deterioration over time. For example, if you said, "I'm getting worse at tennis," you're really saying "I'm getting worse at tennis than I was before." Even if you don't actually utter the whole sentence, you're still comparing your current tennis skills to your previous tennis skills. *Worst*, on the other hand, often accompanies terms that convey exaggeration—like *ever*, *in the world*, and *of all time*. As in: "*Ballistic: Ecks vs. Sever* is the worst movie of all time."

Stink vs. Stank vs. Stunk

Stink vs. *stank* is straightforward: Stink refers to the present, and *stank* refers to the past. *Stank* vs. *stunk* is slightly tougher, as both refer to the past. You use *stank* in reference to an instance of stinking that's already over; e.g., "My shoes stank after I ran the marathon." *Stunk*, meanwhile, is a past participle that must always appear after a

helping verb—in this case, the options are pretty much *has*, *have*, or *had*—and indicates a period of stinking that began in the past and may or may not continue; e.g., "My shoes have stunk ever since I ran the marathon," or "After my shoes had stunk for a month, I finally decided to buy new ones." To make things simple: If you're using *has*, *have*, or *had*, go with *stunk*. Otherwise, it should be *stank*.

O M G

The texting shorthand for "Oh my God!" emerged in an old-fashioned manner: in a letter to Winston Churchill way back in 1917. "I hear that a new order of Knighthood is on the tapis— O.M.G. (Oh! My God!)—Shower it on the Admiralty!!" wrote Lord John Fisher, admiral of the fleet.

How
EDGAR ALLAN
POE
HELPED INSPIRE
SCRABBLE

More than 150 million Scrabble games have been sold since New York City architect Alfred Mosher Butts invented it in the 1930s. Every hour, approximately thirty thousand people start a game, which you can buy in around thirty different languages. It has inspired countless fights about spelling and proper nouns, and has taught people how hard it is to use the letter *q* in a word if you lack access to a *u* as well.

But none of this would ever have happened had Butts not been a fan of Edgar Allan Poe.

In Poe's short story "The Gold-Bug," published in 1843, a character solves a cipher that is based on the popularity of English letters. "Now, in English, the letter which most frequently occurs is e. Afterwards, the succession runs thus: a o i d h n r s t u y c f g l m w b k p q x z," he wrote.

While Poe wasn't *quite* accurate with his assessment of the most and least popular letters, the idea of ranking letters by how much they're used in the English language intrigued Butts. (At that point, he was unemployed, and passed the time by studying games like backgammon, chess, and anagrams.) Because such a ranking didn't actually exist, Butts created his own by tediously counting letters in the *New York Times*, the *New York Herald Tribune*, and *The Saturday Evening Post*. After tallying it all up in a complicated grid, he determined that the letters *e, t, a, o, i, n, s, h, r, d, l*, and *u* were used the most (they totaled 80 percent of letters typically used). Then, he devised his own word game.

Butts named his game Lexiko, then changed the name to Criss-Cross Words. His eventual business partner James Brunot suggested several improvements to Butts's concept, including the color scheme, the bonus for using all tiles in a single play, and yet another new name: Scrabble.

Despite the multiple tweaks to name and gameplay, the game wasn't massively popular until the chairman of Macy's allegedly stumbled upon it while on vacation in 1952, and then ordered thousands of sets for his stores. Scrabble has been a hit with word lovers and board game enthusiasts alike ever since, all thanks to a minor point in a nearly two-century-old short story. It's a plot twist Poe probably never would have imagined.

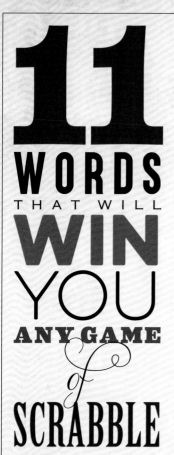

11 WORDS THAT WILL WIN YOU ANY GAME of SCRABBLE

Whether you consider winning at Scrabble a case of extreme luck or supreme spelling ability, here are 11 words that—if conditions are right—will help you trump any opponent.

1. Oxyphenbutazone

DEFINITION: An anti-inflammatory medication used to treat arthritis and bursitis.

CONDITIONS: Possibly the highest-possible scoring word under American Scrabble play—as calculated by Dan Stock of Ohio—has never actually been played . . . and probably never will be (unless you're really, really lucky). That's because it has to be played across three triple word score squares and built on eight already-played (and perfectly positioned) tiles, along with precise words going the other direction (for instance, if *pacifying* gets the *o* in front and becomes *opacifying*; *rainwashing* gets the *b* and becomes *brainwashing*).

POINTS: 1,778

2. Quizzify

DEFINITION: To quiz or question.

CONDITIONS: Not only will you need to draw the game's only *q* and *z* tiles (there's only one of each), but a blank tile, too (in place of the second *z*). Play this verb as your first word across two triple word squares with the *z* on a double letter score square and you've got the game's most valuable eight-letter bingo—but be careful: While it's accepted in most of the world, *quizzify* isn't on the North American word list (but the potentially 401-point *quinzhee* is).

POINTS: 419

3. Oxazepam

DEFINITION: An anti-anxiety drug.

CONDITIONS: All that stress will melt away if you can build on one existing letter, play across two triple word score squares, place the *z* on a double letter score square, and net a fifty-point bingo.

POINTS: 392

4. Quetzals

DEFINITION: The national bird of Guatemala as well as its principal monetary unit.

CONDITIONS: Placement is everything to score this whopper of a word: Building on one letter, use all seven letters on your rack for a fifty-point bingo, with *q* and *s* on triple word score squares and *z* on a double letter score space.

POINTS: 374

5. Quixotry

DEFINITION: A romantic or quixotic idea or action

CONDITIONS: In 2006, Michael Cresta used an already-played *r* and all seven of his tiles across two triple word score squares to earn the North American record for most points ever on a single turn, which aided in a second North American record for the full-time carpenter: the highest-ever individual game score (830 points).

POINTS: 365

6. Flapjack

DEFINITION: A pancake.

CONDITIONS: Placement is a big one for this play. If you can manage to use all your letters to create *flapjack* and ensure it hits two triple word score squares with the *j* on a double, you'll get bingo points and a high score.

POINTS: 356

7. Gherkins

DEFINITION: A small pickle, made from an immature cucumber.

CONDITIONS: In 1985, Robert Kahn paid tribute to the pickle at the National Scrabble Championship in Boston—using an *e* and *r* already on the board—to set a then-record for a non-bingo word score.

POINTS: 180

8. Quartzy

DEFINITION: Resembling quartz.

CONDITIONS: If you're not in North America (where it's not accepted), you can play *quartzy* across a triple word score square with *z* as a double letter score, and get a fifty-point bingo for using all seven letters on your rack.

POINTS: 164

9. Muzjiks

DEFINITION: A Russian peasant.

CONDITIONS: On its own (with no bonuses or extra points), *muzjiks* is worth an impressive twenty-nine points. But exhaust all of your tiles on your first turn to spell it, and you'll earn more than four times that—which is what player Jesse Inman did at the National Scrabble Championships in Orlando in 2008 to earn the record for highest opening score at 126. But he had to use the blank tile for the *u*. If he'd had an actual *u*, he'd have gotten what is theoretically the highest opening score possible.

POINTS: 128

10. Syzygy

DEFINITION: An alignment of three celestial bodies in a system.

CONDITIONS: Forget trying to pronounce it (though, for the record, it's "SIZ-i-jee"). Instead, just remember how to spell it—and that it's worth twenty-one points au naturel. You'll need one blank tile to make up for the lack of *y*s (there are only two in the game). For a higher total, land the *z* on a double letter score square and the final *y* on a triple word score square.

POINTS: 93

11. Za

DEFINITION: Slang term for pizza.

CONDITIONS: Big words are great and all, but two-letter words can also score big—and be especially annoying to your opponent. Build on two *a*s—one directly below, the other directly to the right of a triple letter square—to spell this two-letter delectable across and down.

POINTS: 62

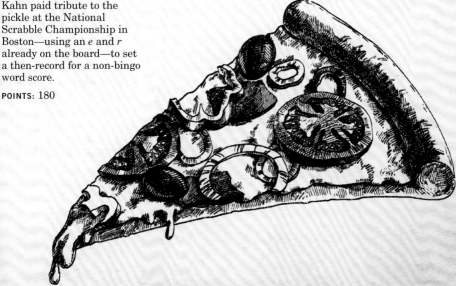

COMMON ENGLISH WORDS *From* NATIVE AMERICAN LANGUAGES

You're probably well aware that *tepee*, *totem*, and *toboggan* are all Native American names for familiar objects, but what about *hickory*, *jerky*, and *tobacco*? Native American languages gave us scores of words for things we frequently use—not to mention the names of many states, rivers, and towns. Here are ten words commonly used in English that were coined by Indigenous groups across the Americas.

Avocado

Sorry, avocado trivia lovers, but the story that this word originally meant "testicle" in Nahuatl, a language spoken by the Aztecs (dialects of which are widely spoken in Mexico today), isn't quite right. According to Nahuatl scholar Magnus Pharao Hansen, the Nahuatl name for the fruit, *ahuacatl*, was also slang for "testicle," but only ever slang. The word *ahuacatl* chiefly described the fruit. It entered Spanish in the late 1600s as *aguacate*, and was eventually anglicized as *avocado*.

Canoe and Kayak

Canoe and *kayak* are both Native American words, but they were coined by different tribes. *Kayak* can be traced back to the Inuit of present-day Greenland, who call the long boat *qajaq*. The word is also present throughout the Inuit-Yupik-Unangan languages. *Canoe*, on the other hand, comes from the Arawakan word *canaoua*. According to the Online Etymology Dictionary, early spellings of *canoe* were *cano*, *canow*, and the Spanish *canoa*, before spelling was standardized in the eighteenth century.

Chocolate

The delicious treat comes to us from nature, but we can thank Indigenous Mesoamericans for this Native American name. The word *chocolate*, like *avocado*, comes from Nahuatl. The Aztecs made a drink from ground cacao seeds called *chikolatl*.

Guacamole

Guacamole stems from two Nahuatl words: *ahuacatl* ("avocado") and *molli* ("sauce"). Mix them together and they make *ahuacamolli*. *Molli*, as fans of chicken mole enchiladas will know, was later spelled *mole* in Mexican Spanish. Tomato (*tomatl*), chili (*chilli*), and chipotle (*chilli* plus *poctli*, meaning "something smoked") are a few other food words that come to us from Nahuatl.

Hammock

This word comes from *hamaca*, whose origins are slightly unclear: It could be from the now-extinct Taíno language (once spoken by Indigenous people in the Caribbean), or from a related Arawakan language. It originally referred to a stretch of cloth and entered the English language via the Spanish (who still call it a *hamaca*).

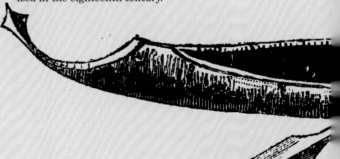

Hurricane

The Maya believed in a "god of the storm," and they called it *Hunraken*. This same word was picked up throughout Central America and the Caribbean to refer to an evil deity. Spanish explorers in the Caribbean changed the spelling to *huracán* and used it to describe the weather phenomenon, and it was finally introduced into English by the sixteenth century.

Opossum

The Native American name of North America's resident marsupial comes from the Virginia Algonquian word *opassum* (alternately spelled *aposoum*), which means "white dog" or "white beast" in the Powhatan language. Skunk, coyote, raccoon, moose, woodchuck, and caribou are a few of the other animals that owe their names to Native American tribes.

Poncho

Indigenous peoples in central Chile who speak Araucanian languages dubbed their shawl-like "woolen fabric" a *pontho*. They were often worn by *huasos*, the cowboys of central and southern Chile. Nowadays, ponchos are commonplace throughout Latin America.

Squash

When English settlers first arrived in North America, they used *squash* as a verb (meaning "to crush something") and, more arcanely, to refer to an unripe pea pod. However, they were unfamiliar with the fruit we now know as squash, according to Merriam-Webster. The Narragansett tribe from present-day New England called it *askútasquash*, which was eventually shortened to *squash* in English.

SEQUOYAH

THE MAN WHO SAVED *the* CHEROKEE LANGUAGE

Born circa the 1760s in what is now Tennessee and trained as a silversmith and blacksmith, Sequoyah, a Cherokee man, was said (according to legend) to have never learned how to read or write in English—but he always knew that literacy and power were intertwined.

During most of Sequoyah's lifetime, the Cherokee language was entirely oral. (A written language may have existed centuries earlier, but the script was supposedly lost as the tribe journeyed east across the continent.) Sometime around 1809, Sequoyah began working on a new system to put the Cherokee language back on the page. He believed that by inventing an alphabet, the Cherokee could share and save the stories that made their way of life unique.

At first, some Cherokee disliked Sequoyah's idea. They saw his attempts to create a written language as just another example of the tribe becoming more like the incoming white settlers—in other words, another example of the tribe losing a grip on its culture and autonomy.

Sequoyah, however, saw it differently: Rather than destroy his culture, he saw the written word as a way to save it. He became convinced that the secret of white people's growing power was directly tied to their use of written language, which he believed was far more effective than collective memories or word of mouth—a belief that was further bolstered after he helped the U.S. Army fight the Creek War in Georgia in 1813. Sequoyah watched soldiers send letters to their families and saw war officers deliver important commands in written form. He found the capability to communicate across space and time profoundly important.

Sequoyah first attempted to invent a logographic system, designing a unique character for every word, but quickly realized he was creating too much unnecessary work for himself. So he started anew, this time constructing his language from letters he found in the Latin, Greek, and Cyrillic alphabets, as well as with some Arabic numerals. He became reclusive, spending hour upon hour working on his alphabet. According to the official website of the Cherokee Nation, people outside his family began whispering that he was meddling with sorcery. By 1821, Sequoyah was too busy to pay the gossip any mind: He was teaching his six-year-old daughter, Ayokeh, how to use the system.

As one story goes, Sequoyah was eventually charged with witchcraft and brought to trial before a town chief, who tested Sequoyah's claims by separating him and his daughter and asking them to communicate through their so-called writing system. By the trial's end, everyone involved was convinced that Sequoyah was telling the truth—the symbols truly were a distillation of Cherokee speech. Rather than punish Sequoyah, the officials asked him a question: *Can you teach us how to read?*

Once accepted by the Cherokee, Sequoyah's eighty-six-character alphabet—which is technically called a *syllabary*—was widely studied. Within just a few years, thousands of people would learn how to read and write, with many Cherokee communities becoming more literate than the surrounding white populations. It wasn't long before the Cherokee language began appearing in books and newspapers: In 1828, the *Cherokee Phoenix* became the first Native American newspaper printed in the United States.

Today, the Cherokee language is considered endangered by UNESCO, but Sequoyah's system remains a landmark innovation—and a source of hope for the future.

DELIGHTFUL
VICTORIAN
Terms
YOU SHOULD BE USING

In 1909, James Redding Ware published *Passing English of the Victorian era, a dictionary of heterodox English, slang and phrase.* "Thousands of words and phrases in existence in 1870 have drifted away, or changed their forms, or been absorbed, while as many have been added or are being added," he wrote in the book's introduction. "'*Passing English*' ripples from countless sources, forming a river of new language which has its tide and its ebb, while its current brings down new ideas and carries away those that have dribbled out of fashion." Ware chronicled many hilarious and delightful words in *Passing English*; we don't know how these phrases ever fell out of fashion, but we propose bringing them back.

Afternoonified

A society word meaning "smart" (as in "fashionable"). Ware demonstrated the usage: "The goods are not 'afternoonified' enough for me."

Arf'arf'an'arf

A figure of speech used to describe drunken men. "[He's] very arf'arf'an'arf," Ware wrote, "meaning that he has had many 'arfs,'" or half-pints of booze.

Back Slang It

Thieves used this term to indicate that they wanted "to go out the back way," in Ware's words.

Bags O' Mystery

An 1850 term for sausages, "because no man but the maker knows what is in them," Ware wrote. "The 'bag' refers to the gut which contained the chopped meat."

Bang Up to the Elephant

This phrase originated in London in 1882, and meant "perfect, complete, unapproachable."

Batty-Fang

Low London phrase meaning "to thrash thoroughly," possibly from the French *battre à fin*.

Benjo

Nineteenth-century sailor slang for "a riotous holiday, a noisy day in the streets."

Bow Wow Mutton

A naval term referring to meat so bad "it might be dog flesh," according to Ware.

Bricky

Brave or fearless. "Adroit— after the manner of a brick," Ware wrote, "said even of the other sex, 'What a bricky girl she is.'"

Bubble Around

A verbal attack, generally made via the press. Ware demonstrated its usage with a sentence from the 1890 novel *The Golden Butterfly*: "I will back a first-class British subject for bubbling around against all humanity."

Butter Upon Bacon

Too much extravagance. Ware included an example sentence: "What—are you going to put lace over the feather—isn't that rather butter upon bacon?"

Cat-Lap

A London society term for tea and coffee that, according to Ware, was "used scornfully by drinkers of beer and strong waters . . . in club-life is one of the more ignominious names given to champagne by men who prefer stronger liquors."

Chuckaboo

A nickname given to a close friend.

Church-Bell

A talkative woman.

Collie Shangies

Quarrels. A term from Queen Victoria's journal, *More Leaves,* published in 1884: "At five minutes to eleven rode off with Beatrice, good Sharp going with us, and having occasional collie shangies (a [Scottish] word for quarrels or rows, but taken from fights between collies) with collies when we came near cottages." (Ware got this term wrong—he spelled it *collie shangles.*)

Cop a Mouse

To get a black eye. "Cop in this sense is to catch or suffer," Ware wrote, "while the colour of the obligation at its worst suggests the colour and size of the innocent animal named."

Daddles

A delightful way to refer to your rather boring hands.

Damfino

This creative cuss is a contraction of *damned if I know*.

Doing the Bear

According to Ware, "courting which involves hugging."

Don't Sell Me a Dog

Popular until 1870, this phrase meant "Don't lie to me!" Apparently, people who sold dogs back in the day were prone to trying to pass off mutts as purebreds.

Door-Knocker

A type of beard "formed by the cheeks and chin being shaved leaving a chain of hair under the chin, and upon each side of mouth forming with mustache something like a door-knocker," Ware wrote.

Enthuzimuzzy

A "satirical reference to enthusiasm" that Ware said was created by Braham the terror (likely John Braham, a famous *tenor* opera singer).

Fifteen Puzzle

Not the game you might be familiar with, but a term meaning "complete and absolute confusion" . . . from the game you might be familiar with.

Fly Rink

An 1875 term for a polished bald head.

Gal-Sneaker

An 1870 term for "a man devoted to seduction," according to Ware.

Gas-Pipes

A term for especially tight pants.

Gigglemug

Ware wrote that a *gigglemug* is "an habitually smiling face."

Got the Morbs

Use of this 1880 phrase indicated temporary melancholy.

Half-Rats

Partially intoxicated.

Kruger-Spoof

Another way to say "lying," from 1896.

Mad as Hops

This term was used to describe someone who was excitable.

Mafficking

An excellent word that meant getting rowdy in the streets.

Make a Stuffed Bird Laugh

According to Ware, this term meant "absolutely preposterous."

Meater

A street term meaning "coward."

Mind the Grease

When walking or otherwise getting around, you could ask people to let you pass, please. Or you could ask them to *mind the grease*, which meant the same thing to Victorians.

Mutton Shunter

An 1883 term for a policeman.

Nanty Narking

A tavern term, popular from 1800 to 1840, that meant "great fun."

Nose Bagger

Someone who takes a day trip to the beach. They bring their own provisions and don't contribute economically at all to the resort they're visiting.

Not up to Dick

Not well? You're not up to dick.

Orf Chump

What you can say when you have no appetite.

Parish Pick-Axe

A prominent nose.

Podsnappery

This term, Ware wrote, describes a person with a "wilful determination to ignore the objectionable or inconvenient, at the same time assuming airs of superior virtue and noble resignation."

Poked Up

Embarrassed.

Powdering Hair

An eighteenth-century tavern term that meant "getting drunk."

Rain Napper

An umbrella.

Sauce-Box

Another term for the mouth.

Shake a Flannin

Why say you're going to fight when you could say you're going to *shake a flannin* instead?

Shoot into the Brown

To fail. According to Ware, "the phrase takes its rise from rifle practice, where the queer shot misses the black and white target altogether, and shoots into the brown i.e., the earth butt."

Skilamalink

Secret, shady, doubtful.

Smothering a Parrot

What you would say if you drank a glass of absinthe neat; the phrase comes from the green color of the booze.

Suggestionize

A legal term from 1889 meaning "to prompt."

Take the Egg

To win.

Umble-Cum-Stumble

According to Ware, this low-class phrase meant "thoroughly understood."

Whooperups

A term meaning "inferior, noisy singers" that could be used liberally today during karaoke sessions.

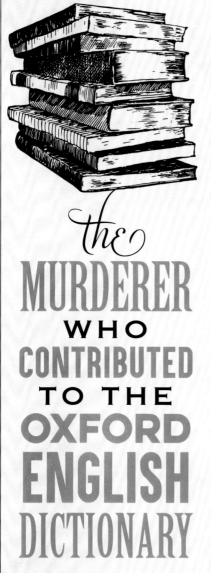

the MURDERER
WHO
CONTRIBUTED
TO THE
OXFORD
ENGLISH
DICTIONARY

O n February 17, 1872, William Chester Minor—a former army surgeon who had been experiencing paranoid delusions—shot and killed a man who Minor claimed had broken into his room. (He hadn't; Minor had pursued his imaginary "attacker" outside and shot a man on his way to work.) Minor was ultimately found not guilty on the grounds of insanity and sentenced to the Asylum for the Criminally Insane, in Broadmoor, England—and from the solitude of his cell, he became one of the most important outside contributors to the most comprehensive reference book in the English language: *The Oxford English Dictionary*.

Unlike your stereotypical glossary, which presents the current usage and meaning of a word, the *OED* tracks a word's evolution: when it entered the language, how its spellings and pronunciations changed over time, when new shades of meaning emerged, etc. Each definition is supported with quotations from books, newspapers, and magazines that show the word being used in that manner, listed in chronological order.

Scouring obscure books for quotations of every word in the English language is no easy feat; it requires the help of hundreds of volunteers. Dr. James Murray, a philologist, published a request for assistance in 1879. Minor, who by that point had been institutionalized at Broadmoor for more than seven years, likely picked up his subscription of *The Athenaeum* and read one of Murray's requests. Minor's cell was filled with towering piles of books, and he quickly got to work.

Instead of copying quotations willy-nilly, Minor flipped through his library and made a word list for each individual book, indexing the location of nearly every word he saw. These catalogs effectively transformed Minor into a search engine. He simply had to reach out to the Oxford editors and ask: *So, what words do you need help with?*

If the editors, for example, needed help finding quotations for the term *sesquipedalia*—a long word that means "very long words"—Minor could review his indexes and discover that *sesquipedalia* was located on page 339 of *Elocution*, on page 98 of *Familiar Dialogues and Popular Discussions*, and so on. He could flip to these pages and then jot down the appropriate quotations. In the 1890s, he sent as many as twenty quotations a day to the subeditors in Oxford. The acceptance rate on his submissions was so high that in the *OED*'s first volume—then called *A New English Dictionary*, published in 1888—Murray added a line of thanks to "Dr. W. C. Minor, Crowthorne." Minor sent in as many as twelve thousand quotes total.

Murray had no idea about his contributor's identity until 1891, when the two exchanged personal letters and agreed to meet at Broadmoor. When Murray arrived, any surprise upon seeing his top contributor confined inside an insane asylum appears to have quickly worn off: The two sat and talked in Minor's cell for hours.

A *Brief History* OF THE PHRASE
Fall off the Wagon

This idiom actually has very little to do with any literal spills. The phrase *on the wagon*—which birthed *off the wagon*—has origins at the turn of the twentieth century and was originally *on the water cart*.

Long before Prohibition, there was a grassroots movement to temper the perceived evils of alcohol. Organizations like the Anti-Saloon League persuaded members to pledge their eternal sobriety to develop better character and set a good example.

Around the same time, it was common for cities to make use of water carts, or water wagons, which were large water tanks towed by horses. The water was used to moisten dusty streets and not really potable. Because of the prevalence of the tank, it became a kind of reference point for those discussing their commitment to sobriety. People said they'd sooner drink from the water wagon than accept a stiff drink. That soon evolved into proclaiming that a person was "on the water wagon."

Once someone hopped on the proverbial water wagon, it followed that a lapse in their devotion would see them fall off the water wagon. As water wagons began to disappear from sight, it simply became "wagon." Whether one was on or off described their current approach to drinking.

Of course, given the right circumstances, it's still possible to fall off the wagon both metaphorically and literally. All you would need is a wagon and way, way too much booze.

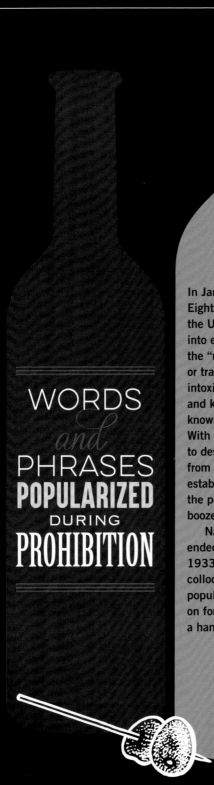

WORDS *and* PHRASES POPULARIZED DURING PROHIBITION

In January 1920, the Eighteenth Amendment to the U.S. Constitution went into effect, prohibiting the "manufacture, sale, or transportation of intoxicating liquors" and kicking off a period known as Prohibition. With it came language to describe everything from drinking establishments to the people who made booze to booze itself.

National Prohibition ended on December 5, 1933, but the colorful colloquialisms it popularized will live on forever. Here are just a handful of them.

Bathtub Gin

A homemade—and usually *poorly* made— gin. It was often concocted in a bottle so tall that it could not be mixed with water from a sink tap and was mixed in a bathtub instead. Though the phrase refers to gin specifically, it came to be used as a general term for any type of cheap homemade booze.

Blind Pig

An illegal drinking establishment (aka a speakeasy) that attempted to evade police detection by charging patrons a fee to gaze upon some sort of exotic creature (e.g., a blind pig) and be given a complimentary cocktail upon entrance. *Blind tiger* was an alternative expression. According to Merriam-Webster, both phrases were used pre-Prohibition, dating back to 1886 and 1857, respectively.

Blotto

Extremely drunk, often to the point of unconsciousness. According to the *Oxford English Dictionary*, this term originated in 1917.

Bootician

Writer H. L. Mencken referred to bootleggers as *booticians*, a word that he said "met a crying need" when he came up with it in 1925: Apparently, the press quickly picked it up, and at least one bootlegger gave his profession as "bootician" when he was arrested in the early 1930s.

Brick of Wine

Oenophiles looking to get their vino fix could do so by simply adding water to a dehydrated block of juice and storing it for a few weeks, at which point it would become wine. (And you thought a *box* of wine was bad!)

Dry

A noun used in reference to a person who is opposed to the legal sale of alcoholic beverages. Bureau of Prohibition agents were often referred to as Dry Agents (though corruption among this crew ran rampant). As an adjective, it describes a place where alcohol is not served.

Giggle Water

This term for champagne originated in 1910. Later, it referred more generally to alcoholic beverages, especially ones made of whiskey or gin.

Hooch

Low-quality liquor, usually whiskey. The term originated in the late 1800s as a shortened version of *Hoochinoo*, a distilled beverage from Alaska that became popular during the Klondike gold rush. The phrase came back into heavy use in the 1920s.

Jake Walk

A *jake walk* is paralysis or loss of muscle control in the leg due to an over-consumption of Jamaican ginger, aka Jake, a legal substance with an alcoholic base. The numbness led sufferers to walk with a distinct gait that was also known as *Jake leg* or *Jake foot*.

Juice Joint

Initially a term for a soda stand, according to the *OED*, *juice joint* dates back to 1927 and came to be used to refer to anywhere booze is served. It became a term for a speakeasy in the 1930s.

White Lightning

According to *Detroit Beer: A History of Brewing in the Motor City*, "white lightning was the whiskey equivalent of bathtub gin. Both were highly potent, illegally made, and poor-quality spirits."

Teetotaler

A person who abstains from the consumption of alcohol. According to Merriam-Webster, the word *tee* was used to emphasize words like *total* and *totally* in the early nineteenth century, but the word *teetotaler* didn't appear until 1834, just a few years after the American Temperance Society was founded. The *tee* here isn't related to the beverage; as Merriam-Webster notes, it's "a reduplication of the letter *T* that begins *total*, emphasizing that one has pledged total abstinence."

Wet

The opposite of dry, a wet is a person who supports the legal sale of alcoholic beverages or a place where liquor is in full supply.

Whale

A heavy drinker.

Why Are Some Liquors Called **Spirits**?

The way your behavior can change after a few shots of tequila might make you feel like you've been inhabited by the spirit of someone who was clearly the life of the party during their corporeal heyday, and one theory suggests that we call some liquors *spirits* because of alcohol's association with one spirit in particular: the Holy Spirit, which, together with God and Jesus, forms the Holy Trinity in most Christian denominations.

This theory is based primarily on certain places in the Bible where the effects of the Holy Spirit are juxtaposed with alcohol's effects. In the New Testament, for example, when Jesus's disciples are "filled with the Holy Spirit" during Pentecost and begin to speak in other languages, some bystanders jokingly write off their strange behavior as a symptom of having drunk too much wine.

A more likely explanation has to do with the etymology of the word *alcohol*, which is thought to have come from either of two old Arabic words. The first option is *al-ghawl*, which literally means "spirit" and is even mentioned in the Qur'an as a spirit or demon that imbues wine with its intoxicating effects.

Though that origin story seems logical enough, the second option, *al-koh'l*, is pretty plausible, too—and more widely accepted. The word *al-koh'l* described an eyeliner made from a black powdery mineral called *stibnite*. Since the method of transforming stibnite into makeup was similar to how people distilled liquids, *al-koh'l* may have gotten co-opted to mean "anything that was distilled." And *spirit*—according to this idea—emerged as an alchemist term to represent volatile substances that got separated in the distillation process.

When the word *alcohol* showed up in English during the sixteenth century, it was used to describe a powder before it became the spirit or essence distilled from some other substance, as in *alcohol of wine*. All things considered, it's not surprising that people eventually just started calling those spirits *spirits*.

From
FARTS TO FLOOZY:
THESE ARE THE
FUNNIEST WORDS IN ENGLISH,
ACCORDING TO SCIENCE

*F*art. *Booty. Tinkle. Weiner.* We know these words have the ability to make otherwise mature individuals laugh, but how? And why? Is it their connotations to puerile activities? Is it the sound they make? And if an underlying structure can be found to explain why people find them humorous, can we then objectively determine a word funnier than *bunghole*?

Chris Westbury, a professor of psychology at the University of Alberta, believes we can. With co-author Geoff Hollis, Westbury published a paper ("Wriggly, Squiffy, Lummox, and Boobs: What Makes Some Words Funny?") online in the *Journal of Experimental Psychology: General.* The pair analyzed an existing list of 4,997 funny words compiled by the University of Warwick and assessed by eight hundred survey participants, whittling down the collection to the two hundred words the people found funniest. Westbury wanted to see how a word's phonology (sound), spelling, and

meaning influenced whether people found it amusing, as well as the effectiveness of incongruity theory—the idea that the more something subverts expectations, the funnier it gets.

With incongruity theory in mind, Westbury was able to generate various equations that attempted to predict whether a person would find a single word amusing. He separated the words into categories—insults, sexual references, party terms, animals, names for body parts/ functions, and profanity. Among the words examined were *gobble, boogie, chum, oink, burp,* and *turd.*

Upchuck topped one chart, followed by *bubby* and *boff,* the latter a slang expression for sexual intercourse. Another equation found that *slobbering, puking,* and *fuzz* were reliable sources of amusement. Words with the letters *k* and *y* also scored highly, and the vowel sound /u/ appeared in 20 percent of words the University of Warwick study deemed funny, like *pubes, nude,* and *boobs.*

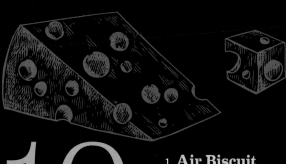

10
WAYS to SAY
FART

Over the course of history, the human race has come up with many delightfully creative ways to describe the act of breaking wind. From regional terms to old-timey phrases, here are a few creative ways to say *fart* that you should work into conversation whenever toots come up.

1. Air Biscuit
According to *Green's Dictionary of Slang*, an *air biscuit* is a super stinky fart or burp. The phrase dates back to the early nineties and originated in the South, but clearly needs to be used everywhere. The act of farting or belching is known as *floating an air biscuit*, by the way.

2. Breezer
A 1920s term for an open-topped car and also an early seventies Australian term for a fart.

3. Bottom Burp
Don't call it a *fart*; call it a *bottom burp*. The phrase gained popularity after it was used on the 1980s British TV show *The Young Ones*.

4. Cheeser
Once a term for a person who made cheese, according to *Partridge's Dictionary of Slang and Unconventional English*, *cheeser* has meant "a smelly fart" since 1811. It's not the only cheese-related fart term, either: Perhaps you've asked "Who cut the cheese?" when you've smelled a particularly nasty odor. According to *Green's*, this phrase for farting came about because of just how smelly some cheeses are, and the *Oxford English Dictionary* dates oral usage back to 1959. *Squeeze cheese* is another delightful phrase, seemingly born of the internet, for a loud fart.

5. Fartick
Use this term, from the early 1900s, to refer to a tiny toot. You can also use the term *fartkin*. Scientists, by the way, have determined that the median volume of a fart is around ninety milliliters.

6. Fizzle
This word, which originated in the sixteenth century, originally meant "to defecate." But by the mid-seventeenth century, *fizzle* (also spelled *fisle*) had acquired an additional meaning: "to fart."

7. Foist
In the late 1500s, the word *foist* was used to describe something that smelled pretty musty; it was also a verb meaning "to break wind silently." In other words, it's a more polite way to describe flatulence that's silent but deadly.

8. Prat Whids
Prat (like *pratfall*) is a sixteenth-century British cant word for the buttocks. *Whid* is a cant word meaning "to speak or tell" or "to lie." So this phrase for breaking wind literally means "buttock speaks."

9. Raspberry Tart
Horse and cart, raspberry tart, heart and dart, and *D'Oyly Carte* are all ways to say *fart*, many originating in England. Welcome to the wonderful world of rhyming slang!

10. Trump
This word, meaning "to fart," dates back to the fifteenth century. It's also been used as a noun since the early eighteenth century. Either way, it's derived from the sound of a trumpet, which makes total sense.

Why Do We Say

Fun though it would be, *PU* does not stand for "Pretty unsavory!," "Putrid, ugh!," or even "Please use (deodorant)!"

In fact, it's not an initialism at all. According to Grammarphobia, the exclamation likely derives from *pew*, an early seventeenth-century word used to voice one's contempt. It's also been spelled *pue*, *peuh*, *peugh*, and even *pyoo*. While all those iterations are technically pronounced as one syllable, the leading theory is that people drew it out over two syllables—"pee-YOO"—for added flair. This is not unlike how you might say "Bee-YOO-ti-ful!" instead of "Beautiful!" when you spot, for example, a fancy pigeon. Since "Pee-YOO!" sounds exactly like the letters *PU*, it's not hard to believe that everyone eventually started thinking that's how it was spelled.

That said, the *pew*-to-*PU* pipeline isn't the only theory behind the expression. It's also been suggested that it comes from the Indo-European word *pu*, meaning "to rot or decay," or the Latin verb *putere*, meaning "to stink." There are quite a few terms with ties to *putere* and other related Latin words (like *putrere*, meaning "to rot," and *puter* or *putridus* for "rotten"). These include, among others, *pus*, *putrid*, and the sixteenth-century noun *putor*, meaning "a bad or unpleasant smell." And those words trace back (along with many words in Indo-European languages, like English's *foul*) to the Proto-Indo-European *pŭ-*, meaning "to rot."

In short, the letters *PU* have been associated with stench for a long time. As for whether the expression *PU* came directly from there or arose in England (or somewhere else) much later, we can't be sure.

When Something Stinks?

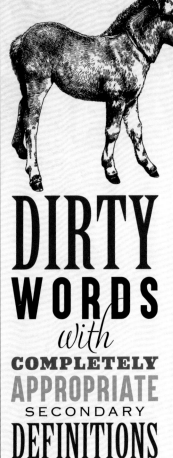

DIRTY WORDS

with

COMPLETELY

APPROPRIATE

SECONDARY

DEFINITIONS

Some words sound dirty but actually aren't. Others *don't* sound dirty, but their etymology suggests otherwise. And then there are those words that usually are considered dirty—though only in certain contexts. From *titty* to *boner*, here are nine inappropriate words whose lesser-known definitions don't ruffle any feathers.

Ass

It's a donkey, it's a derrière, and it's a multi-purpose curse word. But if you're making paper by hand, per the *Oxford English Dictionary*, it's a "curved wooden post" along the rim of your vat that you can place your mold on while it drains. It's sometimes referred to as a *donkey-rest*.

Boner

Boners are slaughterhouse employees responsible for stripping meat from animal bones, as well as cows whose meat is only good for lesser beef products. But to Victorian schoolchildren, *boners* were punches or other bodily blows. In Edmund Lechmere's 1844 drama *The Charter House Play*, for instance, one schoolboy reacts to a classmate's kitchen calamity with this rhyming response:

> *"Poor Scrub! what licks, what boners I foresee; I'm hanged if I a'nt glad it was not me."*

Booby

Primarily in Australia, the *booby* (or the *boob*) is traditionally a prison. You can even boob someone, meaning "put them in prison." *Booby house* is another old synonym for *prison*; it can also refer to a closed compartment or cabin on a ship. And *booby* alone (plus *booby hack*, *booby hut*, and *booby hutch*) also once described an enclosed horse-drawn sleigh common in New England. In 1870, for example, the *Boston Post* mentioned "two elegant new Boobies, nearly finished."

Dildo

Nobody really knows where the word *dildo* came from. But when it first started appearing in print in the late sixteenth and early seventeenth centuries, people were using it in songs and poems as a lilting nonsense word not unlike *la*. Here's an example from Robert Jones's 1601 *Second Book of Songs and Ayres*:

> *"Sweet, now go not yet, I pray;*
> *Let no doubt thy mind dismay.*
> *Here with me thou shalt but stay*
> *Only till I can display*
> *What I will do*
> *With a dildo,*
> *Sing do with a dildo."*

It's unclear whether such songs had anything to do with *dildo* in the sex toy sense, which started cropping up in print around the same time.

Poop

The history of *poop* doesn't just involve feces and ship decks. Back in the sixteenth century, it could mean "to fool or deceive." "Ay, she quickly pooped him; she made him roast-meat for worms," one character says in Shakespeare's *Pericles, Prince of Tyre*. *Poop* was also a twentieth-century military slang term for the latest information—especially if it was confidential or important enough to be memorized.

Prick

If you're not using *prick* as a personal insult or slang for male genitalia, it might just be functioning as a synonym for *pierce* or *poke*. It also once described wine or beer whose flavor had gone sour; as in, "All the wine that pricks," from a 1731 essay by Peter Shaw. *Prick a hare* meant "to track a hare"; and *prick and praise* meant "the praise of excellence or success," per the *OED*.

In the sixteenth and seventeenth centuries, some people even used *prick* as a term of endearment for men—though this trend was almost definitely related to the *prick*-as-*penis* sense. "Ah, ha! are we not alone, my prick? . . . Let us go together into my inner bed-chamber," a character says in Desiderius Erasmus's *Colloquies*, translated in 1671.

Slut

When Samuel Pepys called one of his domestic staff members "a most admirable slut" in a 1660s diary entry, he didn't intend to offend. At the time, *slut* could refer to a scullery maid or any other lowly female servant. It was also just a catch-all term for *female*. "We country sluts of merry Fressingfield / Come to buy needless naughts, to make us fine," one character says in Robert Greene's Elizabethan comedy *Friar Bacon and Friar Bungay*.

Titty

In nineteenth-century England, you might call a cat or kitten a *titty*—or, even better, a *titty pussy*. *Tit* also has a whole host of meanings (some obsolete, some not) that have nothing to do with breasts. As a noun, it could refer to a young or small man, a young or small horse, a tug or pull, a steel rod used in nail manufacturing, and more. To *tit* someone in medieval Scotland, meanwhile, meant to grab them by force or put them to death by hanging.

Twat

Twat, in British slang, can mean to hit someone or something. But in Robert Browning's 1841 verse drama *Pippa Passes*, he used it to describe a nonspecific item— maybe part of a habit— that nuns wear:

> *"Then, owls and bats,*
> *Cowls and twats,*
> *Monks and nuns, in*
> *a cloister's moods,*
> *Adjourn to the*
> *oak-stump pantry!"*

This was strange, considering *twat* had never been used to discuss a nun's garb before, and *Oxford English Dictionary* co-founder Frederick J. Furnivall later wrote to Browning inquiring about the word choice. The poet responded that he'd heard the term in a seventeenth-century ballad called "Vanity of Vanities, or Sir Harry Vane's Picture," which contains these bawdy lines:

> *"They talk't of his having*
> *a Cardinalls Hat,*
> *They'd send him as soon*
> *an Old Nuns Twat"*

As Browning wrote in his letter to Furnivall, "the word struck me as a distinctive part of a nun's attire that might fitly pair off with the cowl appropriated to a monk." The ballad was not, unfortunately, talking about attire.

20 WEIRD OLD WORDS *for* BODILY AILMENTS

Need a better word to describe what ails you? Look no further than this list of old, unusual ways to describe your aches, pains, and whatever else is happening in your body.

1

Acronyx

An ingrown nail, from the Greek words meaning "point" and "nail."

2

Avinosis

The next time airplane turbulence has you reaching for that barf bag, don't say you're airsick—say you're experiencing *avinosis*.

3

Bdelygmia

According to *Mrs. Byrne's Dictionary of Unusual, Obscure, and Preposterous Words*, *bdelygmia* (pronounced "del-IG-me-uh") means "nausea." *A Dictionary of Psychological Medicine* from 1892 defines the word, which has Greek origins, as "an old term used by Hippocrates for a morbid loathing of food."

4

Bromopnea

Bad breath by any other name definitely doesn't smell as sweet. *Bromopnea* comes from two Greek words: *bromos*, meaning "stench," and *pnoe*, meaning "breath."

5

Buccula

This word for a double chin comes from the Latin for "small cheek." Fun fact: You can also call a double chin *submental fullness*.

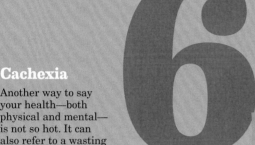

6

Cachexia

Another way to say your health—both physical and mental—is not so hot. It can also refer to a wasting disorder that affects the body.

7

Desudation

Anyone walking around in the summer heat will want to use this word, which dates back to 1728 and means "excessive sweating."

8

Down in the Gills

If you're going through a bout of depression, rather than saying you're down in the dumps, consider using *down in the gills* from 1853.

9

Ecchymosis

A word for a bruise that dates back to the 1500s.

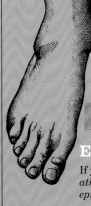

10

Epidermophytosis

If you don't want to call it *athlete's foot*, simply go with *epidermophytosis*.

11

Epistaxis

A nosebleed is much more dramatic when you call it *epistaxis*. It came into English from Ancient Greek by way of Latin.

12

Horripilation

Another word for goose bumps— so-named because they make your skin look like a plucked goose, by the way.

Kakidrosis

Another word for body odor, *kakidrosis* derives from Greek and translates to "bad sweat."

13

14

Lassipedes

Another way to say you have tired feet.

Obdormition

Originally a seventeenth-century word that described falling or being asleep, by the 1850s *obdormition* came to refer to a limb being numb. So when your arm or leg falls asleep, use this fancy word to describe what's happening instead.

Ombrosalgia

If you're a person whose joints start to ache during rain, congratulations— you're suffering from *ombrosalgia*.

Podobromhidrosis

Smelly feet or, as the 1913 book *An Illustrated Dictionary of Medicine, Biology and Allied Sciences* puts it, "offensive sweating of the feet."

Sternutation

Another way to describe a sneeze.

Saprostomous

Saprostomous means "having foul breath" and translates from Greek to "rotten mouth."

Tragomaschlia

This is the medical term for smelly armpits. The word is derived from the Greek word *tragos,* meaning "goat," and *maschale*, or "the armpit."

16 17 18 19 20 5

Why Is It Called the *Placebo Effect*?

Back in the thirteenth century, the term *placebo* didn't call to mind clinical trials, sugar pills, or anything remotely medical. Instead, if you were a member of the Roman Catholic Church, it would likely have made you think of God and death.

Placebo means "I will please" in Latin, and according to the *Oxford English Dictionary*, it's "the first word of the first antiphon of vespers in the Office for the Dead"—an evening prayer that Catholics recited for people who had died. (The full line translates to "I will please the Lord in the land of the living.") Before long, people started using *placebo* to refer to the entire prayer.

By the following century, however, imaginative English speakers had given *placebo* a secondary definition that echoed its literal Latin meaning: If you said someone was singing, making, or playing placebo, you were implying that they were flattering someone in a sycophantic or servile way. You could even just cut to the chase and call the person themselves a *placebo*. We have Geoffrey Chaucer to thank for the earliest known instance of this; in "The Merchant's Tale" (from *The Canterbury Tales*),

he named one of the characters Placebo. Placebo, unsurprisingly, spends a lot of time telling his older brother exactly what he wants to hear, while a third brother, Justinus, gives much better advice.

The word *placebo*—which at that point referred to flattery with the intent to make someone feel good, even if it's not necessarily true—eventually landed in medicine, where it came to define any drug or treatment meant to make someone feel good, even if it technically had no medical potency. But it didn't get there until well into the eighteenth century. "Where a *placebo* merely is wanted, the purpose may be answered by means, which, although perhaps reduced under the *materia medica*, do not, however, deserve the name of medicines," physician Andrew Duncan wrote in his 1770 book *Elements of Therapeutics*.

The full phrase *placebo effect* didn't become common until the early 1900s. The twentieth century also saw the birth of *placebo*'s evil twin—*nocebo* (Latin for "I will harm"), which describes a medically worthless or empty treatment that somehow causes a patient to feel worse. Needless to say, *nocebo* hasn't exactly caught on in the same way that *placebo* has.

10 WAYS TO SAY...

Jabbed with a thorn, scalded by a microwaved dish, or nipped by a "friendly" cat—life is full of ways to provoke an "Ouch!" (from the German *autsch*) from even the most stoic types. If you're in pain but want to avoid a cliché, check out ten alternative interjections to yelp out instead.

1. Argh!

Argh and its variants date to the 1800s but might be best associated with Charlie Brown's complete inability to kick a football.

2. Cussadang!

This regional exclamation from Arizona combines *cuss* and *dang* to create a hybrid yowl.

3. Dagnabbit!

This interjection for annoyance has since taken on a self-aware nod at rural stereotypes, but it still works just fine when your knee hits the IKEA coffee table in your suburban apartment.

4. Feck!

This slang Irish euphemism for another four-letter f-word comes in handy when you want to invoke an expletive without offending anyone.

5. Oof!

People have been simulating the sound a person makes when quickly expelling air through their mouth since the 1700s.

6. Ooyah!

Primarily a Scottish exclamation, *ooyah* can be seen in mid-twentieth-century literature. Don't confuse it for the battle cry of the United States Navy SEALS (*hooyah*) or an exclamation of satisfaction (*booya*).

7. Uff-Da!

Norwegians and Midwesterners like to interject *uff-da* when expressing pain or disgust. *Uff* is a Norwegian exclamation for "oh." *Da* means "there." It's roughly translated to "oh, no" or, "oh, for gosh sakes" and was probably brought to Minnesota (and the script for 1996's *Fargo*) by Norwegian settlers in the 1850s.

8. Wirra!

This Irish expression for pain, regret, or surprise goes back to 1825. Precede it with *oh* to get the full effect: *Oh, wirra, that's one stubbed toe!*

9. Yarooh!

This early-twentieth-century interjection was popularized by fictional British schoolboy Billy Bunter, the creation of author Charles Hamilton. (It's *hooray* spelled backward.) Hamilton would often add extra *o*s to express Bunter's level of discomfort. A real problem might net a simple *yarooh*, while a major infliction warranted a *yarooooh*.

10. Yow!

Australians and New Zealanders use it to indicate amazement, but it's also been used to express pain in English since the early twentieth century.

ANIMAL-RELATED *Words* EVERY PET PARENT SHOULD KNOW

For centuries, dogs were dogs and cats were cats. They did things like bark and drink water and lie down—actions that pet parents didn't need a translator to understand.

Then the internet arrived. Scroll through the countless Facebook groups and Twitter accounts dedicated to sharing cute animal pictures, and you'll quickly see that dogs don't have snouts, they have snoots. Cats, meanwhile, come in a colorful assortment of shapes and sizes ranging from smol to floof.

Pet meme language has been around long enough to start leaking into everyday conversation. If you're a pet owner (or lover) who doesn't want to be out of the loop, here are the terms you need to know.

Blep

If you've ever caught a cat or dog poking the tip of its tongue past its front teeth, you've seen a blep in action. Unlike a derpy tongue (see below), a *blep* is subtle and often gone as quickly as it appears. Animal experts aren't entirely sure why pets blep, but in cats it's been suggested that it may have something to do with the Flehmen response, in which they use their tongues to "smell" the air.

Boof

A low, deep bark—perhaps from a dog that can't decide if it wants to expend its energy on a full bark—is best described as a *boof* (a meaning that dates all the way back to 1906). Consider a boof a warning bark before the real thing.

Bork

According to some corners of the internet, dogs don't bark, they *bork*. Listen carefully next time you're around a vocal doggo and you won't be able to unhear it.

Derp

Unlike most items on this list, the word *derp* isn't limited to cats and dogs. It can also be a stand-in for such expressions of stupidity as *duh* or *dur*. In recent years, the term has become associated with clumsy, clueless, or silly-looking cats and dogs. A pet with a tongue perpetually hanging out of its mouth is textbook derpy.

Doggo

This word isn't hard to decode. Every dog—regardless of size, floofiness, or derpiness—can be a *doggo*. If you're willing to get creative, the word can even be applied to non-dog animals like fennec foxes (*special doggos*) or seals (*water doggos*). The usage of *doggo* saw a spike in 2016 thanks to the internet, and by the end of 2017 it was listed as one of Merriam-Webster's "Words We're Watching."

Floof

Some pets barely have any fur; others have coats so voluminous that hair appears to make up the bulk of their body weight. Dogs and cats in the latter group are known as *floofs*. Floofy animals will famously leave a wake of fur wherever they sit and can squeeze through tight spaces despite their seemingly enormous girth. Samoyeds, Pomeranians, and Persian cats are all prime examples of floofs.

Mlem

Mlems and *bleps*, though very closely related, aren't exactly the same. While *blep* is a passive state of being, *mlem* is active. It's what happens when a pet flicks its tongue in and out of its mouth, whether to slurp up water, taste food, or just lick the air in a derpy fashion. Dogs and cats do it, of course, but reptiles have also been known to mlem.

Pupper

Like *doggo*, *pupper* is self-explanatory: It can be used in place of the word *puppy*, but if you want to use it to describe a fully-grown doggo who's particularly smol and cute, you can probably get away with it.

Smol

Some pets are so adorably, unbearably tiny that using proper English to describe them just doesn't cut it. Not every small pet is *smol*: To earn the label, a cat or dog (or kitten or puppy) must excel in both the tiny and cute departments. A pet that's truly smol is likely to induce excited squees from everyone around it.

Snoot

Snoot was already a dictionary-official synonym for *nose* by the time dog meme culture took the internet by storm. But while *snoot* is rarely used to describe human faces today, it's quickly becoming the preferred term for pet snouts. There's even a wholesome viral challenge dedicated to dogs poking their snoots through their owners' hands.

Sploot

You know your pet is fully relaxed when they're doing a sploot. Like a split but for the whole body, a *sploot* occurs when a dog or cat stretches so their belly is flat on the ground and their back legs are pointing behind them. The amusing pose may be a way for them to take advantage of the cool ground on a hot day, or just to feel a satisfying stretch in their hip flexors. Corgis are famous for the sploot, but any quadruped can do it if they're flexible enough.

Why Do We Call People Blamed for Things **Scapegoats**?

From Marie Antoinette to the cow that reportedly caused the Great Chicago Fire of 1871, history is filled with figures who were single-handedly—yet often undeservedly—held responsible for epic societal failures or misdeeds. In other words, they became scapegoats. But what did goats (who are actually pretty awesome creatures) do to deserve association with this blameable bunch?

The word *scapegoat* was first coined by English Protestant scholar William Tyndale in his 1530 English translation of the Pentateuch, according to David Dawson's 2013 book *Flesh Becomes Word: A Lexicography of the Scapegoat, or, the History of an Idea*. Tyndale, who was deciphering Hebrew descriptions of Yom Kippur rituals from the Book of Leviticus, recounted a ceremony in which one of two goats was selected by lot. A high priest would place his hands on the goat's head and confess his people's sins— thus transferring them to the animal—before casting it out into the wilderness to rid Israel of its transgressions. The other goat would be sacrificed to the Lord.

Tyndale coined the word *scapegoat* to describe the sin-bearing creature, interpreting the Hebrew word *azazel* or *Azazel* as *ez ozel*, or "the goat that departs or escapes." That said, some scholars have disagreed with his interpretation, claiming that *Azazel* actually stands for the name of a goat-like wilderness demon, whom the offering was meant for, or a specific location in the desert to where sins were banished, often thought to be a mountainous cliff from which the scapegoat was cast off and killed.

Over the centuries, the word *scapegoat* got disassociated from its biblical meaning and co-opted as a metaphor to describe a person who receives the blame for any wrongdoing. Now that you know the word's etymology, remember the poor animals that inspired it, and maybe resolve to go a little easier on the next person who ends up having to take the fall for everyone else's mistakes.

50
COLLECTIVE
NOUNS
For
GROUPS OF
ANIMALS

You know which animals move in packs, schools, and herds, but what about a wake, a business, or a flamboyance? Collective nouns—words that indicate a particular group—date back to the fifteenth century, and many of the animal variety can be traced to the *Book of St. Albans*, a manual of sorts for gentlemen published in 1486. (Whether or not they were actually part of popular usage at the time, or simply became popular because of the success of *St. Albans*, is up for debate.) Though the collective nouns on this list may seem a little strange or weird today, at the time they were anything but.

1. An Ambush of Tigers
Since tigers tend to be solitary creatures, a grouping of them would certainly feel like an ambush.

2. A Bale of Turtles
Supposedly, a group of turtles who are cozy in their shells would look like a field of round or squarish hay bales.

3. A Barrel of Monkeys
Not just a game—it's a real term. Monkeys can also congregate as a carload, troop, or tribe.

4. A Battery of Barracudas
Just one barracuda is intimidating, but a *battery* of them? Time to retreat!

5. A Bunch of Worms
Not terribly creative, but when in doubt, just say "a bunch" of whatever.

6. A Business of Ferrets
The *Book of St. Albans* gave ferrets the collective term *busyness* ("besynes"), which today has become *business*.

7. A Cackle of Hyenas
While *clan* is the much more accepted term, there's something very appropriate about *cackle*. And though their laughs and giggles sound entertaining, they're really how spotted hyenas express anger, frustration, and warnings to stay away.

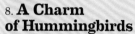

8. A Charm of Hummingbirds
If just one hummingbird is charming, can you imagine how charming a whole group of them would be?

9. A Coterie of Prairie Dogs
While full towns of prairie dogs are called *colonies*, the close-knit, individual family units are called *coteries*.

10. A Covey of Quail
While they can also group as a flock or a bevy, *a covey of quail* sounds much more poetic.

11. A Dazzle of Zebras
They're more commonly called a *herd*, but a *zeal* or *dazzle* of zebras has such a nice ring to it.

12. A Descent of Woodpeckers
Woodpeckers are far more known for their wood-pecking style of foraging for food, but another method some have is to quickly dive-bomb anthills and termite mounds.

13. A Destruction of Cats
A *destruction* refers specifically to a group of wild or feral cats. A group of domesticated cats is a *clowder*.

14. An Exaltation of Larks

An *exaltation of larks* also dates back to the fifteenth century *Book of St. Albans* (which, because of its heraldry section, also happened to be the first book in England to be printed in color).

15. A Family of Sardines

There are more than a dozen fish that can be labeled *sardine* in the supermarket. So in this case, *family* means "a large grouping," rather than "parents and children."

16. A Fever of Stingrays

At the very least, swimming with a fever of stingrays would surely cause your blood pressure to rise.

17. A Flamboyance of Flamingos

Kudos to the creator of this perfect term.

18. A Gam of Whales

Gam is a possible derivative of the word *gammon*, meaning "talk intended to deceive." Considering scientists have only just recently begun thinking they can decipher whale calls, we'd say the gam's gammon is pretty effective.

19. A Gaze of Raccoons

The males are called *boars* and the females *sows*.

20. A Generation of Vipers

A group of snakes is generally called a *pit*, *nest*, or *den*, but they're usually thought of as solitary creatures, so collective nouns for specific types of snakes are more fanciful. A *generation of vipers* likely originates from the King James translation of the Bible, in which Matthew 23:33 reads "Ye serpents, ye generation of vipers, how can ye escape the damnation of hell?"

21. A Harem of Seals

Specifically, when you have a group of females with a dominant male, it's a *harem*. If it's just some breeding seals hanging out, it's a *rookery*.

22. A Hover of Trout

Since trout tend to swim in groups near the bottom of a lake or river, they likely look like they're hovering over the bed of the waterway. Alternately, this collective noun may come from an old term for an overhanging rock where fish—like trout—can hide.

23. An Implausibility of Gnus

This one was coined by James Lipton—yes, the host of *Inside the Actors Studio*—and no one seems to know what he was going for. But it is poetic.

24. A Kaleidoscope of Butterflies

Groups of butterflies can also be called *flutters*.

25. A Memory of Elephants

Sure, a *herd* of elephants is the more common collective, but *memory* is also a term that's used. No idea why a *pack of pachyderms* didn't catch on . . .

26. A Mob of Kangaroos

And just like in human mobs, there's usually a leader (a "boomer," or adult male) who is only in power for a short while before being challenged and defeated by a rival boomer.

27. A Murder of Crows

In the fifteenth century, crows were considered to be omens of death and messengers from the devil—hence this spooky nickname (which doesn't have a basis in fact, by the way).

28. A Muster of Storks

Muster can also be used for groups of peacocks/peafowl (though an *ostentation* of peacocks is much more illustrative).

29. A Mutation of Thrush

An ancient and medieval belief that thrushes shed and regrew their legs each decade led to the collective term of a *mutation of thrush*.

30. A Parliament of Owls

It's unclear when this phrase was invented, with examples dating to the late nineteenth century. But its origin is likely an allusion to Chaucer's poem "The Parliament of Fowls," alongside the use of *parliament* as a collective noun for rooks.

31. A Pod of Pelicans
They can also be called a *squadron*.

32. A Prickle of Porcupines
Could this term be any more apt?

33. A Raft of Otters
According to the *Oxford English Dictionary*, many aquatic animals, such as ducks or puffins, also form rafts.

34. A Rhumba of Rattlesnakes
Because, perhaps under circumstances that didn't involve a large number of snakes, that many rattles in one place would make you want to dance.

35. A Rout of Wolves
While *pack* is definitely the better-known term today, a very old term for wolves is *rout*, a word that ultimately came from the Middle French for "company."

36. A Run of Salmon
A salmon run isn't just the mass migration of salmon up the river—a *run of salmon* is also the name of a grouping of the fish.

37. A Scold of Jays
Jays also hang in *bands* and *parties*.

38. A Scourge of Mosquitoes
They're more commonly called a *swarm*, but a *scourge* sounds just as accurate.

39. A Scurry of Squirrels
Scurries are fairly unusual, because squirrels are not pack animals by nature, so the more commonly used *dray* refers to a nest consisting of a mother squirrel and her young.

40. A Shiver of Sharks
The term *shiver* applies a bit more to nervous humans when they see a large group of sharks, which is perhaps why the term has caught on in recent years.

41. A Shrewdness of Apes
This term has been around since the late 1400s—at the time, *shrewdness* referred to the mischievous nature of apes, though knowing now how intelligent they are, the term still works.

42. A Siege of Herons
When herons pick a new lake or river to hang out at, the fish there certainly feel under siege.

43. A Skein of Geese
A *skein* is used specifically when geese (or other wild birds) are flying, while the alliterative *gaggle* is the term for grounded or domestic geese.

44. A Skulk of Foxes
This term likely came about because mother foxes raise their young while burrowed underground.

45. A Sleuth of Bears
This isn't a reference to any detective work bears may or may not do—it's derived from the Old English word for *sloth*, meaning "slow" (and *sloth* itself is sometimes used as a collective noun as well).

46. A Stubbornness of Rhinoceroses
They can also collectively be called a *crash of rhinos*.

47. An Unkindness of Ravens
Ravens aren't exactly friendly fowl. They often gang up on their prey or animals that enter their space. And because of the impression that they're an ominous presence, an unkindness of ravens can also be called a *conspiracy*.

48. A Wake of Vultures
When it comes to vultures, a *wake* specifically refers to a group feeding on a carcass. The less morbid terms *kettle* and *committee* are reserved for groups that are flying and resting in trees, respectively.

49. A Walk of Snails
Considering that walking is one of the things a snail cannot do, this seems like an unusual choice. Perhaps the lesser-known (but still accepted) *escargatoire* would be more accurate.

50. A Wisdom of Wombats
Wombats have large brains and are incredibly playful, which is often viewed as a sign of intelligence.

A *Brief History* OF THE PHRASE

...And the Horse You Rode In On

Horses may no longer be the dominant form of transportation in the U.S., but the legacy of our horseback-riding history lives on in language. When telling people off, we still use the phrase *and the horse you rode in on*. These days, it's rare for anyone you're telling to go screw themselves to actually be an equestrian, so where did *and the horse you rode in on* come from, anyway?

Well, let's start with the basics. The phrase is, essentially, an intensifier, one typically appended to the phrase *fuck you*. As the public radio show *A Way with Words* put it, it's usually aimed at "someone who's full of himself and unwelcome to boot." Co-host and lexicographer Grant Barrett explained that, "instead of just insulting you, they want to insult your whole circumstance."

The phrase can be traced back to at least the 1950s, but it may be even older than that, since, as Barrett notes, plenty of crude language didn't make it into print in the early twentieth century. He suggests that it could have been in wide use even prior to World War II.

In 1998, William Safire of the *New York Times* tracked down several novels that employed the term, including *The Friends of Eddie Coyle* (1972) and *No Bugles, No Drums* (1976). The editor of the latter book, Michael Seidman, told Safire that he heard the term growing up in the Bronx just after the Korean War, leading the journalist to peg the origin of the phrase to at least the late 1950s. It seems that even in a world where almost no one rides in on a horse, insulting a person's steed is a timeless burn.

Where Does the Term **Double Dog Dare** Come From?

You needn't have been on the receiving end of a double (or triple) dog dare to understand its implications for any self-respecting twentieth-century schoolchild. All it really takes is one viewing of 1983's *A Christmas Story*.

In the film, probably set in 1939, Ralphie watches in horror as his friend Flick valiantly resists a double dare and then a double dog dare before finally caving to the pressure of the dreaded triple dog dare. (The dare itself is for Flick to lick a frozen flagpole, with disastrous but not altogether surprising consequences for his tongue.) "The exact exchange and nuance of phrase in this ritual is very important," an adult Ralphie narrates over the action.

It's not hard to guess why *double* got added to *dare* in this age-old schoolyard custom. It automatically heightens the situation—and the peer pressure—without actually altering the stakes themselves. But what do dogs have to do with it?

Unfortunately, nobody really knows. What we do know is that kids have been double dog daring each other at least since the late nineteenth century. On his blog The Big Apple, Barry Popik unearthed a number of references to *double dog dare* from the 1890s. One of them comes from the 1896 book *The Child and Childhood in Folk-Thought*, in which Alexander Francis Chamberlain reports a certain "scale of challenging" used by children in Kentucky: "I dare you; I dog dare you; I double dog dare you. I dare you; I black dog dare you; I double black dog dare you."

Dog does have a few definitions that aren't completely out of step with the connotation of the phrase. It can mean to keep at something or pursue someone persistently, and you might indeed feel a bit hounded if your playground rival hits you with a progression of double and triple dog dares after you've refused a regular one. *Dog* has also long been used as a stand-in oath for *God* and *damn* (separately). Whether nineteenth-century kids were thinking about the lexical history of the word *dog* when they started issuing double dog dares is anyone's guess. It's possible, as Michael Quinion posited on his World Wide Words blog, that thanks to all that alliteration, it just sounded good.

Why Do We Call It a **Piggyback** Ride?

The phrase *piggyback ride* can trace its roots to a sixteenth-century phrase that merely implies that someone's back is involved and has nothing to do with pigs at all: *pick pack*. Back then, the word *pick* could also mean *pitch*, so the leading theory is that *pick pack* originally referred to a pack pitched on your back for ease of transport. After a while, people started using it to describe other things—including people—carried on your back.

Though the evolution of *pick pack* to *piggyback* isn't exactly a straight (or even solid) line, what we do know is that somewhere along the way, *pack* got changed to *back*. This is likely because *pack* was so easy to mishear as *back*, especially considering that a back was integral to every pick pack operation.

The *pick*-to-*pig* update is also thought to have occurred simply because the words sound so similar. And it happened quite a while ago:

According to the *Oxford English Dictionary*, the earliest written mention of *pig back* dates all the way to 1736. As for how *pig* became *piggy*, that, too, can probably be chalked up to miscommunication. *Pick pack*, *pick back*, and *pig back* spawned *pick-a-pack*, *pick-a-back*, and *pig-a-back*—the last of which seems to have been mistaken often enough for *piggyback* that it eventually stuck, which happened around the mid-nineteenth century.

And if "*pick* sounds like *pig*" just doesn't seem adequate to explain how swine got swapped into the phrase, *A Dialogue in the Devonshire Dialect*, published in 1837, offers a different one. In its glossary, the term *pig-a-back* is defined as being "said of schoolboys that ride on one another's backs, straddling, as an Irishman would carry a pig." So while piggyback rides never really referred to people riding on pigs, some of them *may* have involved pigs riding on people.

The UNEXPECTED ORIGIN OF FEELING ONE'S OATS

When someone wanders outside the boundaries of maturity, we tend to say that they're *feeling their oats*. The phrase isn't really intended to refer to the tactile act of rubbing oats, but experiencing the effects of ingesting them. As a horse. It appears the term first began turning up in print in the 1800s, though it's not known how long ago it was being bandied about.

Horses typically get oats when they need some quick energy from starches and sugars, though there's a good amount of protein and B vitamins in there, too. Unlike other starches, horses can munch on oats raw. Then, presumably, they tear it up. This is especially true of racehorses, who might consume up to 35,000 calories a day, some of them in the form of oats or processed feed with more fats and fiber.

Not all horses do well with oats, however. Some may not produce enough of the amylase enzyme needed to break them down properly, or the horse might have an allergy. In those cases, you wouldn't want a horse to be feeling their oats.

The related phrase *sow your wild oats* also stems from carbohydrates. In this case, wild oats don't really need to be sown, as they grow easily. To *sow wild oats* is to exhibit some needless frenzy of activity. So go ahead and feel those oats, sow them, or do whatever else you're inclined to do.

WHAT IN THE WORD?

Walrus

The etymology of the word *walrus* is a bit hard to pin down definitively. In fact, a onetime employee of the *Oxford English Dictionary* handwrote a number of versions of the word's origins—six of which survive in the archives. That *OED* employee was one J.R.R. Tolkien, and his favored explanation went back through Dutch to the Old Norse word *rosmhvalr*.

FASCINATING
PRISON
SLANG
TERMS

The big house. The pokey. Going off for a government vacation.
Taking a trip to Club Fed. Many euphemisms exist for a state or
federal prison stay—and once inside, inmates have
to adopt a whole new jargon to navigate incarcerated life.
Linguist Julie Coleman told *PBS NewsHour* that prison is
virtually ideal for new slang to flourish: People are stuck in
one place and talking, often hoping to avoid detection
by eavesdropping guards. Devising new twists on language
and communication is a necessity. Check out some of the slang
terms that have made up felonious discourse behind bars.

All Day

Caught a life sentence? You're in prison *all day*, a term used by those incarcerated in Australia as far back as 1910. If you have a life sentence without parole, you've got *all day and a night*. If you're only in for a year, then you're doing a *bullet*.

Bean Slot

When it's mealtime and you can't leave your cell, guards may deliver your food via the *bean slot*—that mail slot–esque opening that allows a tray to be slipped in and out.

Buck Fifty

If one person who is incarcerated assaults another with a weapon (like a shank) and creates a huge wound, it's known as a *buck fifty* because it might take one hundred and fifty stitches to close it up.

Car and Cadillac

No, people who are incarcerated do not have access to automobiles. A *car* in prison slang refers to a group of imprisoned people. If you're new, you'll want to see if you can find a car that's a good fit. But if you hear someone refer to a *Cadillac*, they're referring to a coffee with cream and sugar.

Duck

A *duck* in prison is bound to ruffle some feathers. It typically refers to a corrections officer who sympathizes with and passes along information to imprisoned people.

Fish

When a person convicted of a crime first arrives in prison, they're designated a *fish*. While it could refer to their fresh status—as in *fresh fish*—it might also stem from the smelly, cheap ink once used to stamp an inmate's booking numbers on their uniform. *Green's Dictionary of Slang* dates the term's published use back to 1933, when the memoir *Limey: An Englishman Joins the Gangs* by James Spenser was published: "The fish uniform is the pauper's badge in San Quentin. It is the outward proof that the poor guy who wears it has no friends."

Gassing

When people who are imprisoned want to seek retribution against a corrections officer but can't quite get hold of them, an inmate might resort to *gassing*, or throwing urine or feces at them from behind bars.

Jody

When someone hooks up with an imprisoned person's wife or girlfriend, they're known as a *Jody*. The term may have originated with the military, when enlisted men worried that a Jody would sweep their loved ones off their feet while they were away.

Keister

When someone who is incarcerated has a prohibited item and no place to hide it, they might *keister* (or *keester*) it, inserting it into their rear for safekeeping (*keister*, of course, being a slang term for the butt . . . though originally, it was a word for a suitcase). *Green's* dates it back to 1992.

While one would think a cavity search would negate any keistering, it is possible to shove contraband deep enough to be missed during an inspection. One inmate in Lake County Correctional Facility in Florida managed to keister a cell phone as well as an MP3 player (and headphones), some marijuana, tobacco, and $140 in cash in 2011. Officials became suspicious when they noticed a marijuana odor coming from his cell.

Kite   Instead of a recreational activity, *kite* refers to a note passed between people who are incarcerated: "I hear we're getting a new warden," one might say. "I'll fly you a kite." A *kite-box* is a kind of suggestion box housed in a prison where messages can be left for staff, which is probably why it's also known as a *snitch box*.

Ninja Turtles   When correctional officers don riot gear, they have been said by some to bear a fleeting resemblance to the Teenage Mutant Ninja Turtles.

Porcelain Termite   When a person who is incarcerated gets upset and starts to destroy fixtures like toilets or sinks, they're dubbed a *porcelain termite*. The phrase got national recognition with the publication of Pete Earley's *The Hothouse: Life Inside Leavenworth Prison* in 1992.

Pruno   *Pruno* refers to moonshine made by fermenting bread, water, and fruit or fruit peelings in a bag and then hiding it—sometimes in a toilet. *Green's* dates its use as far back as 1918.

Pumpkin   People convicted of a crime who sport orange correctional apparel during processing or while incarcerated are sometimes called *pumpkins*. If enough of them are together in an intake area, you've got a *pumpkin patch*.

Road Dog   When people who are incarcerated form a tight bond of friendship, they're considered *road dogs*. The term can also refer to people who have recreational time together or were friends while outside of prison.

Shank   At various times throughout history, *shank* has been used to describe part of the leg, part of a tobacco pipe, or a portion of a harpoon—and in a 2019 draft addition to the *Oxford English Dictionary*, it was noted as slang for "a makeshift knife."

Shot Caller   Originally used in the legal field, *shot caller* took on a new meaning in the prison system: It refers to an incarcerated person who calls the shots, or hands down the orders, to underlings.

Two-For-Three   Prison is often home to haggling and bargaining in lieu of cash, so people who are incarcerated have to come up with creative ways to navigate commerce. A *two-for-three* is an offer to hand over two of something—like bags of chips—in exchange for three at a date to be determined.

Why Do We Use the Word *Mug* as a Synonym for *Face*?

Get caught breaking the law, and you'll likely be hauled down to the police station so officers can snap a few photos of your face. The reason we call those images *mug shots* is because the word *mug* is slang for "face."

While there's no definitive trail of evidence to prove how *mug* first took on that meaning, most signs point to the Toby jugs of eighteenth-century Britain. According to the American Toby Jug Museum in Illinois, the original Toby jugs were ceramic pitchers shaped and painted to resemble a rotund, happy man in period attire smoking a pipe and holding a glass of ale.

As for who Toby actually was, it's still up for debate. Some people believe he was inspired by Sir Toby Belch, the boisterous party animal from William Shakespeare's *Twelfth Night*. Others think he was modeled after Henry Elwes, one of Yorkshire's most infamous drinkers from the era. Elwes was fondly nicknamed "Toby Philpot" (or "Fillpot") and immortalized in a drinking song called "The Brown Jug."

"In boozing about 'twas his pride to excel, and amongst jolly topers he bore off the bell," the song says of Toby, who's described as "a thirsty old soul" who sits "with a friend and a pipe, puffing sorrow away." Toby dies suddenly, and his body eventually deteriorates into the clay beneath the grave. The story ends after a potter happens upon that patch of clay and uses it to make a brown jug for ale.

As time progressed, potters started producing receptacles that bore the likenesses of other people and characters, too. While the original Toby jugs depicted a whole man and featured a spout for pouring liquid, many later iterations were drinking mugs that showed only the subject's face. These faces were somewhat caricaturish, which may explain why the word *mug* is often used to describe an unattractive face, a funny facial expression, or even a foolish person. Since not many suspects manage to look their best in a mug shot, the colloquialism seems especially apt.

WORDS COINED *by* AUTHORS

The subject of words coined by authors can often be a tricky one, since there's a difference between a writer *inventing* a word and just being the first one to have been recorded using it. Here, though, are some words we can reasonably believe were created by notable scribes.

Astronaut

The word *astronaut* actually predates the real-life profession. It was used to refer to a spaceship, not a person, in Percy Greg's *Across the Zodiac* in 1880. When referring to a person who explores space, a similar word in French, *astronautique*, was coined by science fiction writer J.-H. Rosny aîné in 1927. The word's Greek roots give it the literal, if still quite poetic, meaning of something like "star sailor."

Bedazzled

We owe a number of words to the Bard, including *bedazzle*, meaning "to confuse with a bright light." Shakespeare first used it in *The Taming of the Shrew*: "That haue bin so bedazled with the sunne."

Chortle

Lewis Carroll's "Jabberwocky" has a character *chortle* in joy. It seems Carroll combined chuckling and snorting to build a new, intuitively understood verb.

Cyberspace

Author William Gibson first gave us the word *cyberspace* in a 1982 story that appeared in *Omni* magazine, and brought it back two years later in his novel *Neuromancer*. (He was not, however, the first to actually use it: Gibson told *TIME* that he later found out *cyberspace* had already been used in Scandinavian abstract art—in a sense that had nothing to do with technology.) His first drafts of the word were *infospace* and *dataspace*.

Factoid

Today, *factoid* is often used to mean a short, somewhat trivial fact. When Norman Mailer coined the term, though, he explained it as "facts which have no existence before appearing in a magazine or newspaper . . . not so much lies as a product to manipulate emotion in the Silent Majority."

Hobbit

Philologist and *Lord of the Rings* author J.R.R. Tolkien coined or redefined a number of words in building out his fantasy worlds, but one of his most famous creations may not have been entirely his. The author himself said he coined the word *hobbit* in a moment of inspiration, and his son Michael recalled hearing his father use the word in stories he invented for his children. Later in life, though, Tolkien expressed a degree of doubt—after all, it would have been easy to have once seen or heard the word and then unconsciously incorporate it into his personal vocabulary.

Pre-Tolkien uses of *hobbit* were eventually discovered, including in *The Denham Tracts*, a compendium of

British folklore collected in the mid-1800s, in which they were listed as a type of supernatural creature. Whether this was a case of parallel thinking or unintended influence may be impossible to say, but—befitting a philologist such as Tolkien—the author eventually created his own retroactive etymology for *hobbit*, deciding that it derived from *holbytla*, from Old English roots meaning "hole-dweller."

Nightlife

The term *nightlife* doesn't require a ton of explanation—it's life that happens at night—but it's neat to realize that the word's first known appearance in English was in Herman Melville's *Pierre; or, The Ambiguities*. Melville describes his character, Pierre, looking for a cab late at night. He turns off a side street and, "find[s] himself suddenly precipitated into the not-yet-repressed noise and contention, and all the garish night-life of a vast thoroughfare."

Pandemonium

John Milton constructed the word *pandemonium* out of the Greek root *pan-*, or "all," and *daemonium*, from the Latin for "evil spirit." The pandemonium in *Paradise Lost* was a "place for all the demons," which makes sense as a name for what was basically the capital city of hell. It was the opposite of a pantheon, or place for all of the gods. *Pandemonium* was used in something more like its modern context in the *Cheltenham Chronicle* in 1819, when a writer invited his audience to "Let any man, in his senses, take a view of the riot—the confusion—the fury—the pandemonium of hatred, discord, and all bad feeling, let loose in the late contest for Westminster."

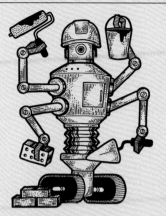

Robot

In his 1920 hit *RUR*, or "Rossum's Universal Robots" in translation, Karel Čapek needed a word for the mechanical beings who go on to world domination in his story. After originally toying with the idea of using the Latin *labori*, or "labor," as a departure point for labeling his soulless workers, Čapek's brother pointed him to the word *robota*, a term that, in Czech, is used in regard to serfdom. And it's actually in regard to the Central European system of serfdom that English had picked up the word *robot* decades earlier. That explains this wonderful line from a discourse about politics in 1855, long before the word was applied to mechanical beings: "The Austrian government has suppressed the robot."

Scaredy-Cat

This word for a coward was coined by Dorothy Parker in the 1933 short story "The Waltz." She may have taken inspiration from '*fraidy cat*, which according to the *Oxford English Dictionary* began showing up in slang dictionaries around 1910.

Spring Clean

According to the *OED*, the first use of the term *spring clean* dates back to an 1848 letter sent by *Jane Eyre* author Charlotte Brontë (who also coined the term *Wild West*): "I hope by this time you have got your 'Spring Clean' over and are more settled," she wrote. The term *spring cleaning*, however, dates to a few years before that.

Tattarrattat

At twelve letters, this word—coined by James Joyce in *Ulysses* and meaning "a knocking at the door"—is likely the longest palindromic word in English.

What Does *Sic* Actually Mean? (and How to Use It Correctly)

You're perusing a news article when there, right in the middle of a quote, is the word *sic* encased in brackets. Since this is far from the first article you've ever read, maybe you already know what *sic* signifies: that the word or phrase directly preceding it hasn't been altered from the original quote—even though it might be misspelled or simply a strange word choice.

But why *sic*? The shortest possible answer to that question is this: because Latin.

Like *e.g.* (*exempli gratia*), *mea culpa* (see page 150), and countless other terms, *sic* is just another word we've borrowed from the supposedly dead language (for more on that, see page 155). It literally means "thus" or "so" (as in *sic semper tyrannis*, "thus ever to tyrants"), but that hasn't stopped people from coming up with a slew of "backronyms" that describe it in slightly more detail: "spelling is correct," "said in copy," "said in context," etc. Though *sic* isn't a new device, English writers only started using it around the late nineteenth century, according to the *Oxford English Dictionary*.

Sic is often inside brackets or parentheses and may or may not be italicized. As for when you might want to use it, there are a couple different scenarios. One is when a quote features a typo, a misspelling, or a grammatical error. Once you've dropped *sic* to call attention to the error the first time, you don't have to include it if the same error appears in a later quote from the same source.

Sic can also come in handy if you're writing something that the reader might accidentally interpret as a mistake. Merriam-Webster cites the comic book *Funny Aminals* as an example: The misspelling of *animals* is intentional, but someone unfamiliar with it could easily just think you, the writer, made a typo.

Convenient as *sic* may seem in theory, some consider it a problematic device. As the *Columbia Journalism Review*'s Merrill Perlman noted in 2014, *sic* "can come off as snarky," and some outlets recommend using it sparingly or not at all. In 2019, the *Associated Press Stylebook* announced that it would henceforth retire *sic* for good. Instead, their experts recommend simply paraphrasing a quote if that's the best method "to convey information in the clearest way possible."

If the quote contains a grammar or spelling error (typos included), you can also use brackets to fix it directly. For example, if a source says "Using *sic* make the writer seem insufferably smug," you could update "make" to "make[s]" without employing *sic* and proving your source's point.

The ORIGINS OF 8 LITERARY CLICHÉS

Worn-out phrases can make a reader roll their eyes, or worse—give up on a book altogether. Clichés are viewed as a sign of lazy writing, but they didn't get to be that way overnight; many modern clichés read as fresh and evocative when they first appeared in print, and were memorable enough that people continue to copy them to this day (against their English teachers' wishes). From Shakespeare to Dickens, here are the origins of common literary clichés.

1. Add Insult to Injury

The concept of adding insult to injury is at the heart of the fable "The Bald Man and the Fly." In this story—which is alternately credited to the Greek fabulist Aesop or the Roman fabulist Phaedrus, though Phaedrus likely invented the relevant phrasing—a fly bites a man's head. He tries swatting the insect away and ends up smacking himself in the process. The insect responds by saying, "You wanted to avenge the prick of a tiny little insect with death. What will you do to yourself, who have added insult to injury?" Today, the cliché is used in a less literal sense to describe any action that makes a bad situation worse.

2. Albatross Around Your Neck

If you studied the Samuel Taylor Coleridge poem "The Rime of the Ancient Mariner" in English class, you may already be familiar with the phrase *albatross around your neck*. In the late-eighteenth-century literary work, a sailor recalls shooting a harmless albatross. The seabirds are considered lucky in maritime folklore, so the act triggers misfortune for the whole crew. As punishment, the sailor is forced to wear the animal's carcass around his neck:

"Ah! well a-day! What evil looks Had I from old and young!
Instead of the cross, the Albatross About my neck was hung."

Today, the image of an albatross around the neck is used to characterize an unpleasant duty or circumstance that's impossible to avoid. It can refer to something moderately annoying, like an old piece of furniture you can't get rid of, or something as consequential as bad luck at sea. Next time you call something an *albatross around your neck*, you can feel a little smarter knowing you're quoting classic literature.

3. Forever and a Day

This exaggerated way of saying "a really long time" would have been considered poetic in the sixteenth century. William Shakespeare popularized the saying in his play *The Taming of the Shrew* (probably written in the early 1590s and first printed in 1623).

Though Shakespeare is often credited with coining the phrase, he wasn't the first writer to use it. According to the *Oxford English Dictionary*, Thomas Paynell's translation of Ulrich von Hutten's *De Morbo Gallico* put the words in a much less romantic context. The treatise on the French disease, or syphilis, includes the sentence: "Let them bid farewell forever and a day to these, that go about to restore us from diseases with their disputations." And it's very possible it's a folk alteration of a much earlier phrase: *Forever and aye* (or *ay*—usually rhymes with *day*) is attested as early as the 1400s, with the *OED* defining *aye* as "ever, always, continually"—meaning *forever and aye* can be taken to mean "for all future as well as present time."

He may not have invented it, but Shakespeare did help make the saying a cliché; the phrase has been used so much that it now elicits groans instead of swoons. Even he couldn't resist reusing it: *Forever and a day* also appears in his comedy *As You Like It*, written around 1600.

4. Happily Ever After

This cliché ending line to countless fairy tales originated with *The Decameron*, penned by Italian writer Giovanni Boccaccio in the fourteenth century. A translation of the work from the 1700s gave us the line, "so they lived very lovingly, and happily, ever after" in regard to marriage. In its earlier usage, the phrase wasn't referring to the remainder of a couple's time on Earth. *The ever after* once referred to heaven, and living *happily ever after* meant "enjoying eternal bliss in the afterlife."

5. It Was a Dark and Stormy Night

Edward Bulwer-Lytton's 1830 novel *Paul Clifford* opens with "It was a dark and stormy night." Those seven words made up only part of his first sentence, which continued, "the rain fell in torrents—except at occasional intervals, when it was checked by a violent gust of wind which swept up the streets (for it is in London that our scene lies), rattling along the house-tops, and fiercely agitating the scanty flame of the lamps that struggled against the darkness."

Regardless of what came after it, that initial phrase is what Bulwer-Lytton is best remembered for today: an infamous opener that has become shorthand for bad writing. No artist wants to be known for a cliché, but Bulwer-Lytton's legacy as the writer of the worst sentence in English literature may only be partially deserved. Though he popularized "It was a dark and stormy night," the phrase had been appearing in print—with that exact wording—decades before Bulwer-Lytton opened his novel with it.

6. Little Did They Know

The cliché *little did they know*, which still finds its way into suspenseful works of fiction today, can be found in works published in the nineteenth century, according to writer George Dobbs in a piece for *The Airship*, but was truly popularized by adventure-minded magazines in the 1930s, forties, and fifties. The phrase was effective enough to infect the minds of generations of suspense writers.

7. Not to Put Too Fine a Point on It

Charles Dickens is credited with coining and popularizing many words and idioms, including *flummox*, *abuzz*, *odd-job*, and—rather appropriately—*Christmassy*. The Dickensian cliché *not to put too fine a point upon it* can be traced to his mid-nineteenth-century novel *Bleak House*. His character Mr. Snagsby was fond of using this phrase meaning "to speak plainly."

8. Pot Calling the Kettle Black

The earliest recorded instance of this idiom appears in Thomas Shelton's 1620 translation of the Spanish novel *Don Quixote* by Miguel de Cervantes. The line reads: "You are like what is said that the frying-pan said to the kettle, 'Avant, black-browes.'" Readers at the time would have been familiar with this imagery. Their kitchenware was made from cast iron, which became stained with black soot over time. Even as cooking materials evolved, this metaphor for hypocrisy stuck around.

The JAPANESE TERM FOR WHEN YOUR BOWELS SPRING TO LIFE in BOOKSTORES

In the mid-1980s, a woman named Mariko Aoki sent a letter to Japan's *Hon no Zasshi*, or *Book Magazine*, explaining a puzzling condition: Whenever Aoki entered a bookstore, she suddenly had to use the bathroom. The magazine printed the letter in its February 1985 issue, and it soon became clear that Aoki wasn't alone. Other readers mailed in letters detailing similar experiences, and *Hon no Zasshi* published a lengthy feature article called "The Phenomenon Currently Shaking the Bookstore Industry!"

While the condition—now known as the *Mariko Aoki phenomenon*—hasn't been scientifically proven, a handful of small studies conducted in Japan have suggested that it occurs all over the country, and it's between two and four times more common in women than in men. People who work in bookstores might have built up an immunity to it, and few cases have been documented in children. That said, without research on a larger scale, it's impossible to view these trends with any degree of certainty.

There's a lack of evidence to support the theories that could explain the Mariko Aoki phenomenon, too, though it's still entertaining to ponder them. One hypothesis is that the ink or paper used in the manufacturing of some books could contain a laxative agent, while another idea is that our societal habit of reading on the toilet has conditioned our bodies to induce a defecatory development whenever we open a book. It has also been suggested that all the bending and squatting we do while scanning shelves and pausing to read a few pages could move things along in our intestines. Yet another theory alleges we're subconsciously overwhelmed by all the information we encounter in a bookstore, and the urge to empty our bowels is a psychosomatic attempt to escape all this data.

Next time you're waiting in line at a bookstore bathroom, why not pass the time by discussing the merits of each theory with your fellow Mariko Aoki–sensitive patrons?

When *A Clockwork Orange* Author Anthony Burgess Wrote a Slang Dictionary

Fans of Anthony Burgess know that the famed English author loved playing with language. While writing his seminal novel *A Clockwork Orange* (1962), Burgess invented a teenage slang called *Nadsat*, which he peppered with anglicized Russian words. And in 2017, more than twenty years after Burgess's death, archivists in Manchester, England, rediscovered another sign of his fascination with words: an unfinished slang dictionary.

First commissioned by Penguin Books in 1965, the dictionary contains several hundred entries. The International Anthony Burgess Foundation—an educational charity in Burgess's birth city of Manchester—rediscovered the work among the author's personal objects, at the bottom of a box containing old bedsheets.

Working on the dictionary was both time-consuming and linguistically challenging, so Burgess abandoned the project instead of completing it as a full-length reference work. What remained of the endeavor were hundreds of six-by-four-inch slips of paper, on which Burgess had typed each entry.

The work offers insight into Burgess's interest in language and tells us about his life experiences. But it's simply not a great dictionary, according to slang lexicographer Jonathon Green: It included words like *writer's block* and proper names like *The Beatles*, which are not slang. Green theorized to the *Guardian* that Burgess soon realized he was in over his head, and chose to abandon the project instead of setting himself up for failure. "Smart as he was, with an understanding of linguistics and language, I don't think he could have allowed himself to do a second-rate [dictionary]," Green said. "If he didn't stop everything else, that's what he would have turned out with."

TALKING LIKE MY GENERATION:
SLANG TERMS
USED BY
GEN XERS,
MILLENNIALS,
and GEN Z

Gen X, the demographic born between the years 1965 and 1980, was often depicted as relaxed, cynical, and music-loving at their cultural peak in the 1980s and nineties. Meanwhile, Millennials are no longer synonymous with *kids these days*: The generation was born between 1981 and 1996, making the youngest Millennials twenty-seven and the oldest forty-two in 2023. And the cohort known as Gen Z? They're just getting started. Each of these generations has their own manner of speaking, slang that sets them apart from the generations that came before and after. Here are some terms you should know.

	GEN X	MILLENNIAL	GEN Z
Adulting		X	

Filing taxes, doing laundry, and on some days, preparing a meal that requires more steps than pouring cereal in a bowl are all things that qualify as *adulting*. *Adult* was first used as a verb (literally meaning "to mature") as early as 1909. The word as it's used today, meaning "to conduct oneself like an adult," first appeared on Twitter in 2008. As the youngest Millennials entered young adulthood over the next decade, the term exploded in popularity.

Though it often appears in a tongue-in-cheek context, *adulting* has been used to reinforce negative stereotypes of Millennials being lazy and immature. Now that the youngest Millennials are approaching their thirties, most of them (hopefully) know how to behave like adults—but that doesn't mean they have to enjoy it.

	GEN X	MILLENNIAL	GEN Z
Bae		X	

Bae is a term of endearment that has roots in African American Vernacular English (AAVE; also known as African American Language, or AAL). Originally, it was used to refer to a significant other. By 2014, brands were using the slang term to shill their products (as in "Mountain Dew is the bae"), making it hard to use it unironically.

	GEN X	MILLENNIAL	GEN Z
Bussin			X

Bussin, which may be an offshoot of *bustin'*, began as AAVE. It's specifically meant to describe delicious food, which is how TikTok user @chinaglivens used it in a March 2021 video about hot sauce on fried chicken. The sound went viral, which helped popularize the phrase among a broader audience.

    These days, it's not uncommon to hear or see *bussin* in reference to something that isn't edible; Nicki Minaj uses it to describe a whole host of things in her 2022 song "Bussin." Some Black Americans argue that non-Black people shouldn't be using the term at all—or at the very least, that it shouldn't be taken out of its culinary context.

	GEN X	MILLENNIAL	GEN Z
Cheugy			X

Millennials had the word *basic*, and Gen Z has *cheugy*, a term invented by Los Angeles–based software developer Gaby Rasson when she was a high school student in 2013. The term, which took off in 2021 after Hallie Cain posted a TikTok about it, describes anything that's slightly off-trend, outdated, or cringey, such as: being a Disney adult; the word *adulting*; decor that features trite or punny sayings; and whatever else any nearby Gen Zer tells you is cheugy. It's up to interpretation. (And according to some Gen Zers, it's actually a Millennial plot to make Gen Z look bad and not a word that's actually used much at all.)

	GEN X	MILLENNIAL	GEN Z
Chill Pill	X		

When a Gen Xer tells you to *take a chill pill*, they're telling you to relax already. The phrase first popped up in the early eighties.

	GEN X	MILLENNIAL	GEN Z
Cool Beans		X	

Cool beans can be used interchangeably with *cool* to express approval; what the inclusion of *beans* adds to the interjection is unclear. According to Merriam-Webster, this slang term dates back to 1985, when the oldest Millennials were just four years old. But though they may not have coined the phrase, the generation definitely popularized it in the 1990s and 2000s.

	GEN X	MILLENNIAL	GEN Z
Dude	X		

To be called a *dude* when the term first popped up in the 1870s was *not* a good thing: It was an insult for men who dressed to the nines (likely derived from Doodle of "Yankee Doodle Dandy" fame), or a city slicker who tried to make it out in the rural American west (New York City resident Theodore Roosevelt was called a *dude* when he showed up in the Dakota territories well before his presidency, for example). By the late 1960s, it was being used to refer approvingly to a cool person, but it wasn't until Gen X got ahold of it that *dude* was used as an interjection to show a person's approval, surprise, or other strong emotion.

	GEN X	MILLENNIAL	GEN Z

Ghosting

		X	

As more of their dating lives moved online, Millennials coined this term for a phenomenon that was specific to their generation. *Ghosting* means abruptly cutting off communication with someone in your life without warning. This behavior existed before the Tinder era, but now that many people have their phones on them at all hours of the day, it feels harder to brush off.

Gnarly

	X		

It's probably not a surprise that *gnarly* is related to *gnarled*. The word originated in the 1970s as a surfing term meaning "treacherous or difficult," perhaps in reference to rough seas. It can be used for things both awesome and scary, and was popularized by *Fast Times at Ridgemont High* (1982).

Headbanger

	X		

The term *headbanger* has been around since at least the 1930s, when it was mostly used to refer to babies who shook their heads repeatedly. But then Gen X found a new way to rock out to grunge, alt-rock, and heavy metal, and *headbanger* came to refer to people who either engaged in headbanging or were fans of music they could headbang to.

Hits Different

			X

There are a couple main ways to use *hits different*. One is to describe something that simply feels better under certain conditions—e.g., waking up on Christmas morning hits different (than waking up on a regular Wednesday). Another is to describe something that you experience or interpret differently now that new information has come to light—it's this sense that went viral in 2019 when YouTube duo Daniel Howell and Phil Lester both came out as gay, prompting their stans (more on that term in a bit) to revisit their older content and read into those interactions.

Humblebrag

		X	

If you feel self-conscious bragging about your achievements, you can always fall back on the humblebrag. Announcing an important accomplishment in a casual or self-deprecating tone lets you boast about it without coming off as conceited (at least that's the intention).

Social media provided the ideal platform for the humblebrag around the same time Millennials started reaching important milestones. The Millennial sayings *I did a thing* or *I made a thing* are classic examples of humblebragging. If you choose to indulge in this behavior, do so with caution: A study published in 2018 suggested that humblebragging may make people dislike you.

	GEN X	MILLENNIAL	GEN Z
IYKYK			X

An acronym for *if you know, you know*, IYKYK usually goes along with content shared without context—be it a video taken at a party that only other attendees will understand, or a certain nineties childhood memory for which everyone except other nineties kids would need an explanation. It's not clear exactly where the abbreviation came from, but Pusha T popularized the full phrase with his 2018 song "If You Know You Know."

	GEN X	MILLENNIAL	GEN Z
Lowkey		X	X

People have been putting the words *low* and *key* together to describe something muted or understated for decades. But Millennials (and some Gen Zers, too) were the first to drop the hyphen and also use the phrase as an adverb, rather than an adjective or a noun.

In the twentieth century, you might talk about a "low-key song" or a "low-key painting." Today, you can be "lowkey excited" for an event or say that you "lowkey need a break" from social media. In other words, *lowkey* is basically a stand-in for other adverb qualifiers like *slightly* and *kind of*. It's less about implying that you're only a little excited about something, for example, and more about conveying that you're actually really excited—but you're only showing it a little.

	GEN X	MILLENNIAL	GEN Z
No Cap			X

If someone punctuates a piece of information with *no cap*, it means they're not lying or exaggerating. According to Genius, the first mention of the phrase in rap lyrics came from Chief Keef and Gino Marley's 2011 song "Just in Case," and other hip hop artists like Migos have mentioned it on more recent tracks, too.

But before there was *no cap*, there was *high cap* or *high cappin'*—which rappers like Too Short and Willie D started using in songs during the eighties; the latter noted that *capping* could be used either in an insulting way or in a bragging way. The term may have grown out of playing the dozens, a decades-old game in Black communities where two people try to out-roast each other. Not only are the insults often exaggerated or untrue, but the game was known in some circles as *capping*.

	GEN X	MILLENNIAL	GEN Z
Sending Me			X

Today, anything can be *sending you*, meaning it thrills or excites you. But when the phrase originated around the 1930s, it was most often applied to music that caused strong emotions in a listener, according to the *Oxford English Dictionary*, and was being used to apply to things beyond music by the late 1950s.

	GEN X	MILLENNIAL	GEN Z
Stan			X

Eminem coined this term in his 2000 song "Stan," in which a guy named Stan takes his Eminem obsession to the extreme. The following year, Nas helped broaden its meaning to "any overly obsessed fan" when he mentioned *Stan* in his iconic Jay-Z diss track "Ether." Despite those early beginnings as a putdown, *stan*—lowercase, these days—has now been reclaimed by masses of Swifties, Barbz, and other members of specific fan bases who are proud to wear their stan-dom on their sleeves. You can also use *stan* as a verb, a trend that started around 2008.

Sus			X

Sus—an abbreviation for *suspect* or *suspicious*—describes suspicious behavior. It was popularized by players of the 2018 online game Among Us, in which the crew members of an alien spacecraft try to determine who the impostors are (or die trying). But according to the *Oxford English Dictionary*, English speakers have been using *sus* in this way since at least the 1950s, and its origins in law enforcement date back to the 1930s.

Tea			X

Tea as slang for *gossip* didn't originate from Kermit the Frog's "But that's none of my business" meme or any other tea-related internet content. As Merriam-Webster explains, the term comes from the eighties and nineties Black drag scene, and it wasn't just used for gossip about others. When transgender performer the Lady Chablis mentions her *T* in John Berendt's 1994 nonfiction book *Midnight in the Garden of Good and Evil*, she's referring to her own personal information. In her 1997 autobiography, she specified that *T* stands for *Truth*. *T* and *tea*— for personal truths and others' secrets—were both used during the nineties, but today *tea* reigns supreme.

To the Max	X		

This phrase that indicates doing the absolute most debuted in the early 1970s (likely in an issue of *Playboy* magazine, in which a person was described as "cool to the max"), but really became popular in the 1980s.

	GEN X	MILLENNIAL	GEN Z
Totes		X	

Not to be confused with canvas bags, *totes* is an abbreviated form of *totally*. It appears in the phrase *totes my goats* (a phrase that has multiple alternative spellings) as an enthusiastic expression of agreement. Paul Rudd had a huge impact on Millennial vocabulary when his character uttered the exclamation in the 2009 comedy *I Love You, Man*.

	GEN X	MILLENNIAL	GEN Z
Vibe	X		

Places could be vibing—aka have an exciting energy—as early as the late 1960s, but by the following decade, the term was being used a bit differently: To *vibe* meant to channel energy that you were feeling. You could send out vibes (both good and bad), and receive them, too.

	GEN X	MILLENNIAL	GEN Z
Yas			X

Though it became mainstream Millennial slang in the 2000s, *yas* originated in its modern usage with queer, POC subcultures in the 1980s. The playful take on the interjection *yes!* was commonly heard at balls, where competitors (often in drag) would strut down the floor showing off their fiercest looks. The ballroom scene gave us many words that have been appropriated by the larger culture, including *werk*, *shade*, and *serving*.

	GEN X	MILLENNIAL	GEN Z
Yuppie and **Dis**	X		

Yuppie was derived from the acronym YUP, for "young urban professional." Though the *OED* notes the term is playful, it can also be a dis (or diss), an insult used to express contempt, and another term given to us by Gen X.

How Do GENERATIONS GET
THEIR
NAMES?

There is no single or even typical way that generations historically get their names, because lumping everyone who's roughly the same age together is a relatively new phenomenon. Some social historians trace the practice back to Ernest Hemingway's 1926 novel *The Sun Also Rises*, which in the epigraph quotes Gertrude Stein saying, "You are all a lost generation" (though she may not have originated the phrase). A more convincing progenitor might be a 1951 *TIME* article that read "today's younger generation . . . does not issue manifestoes, make speeches or carry posters. It has been called the 'Silent Generation.'" While *Silent Generation* was popularly used in the 1950s to describe the teenage/young adult crowd born in the early twenties to early thirties, these days, we generally use the phrase to refer to those born from 1928 to 1945. (Considering that people like Martin Luther King Jr. were supposedly of the Silent Generation under either definition, *TIME* was quite wrong in their criticism of that cohort.)

Eventually, the U.S. Census Bureau started to refer to the years after World War II (now 1946–1964) as a "Post-War Baby Boom" due to births rocketing up from around 3 million a year to more than 4 million a year. As the kids born in this boom started to grow into adults (and thus, consumers), ad agencies found traction by marketing their products to so-called Baby Boomers. This would be the first (and so far last) time a generation's "official" name would come from a government organization.

Eventually, the Baby Boomers got older and were thus less appealing to companies with something to sell. The ad agencies wanted another catch-all term for the new members of their target age group and began shopping around different terms. The media and researchers also got in on the fun.

Generation X, one term that had been applied to Baby Boomers in an article in *The Observer*, ended up becoming associated with the post-Boomer generation—but not until 1991, when Douglas Coupland published the book *Generation X: Tales for an Accelerated Culture*.

Around that same time, *Generation Y* was being floated by several newspapers and magazines in the early nineties for the generation after Gen X—but it didn't catch on. Instead, the 1991 book *Generations*, by Neil Howe and William Strauss, gave us *Millennials*, so-called because the oldest members of the cohort would be graduating high school in the year 2000.

As for the current generation growing up: They first went by *Generation Z* before the Pew Research Center tried to redefine them as *Post-Millennials*—and now they're just plain *Gen Z* and sometimes *Zoomers*.

Irregardless:

EVERYTHING YOU NEED TO KNOW *about* THE WORD THAT DRIVES YOU NUTS

Since time immemorial (or at least as long as Twitter has existed), pedants have taken pleasure in pointing out that *irregardless* is a redundant form of the word *regardless*. The suffix *-less* already means "without," so adding the prefix *ir-*, which means basically the same thing, creates a lexical abomination roughly akin to "without without regard." Defining *irregardless* as "not without regard" would make a bit more sense, but that's not how people use it. They just use it as a synonym for *regardless*.

Irregardless is in most major dictionaries—and it's been there for some time. Merriam-Webster added the word to its unabridged edition way back in 1934, and its current editors recently published a blog post justifying its long-standing inclusion, noting that it doesn't matter that that the word is unnecessary, or that people view it as nonstandard. The dictionary's job, they argued, is to define all parts of language, unnecessary, nonstandard, or otherwise.

While some sources argue for a prescriptivist understanding of language and usage, where an authority prescribes how words *ought* to be used, Merriam-Webster takes the opposite stance: Theirs is a descriptivist understanding of what a dictionary is meant to do—to describe how language is actually used. Which explains why *unthaw* has an entry in Merriam-Webster's dictionary, too. Its definition is a single word—"thaw."

The Twentieth Century's Best Slang, Decade by Decade

The word *slang* is shrouded in mystery. We know that it emerged from cant—the language of criminals and other "disreputable characters"—in the mid-1700s and referred to the words used by groups of lower-class people, but beyond that, its etymology is unknown. Soon, it came to mean the vocabulary used by particular professions and then more broadly to informal, colloquial language that used words—old and new—in a unique or unusual way.

Many slang terms never made it into mainstream dictionaries, but lexicographers did their best to commit the words to paper, giving us volumes like *A Classical Language of the Vulgar Tongue* by Francis Grose, *Slang and Its Analogues Past and Present* by John Stephen Farmer and William Ernest Henley, *A Dictionary of the Underworld* and *A Dictionary of Slang and Unconventional English* by Eric Partridge, and *Green's Dictionary of Slang* by Jonathon Green, aka "Mister Slang." Green worked on his dictionary for a whopping seventeen years; it covers slang from 1500 onward and currently has 135,000 definitions (and counting).

Every language, every culture, every era has its own slang, and as these terms come and go, language expands and becomes *more* colorful. But, as Green told *TIME*, "What slang really does is show us at our most human." Here are a few of our favorite English slang terms of the twentieth century. Hang on to your tighty-whities, hop in your automobubble, and let's motor!

Ampersand

Yes, an ampersand is a punctuation mark, but in the 1900s, it was also slang for the butt—or, as *Slang and Its Analogues Past and Present* put it, "the breech; or posteriors." Why? Because way back when, the ampersand was often the twenty-seventh letter of the alphabet, coming *behind* all the other letters. Plus, it has nice curves.

Automobubble

The first automobiles hit the road in the late 1800s, and slang terms describing them weren't far behind. In the early 1900s, *automobubble* and *automobuzzard* were two informal ways to refer to a car; according to *Green's Dictionary of Slang*, the former may have been coined in a 1902 *Johnny Wise* comic strip. (By the way, the term *ambulance-chasing* in reference to lawyers dates back to this era.)

Goop

These days, any mention of the word *goop* likely brings to mind two things: a gross liquid substance or Gwyneth Paltrow (and maybe her company's vagina-scented candles). But back in the 1900s, *goop* (which might be a variant of *goof*) was a slang term for a foolish person.

Strop One's Beak

Slang had plenty of ways to refer to doing the deed that didn't involve mentioning the word *sex*—in 1611, it might have been *fadoodling*; in 1843, *horizontal refreshment*. In 1900, a man engaging in some hanky-panky could have said he was *stropping his beak*: *Strop* was a verb meaning "to sharpen," and *beak* was slang for "penis."

Ack Emma and Pip Emma

If someone said they planned to catch the train at seven o'clock pip emma, they meant 7 P.M. Early-twentieth-century telephone operators used *pip emma* to signal *P.M.*, and *ack emma* to signal *A.M.* Eventually, both phrases entered the public lexicon as alternatives to *afternoon* and *morning*.

San Fairy Ann

San fairy ann or *san ferry ann* is the early-twentieth-century equivalent of saying "Whatever!"—implying you either don't care at all or you've simply come to terms with something, whether you like it or not. English-speaking World War I soldiers created the phrase by phoneticizing the French expression *ça ne fait rien*, meaning "it doesn't matter."

Crivens

To express surprise or fright in the 1910s and beyond, you could skip the boring old *Oh my!* in favor of the much more colorful *Crivens!* The interjection—like *Crikey!* before it—was probably coined as an alternative to *Christ!* In the case of *crivens*, according to the *Oxford English Dictionary*, the latter half may have come from *Heavens!*

Swizz

These days, you might say "What a bummer!" to express disappointment over an unfair or regrettable situation. In the 1910s, you'd exclaim "What a swizz!" or "What a swizzle!" instead. *Swizzle* in this context is believed to be a creative adaptation of the word *swindle*. (Dating back to the early nineteenth century, *swizzle* also referred to an alcoholic beverage. Its origin is unclear, but it could be related to switchel, a classic sweet drink often containing molasses and ginger.)

1910s

Knee Dusters

As technology exploded in the early twentieth century, fashion underwent a revolution of its own. The flappers of the 1920s raised hemlines to heights previously considered indecent. These short (at least for the time) dresses were given a descriptive nickname: *knee dusters*.

Scofflaw

Scofflaws weren't in short supply in the 1920s. The word—which describes a person who proudly flouts the law—entered the lexicon with help from a man named Delcevare King in 1924. That year, King held a contest to pick a name for the rule-breakers who imbibed during Prohibition. Throughout the decade, *scofflaw* was applied to people who drank alcohol in addition to indulging in other illicit activities.

Texan Road

A variant of *Texen Road*, this was part of a trend of "Ka-cab—Ka-lat," or backtalk, as is evidenced by this example exchange from a 1923 Northern Irish newspaper: "For instance, one shop-boy would ask another, 'Where's the retsam?' and the reply would come like lightning 'Texen Road.'" The phrase meant "next door."

Zozzled

As long as they have produced alcohol, humans have come up with creative terms for getting drunk (or sloshed, hammered, etc.). The 1920s gave us one of the more delightful euphemisms for intoxication: *zozzled*. It's one of many pieces of drinking lingo that was popularized during Prohibition, but unlike *hooch* and *plastered*, *zozzled* didn't become a permanent part of the language.

1930s

Abyssinia

Squeeze the phrase *I'll be seeing you* into one word and you wind up with *abyssinia*, a breezy way to say goodbye that was popularized by teens of the 1930s. Though obsolete now, it was a favorite of *A Clockwork Orange* writer Anthony Burgess, who included it in his unpublished dictionary of slang, describing it as "so Joyceanly satisfying that it is sometimes hard to resist."

Hooverville

It should come as no surprise that much of the slang that cropped up during the 1930s had its roots in the Great Depression. The best known was *Hooverville*, a nickname for the shanty towns built by the ever-growing number of unhoused people that sprang up in cities like Manhattan and Seattle. Named for Herbert Hoover, the sitting president who was widely blamed for the Depression, the derisive term was as popular as it was politically damaging.

Boondoggle

In the late 1920s and early 1930s, *boondoggles* referred to brightly colored lanyard bracelets made by the Boy Scouts. In 1935, the term took on a more derisive meaning when the *New York Times* reported that the federal Works Progress Administration spent more than $3 million on various activities for the unemployed, including dance lessons and the "making of 'boon doggles.'" The lessons were given to unemployed teachers in the hope that they could then instruct children in poor areas, but critics found it to be a waste of taxpayer money. Now, if something is a *boondoggle*, it usually means it's an unnecessary, wasteful expense, mainly perpetrated by the government.

Ameche

Actor Don Ameche's portrayal of Alexander Graham Bell in a 1939 biopic earned him more than just praise from critics—it also led to *Ameche* becoming a slang term for "telephone" during the beginning of the 1940s.

Dead Hoofer, Maroon, and Lemonette

So much of the slang from the 1940s came from teenagers, and there were definitely a few terms you didn't want hurled your way. Chief among these was *dead hoofer*, meaning you were a bad dancer. Then you had *maroon*, meaning "stupid," and *lemonette*, a girl who wasn't a good companion.

Salt and Pepper

There's no shortage of terms for marijuana, and *salt and pepper* is among the most delightful (and head-scratching). It's not clear how it came into existence, but it was given validity by jazz musician Mezz Mezzrow, who used it in his 1946 memoir, *Really the Blues*. That same memoir also gave birth to *Mezzroll*, which is another term for a generously filled marijuana cigarette. The 1940s propagated a plethora of other pot-related synonyms as well, including *yesca*, *birdwood*, and *panatella*.

Snafu

Snafu is an example of military slang that eventually made its way into civilian life. And while it may seem like a made-up word devised by homesick troops, it's actually an acronym that stands for "situation normal: all fouled up." (Though you're free to substitute the more profane f-word for *fouled*.) According to the *Oxford English Dictionary*, *snafu* was originally intended as a phrase that denoted a soldier's "acceptance of the disorder of war and the ineptitude of his superiors."

1940s

Passion Pit

Drive-in movie theaters were at their peak in the 1950s, with more than 4,000 of them spread across the United States by the end of the decade. But it was more than just a spot to go and see a cheap B-movie with your friends—drive-ins were also *the* place for teens in heat to bring a date. And thanks to all of those high school sweethearts locking lips behind the wheels of their Ford Thunderbirds, these outdoor theaters quickly became known as *passion pits*.

Atomized, Bagged, Incognitoed, and Skunky

There are countless synonyms you can try for *drunk*. To do so in an authentically 1950s way, you can use slang terms like *atomized*, *bagged*, *incognitoed*, or *skunky*.

Squaresville, Cubesville, and Endsville

If you really wanted to ramp up your slang game in the fifties, all you needed to do was slap a *-ville* at the end of a well-known term. For example, you could take *square* and *cube*, which were both used to describe a boring person, and amplify them to encompass an entire fictional town full of dullards. That ho-hum co-worker of yours who barely says a word? He's from squaresville, daddy-o. Your uncle who keeps telling you to get a haircut? He's the mayor of cubesville.

On the other end of the spectrum, there was *endsville*, which the *Oxford English Dictionary* describes as a fictional place full of all the good things (and people) in life—like a town where your favorite bands and restaurants reside.

1950s

1960s

A-Go-Go

In French, *à gogo* translates to "galore," so the famous Parisian discotheque Whisky à Gogo literally means "Whisky Galore." The spot was so popular among cool, stylish youths that English speakers started using *a-go-go* to describe anyone or anything that was also cool and stylish—or just as lively as the place itself. Other clubs named Whisky a Go Go began cropping up in the U.S., too, most notably in Los Angeles.

Bogart

Humphrey Bogart's film performances made such an impression that his surname became slang in two separate senses during the 1960s. One, popularized by Black Americans, meant "to coerce" or "to intimidate"—inspired by Bogart's habit of playing tough guys. To bogart a (marijuana) joint, meanwhile, meant to selfishly hog it. This sense was a nod to how often Bogart smoked cigarettes on screen (and his tendency to take especially long drags).

Noodge

If someone tells you to quit noodging, they want you to stop pestering or complaining. The word evolved from the Yiddish word *nudyen*, meaning "to bore or pester." And if you tend to pester or complain fairly often, you might get labeled a *nudnik*—a Yiddish term for an annoying person, which gained popularity in the early twentieth century.

Kidult

Kidult, a portmanteau of *kid* and *adult*, defined a rising subset of entertainment—chiefly TV shows and movies—aimed at both children and adults. Grammatically speaking, *kidult* was a multi-purpose term. You could call *The Flintstones*, for example, a *kidult show* or just a *kidult*. You could even refer to the viewers of these shows themselves as *kidults*.

Burnout

In the 1940s, *burnout* was an aerial term for when a jet's engines gave out, but beginning in the seventies, *burnout* turned into a noun that referred to someone heavily abusing drugs. It was also coined as a verb by psychologist Herbert Freudenberger, who wanted a term to describe the effects of his extreme work stress.

Couch Potato

Spending too much time in front of the television could net you a label of *couch potato*. According to *Green's*, the term was coined in 1976 and may have come from another TV-related dis, *boob tuber*. (For more on the phrase *boob tube*, see page 132.)

Deep-Six

When you want to be rid of something, you can deep-six it. The *Oxford English Dictionary* speculates that the term may come from the notion of being buried at sea in six fathoms of water. While its use dates back to the 1920s and referred to a grave, the phrase was resurrected in the 1970s, thanks to coverage of Watergate and testimony that someone was asked to deep-six incriminating documents. It was a peculiar enough term at the beginning of the decade that fans of Ann Landers wrote in asking what she meant by the phrase in reference to a reader's lying husband (she clarified that she "wasn't recommending homicide").

Space Cadet

Once a literal term for a person engaged in space travel, in the seventies *space cadet* evolved to describe someone neurologically affected by excessive drug use and detached from reality. Sci-fi legend Robert Heinlein also used it as the title of a 1948 novel.

Guilt Trip

If you've ever felt remorse over something you did—or didn't—do courtesy of someone else's shaming, you've had a guilt trip laid upon you. The *OED* dates the phrase back to 1972's *Any Minute I Can Split*, a novel by Judith Rossner, where a character states that "nobody's sending me on any guilt trip over my money." It had, however, been used earlier in print in 1970 by Bernardine Dohrn of the Weather Underground radicals group.

Lame-O

If you knew someone to be a social disappointment or otherwise a bit of a dweeb, you might consider them a lame-o. The phrase got some public airtime during a 1977 episode of *Saturday Night Live*.

Tighty-Whities and Wedgie

Formerly a term for a shoe with a thick sole, *wedgie* took on more sinister connotations in the 1970s. When grabbing someone's tighty-whities (a slang term for underwear that dates back to 1978), you can deliver a wedgie—pull that underwear right up into their butt crack.

Bod

Bod dates all the way back to the eighties—the 1780s, according to the *OED*. A clipped form of *body*, it also refers more generally to a person, and in the early days may have been a shortened form of *bodach*, a Scottish word for a specter. On college campuses in the 1960s, it came to mean "an attractive person." And when a girl asks Ferris "How's your bod?" in 1986's *Ferris Bueller's Day Off*, what she's actually asking is: "How are you feeling?"

Gag Me With a Spoon

This expression of disgust, dating back to 1982, apparently had other forms as well: Gag me with a blowdryer, a snow shovel, the phone book (remember those?!).

Grody

Initially written in the mid-1960s as *groaty*, this term basically describes something that is slovenly, dirty, or super gross. If something is truly terrible, you might describe it as *grody to the max*.

Motor

A verb meaning "to leave quickly." Curious about how to use it in a sentence? Look no further than this quote from the 1989 movie *Heathers*: "Great paté, but I gotta motor if I want to be ready for that party tonight."

Tubular

Tubular, from the Latin *tubulus*, began its life in the 1680s as a word for things that were shaped like a tube. But in the 1980s, it took on a new meaning entirely— this one related to waves. According to the *OED*, surfers in the U.S. used it to refer to hollow, cresting waves perfect for riding, and soon, it was used to discuss anything that was pretty much perfect.

Wastoid

A slang term for a person who does so many drugs that they've essentially become worthless. The term was coined by John Hughes, who used it in 1985's *The Breakfast Club*: Listen for when Andrew tells Bender, "Yo, wastoid, you're not going to blaze up in here." It's also frequently used in the first season of *Stranger Things*.

1980s

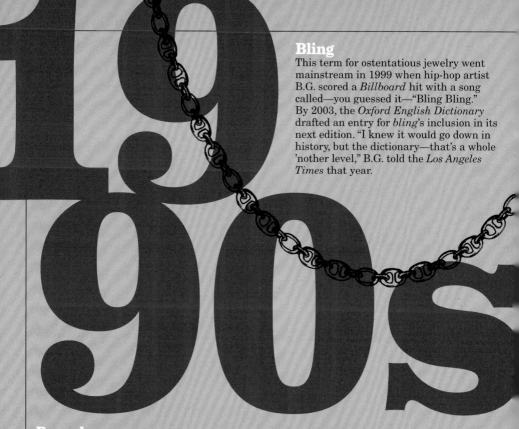

1990s

Bling

This term for ostentatious jewelry went mainstream in 1999 when hip-hop artist B.G. scored a *Billboard* hit with a song called—you guessed it—"Bling Bling." By 2003, the *Oxford English Dictionary* drafted an entry for *bling*'s inclusion in its next edition. "I knew it would go down in history, but the dictionary—that's a whole 'nother level," B.G. told the *Los Angeles Times* that year.

Booyah

An exclamation originally used to emphasize suddenness or surprise, *booyah* became forever associated with brilliant sports plays thanks to the late Stuart Scott, an innovative ESPN anchor, who punctuated his commentary with it and many other catchphrases. If you drained a three-pointer, scored a touchdown, or hit a home run in the 1990s, you or a teammate likely shouted, "Booyah!"

Buzzkill

It wasn't in the Scrabble dictionary until 2014, but according to Merriam-Webster, *buzzkill*—a person who makes others feel bad or depressed—was first used in 1992, four years before the short-lived MTV prank show that bore its name.

Chillax

Chillax has had a long post-nineties afterlife, but according to the *OED*, it began in a very nineties way: in an online forum discussing the nascent oeuvre of Quentin Tarantino in December 1994, just two months after the release of *Pulp Fiction*. (Word Histories tracked down an earlier citation—*chillaxin*— in a 1992 newspaper.)

Jiggy

Though *jiggy* has been a slang term for nervous energy since the 1890s, it only acquired its connotations of dancing, fun, and sex from one place: Will Smith's 1997 hit "Gettin' Jiggy Wit It."

Noob

No list of nineties slang would be complete without one from the then-newfangled commercial internet. This term for a beginner made its first appearance in 1995, in a Usenet forum devoted to the band Phish. If you didn't know what *ASL* stood for on ICQ, you were likely a *noob*.

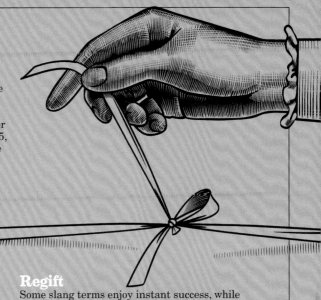

Not!

Saturday Night Live has been a font of jokes, catchphrases, and now memes for nearly half a century. One of its most popular contributions to the way people talked in the nineties was the exclamation *Not!* which debuted in a "Wayne's World" skit in 1989 and was the American Dialect Society's word of the year in 1992. Adding it to the end of any declaration immediately negates what you just said in the funniest way possible. Not! (Being on the receiving end of a "Not!" was, needless to say, not so funny.)

Regift

Some slang terms enjoy instant success, while others must wait a while to find their moment. The first recorded use of *regift* as a noun was four hundred years ago during the time of Oliver Cromwell. But it was only in 1995 that the term found real popularity thanks to an episode of *Seinfeld*. The actor who played the "regifter" in question also later rose to fame; he was played by a young Bryan Cranston.

Skeezy

An internet newsgroup was the first place that this term for something distasteful appeared, according to the *OED*. It was used to describe Axl Rose's pants at 1992's Freddie Mercury tribute concert: "If you were performing in a benefit concert for the lead singer of Queen . . . wouldn't you dress up a little more than skeezy pants and football net-jersey?"

Spousal Unit

In the nineties, you could use this gender-neutral term for your romantic partner (legal or otherwise). The only problem was that in tax law, *spousal unit* refers to the couple, not the individual. It wound up on Lake Superior State University's Banished Words List in 1992.

Way Harsh

When Tai declares that Cher is "a virgin who can't drive" in 1995's *Clueless*, Cher shoots back, "That was way harsh, Tai"—*way harsh*, in this context, meaning "very rude." *Clueless*, by the way, is such a rich repository of nineties lingo that it received seventy-four citations in *Green's Dictionary of Slang*.

Awesomesauce

This word built off the 1989 term *weak sauce*, which referred to something that was worthless or stupid. *Awesomesauce*, on the other hand, meant exactly the opposite, and first popped up in the alt.tv.kids-in-hall Usenet group in September 2001 (it was used in a post about a Taco Bell ad). A similar word, *amazeballs*, debuted in 2008.

Y2K panic may have amounted to nothing, but entering a new millennium—where the internet rose to primacy, little computers that could also make phone calls *and* take photos proliferated, and social media and streaming services took off—gave us plenty of fascinating new slang terms. Here are a few of our favorites.

Bromance

This portmanteau of *bro* and *romance* can be traced back to the April 2001 issue of *TransWorld Surf* magazine.

Debbie Downer

It wasn't long after Rachel Dratch debuted this iconic character in a May 2004 episode of *Saturday Night Live* that *Debbie Downer* entered the vernacular to refer to a seriously negative person. (A similarly alliterative name, *Negative Nelly* or *Nancy*, emerged in the 1930s.)

Dumpster Fire

Once used to refer to an actual fire in a dumpster, the term *dumpster fire* took on a less literal meaning in 2008, when it was used for the first time to refer to a seriously disastrous situation in a pro-wrestling Usenet group. But it wasn't about what you think. *Dumpster fire* was used to describe the animated movie *Shrek the Third*: "*Shrek 3* was a dumpster fire, don't get me started."

Headdesk

A cousin of the nineties term *facepalm*, *headdesk*—banging your head on the table repeatedly in a dramatic fashion—first appeared in a Usenet group in 2002. As the *Oxford English Dictionary* notes, it's not often meant literally, but instead as a kind of a joke about the nature of communication on the internet.

Mukbang

This word, which first popped up in English in 2013, is from Korean and derived from the words *meok*, meaning "to eat," and *bang*, a shortening of *bangsong*, "broadcast." Aptly, a *mukbang* is a video in which someone chats while chowing down on tons of food.

Nomophobia

Combining *no* with the *mo* in mobile and *phobia*, *nomophobia* is all about the anxiety associated with not having access to your phone. It first appeared in print in the *Daily Mail* in 2008.

Photobombing

In theory, the act of photobombing has been around for a long time, but the term itself didn't come about until 2008, when it popped up on a blog in the U.K.

Sharenting

Since 2012, this portmanteau of *share* and *parenting* has referred to a parent sharing information about their kid—whether it be news updates or adorable photos—on social media. The term gave birth to the term *oversharenting*, which is exactly what it sounds like (and can also refer to sharing parenting responsibilities).

Showrooming

Showrooms, of course, are rooms where things you can purchase are displayed; we typically think of them in terms of things like cars or appliances. That usage dates back to 1616. In 2009, a clever soul on Twitter added *-ing* to *showroom* to give us *showrooming*, or going to a store to check out merch before buying it online, where the price is usually lower.

"I hope, sir, that we are not mutually Un-friended by this Difference which hath happened betwixt us," clergyman Thomas Fuller wrote in 1659, marking the debut of the verb *unfriend*. Today, the more familiar use describes removing someone from your list of social media mutuals.

WHERE DID THE
AMPERSAND
SYMBOL COME FROM?

The symbol we know as the *ampersand* can be traced as far back as some graffiti on a Pompeian wall around the first century CE. It wasn't called an *ampersand* at the time—it was just a ligature of the cursive letters *e* and *t* forming the Latin word *et*, which means "and." (This is why *etc.* is sometimes written *&c.*)

At first, & had competition for use, as shorthand *et*—the "Tironian et" (7)—is said to have been created maybe a hundred years before as part of Cicero's secretary Tiro's extensive shorthand system, the *notae Tironianae*. Although it persisted into the Middle Ages, eventually the entire *notae Tironianae* fell out of use, leaving & to evolve and spread along with the language.

By the early nineteenth century, & was often treated as the twenty-seventh letter in the alphabet, coming right after *z*. Without a title yet, it was still read as just *and*, which made reciting the end of the alphabet a little confusing—*x, y, z,* and *and*. Kids started inserting the phrase *and per se and* to distinguish it, and over time, this all got blended together to sound more and more like *ampersand*.

The mondegreen name for the centuries-old symbol first appeared in the 1790s. More than 200 years later, this little piece of punctuation has got a whole day—September 8—dedicated to celebrating its history and continued use.

WILD ABOUT
WORDLE:
Why
WE LOVE IT

F ollowing tumultuous affairs with games like Candy Crush came the time-killing pastime Wordle, a game created by software engineer Josh Wardle in late 2021. What began as a simple game for Wardle's partner and later for his family and friends in a WhatsApp group has millions of players today—and ideas have emerged about why it's proven to be such an addictive diversion.

Winning Wordle isn't complicated: It's a simple game in which players are tasked with guessing a five-letter word. If you type *bikes*, for example, Wordle will let you know which letters are already in the correct position by turning the boxes green; yellow means the letters are in the word, but not in the right positions; gray letters aren't present at all. It's *Wheel of Fortune* meets a crossword puzzle.

According to University of Utah professor C. Thi Nguyen, Wordle has taken off in part because of how easy it is to share your achievements on social media. (Naturally, Nguyen shared his thoughts in a Twitter thread.) Because you have six tries to guess the daily word—which is the same for everyone playing—you can rate yourself against others. And you can do it without spoiling the answer by sharing the color-coded grid. Guess the word in fewer tries and you have some online cachet.

Tweeted brags are just one component. These types of games with a clear reward stimulate the release of dopamine, the brain's pleasure chemical, and are also relatively low-tech. Users aren't being sold anything or being asked to buy something to enrich the playing experience. It's just a simple language puzzle that can only be played once daily.

The
SECRET TO
WINNING
WORDLE

Working out the daily Wordle requires a healthy dose of luck. A player's chances of winning early in the game depend on what the word is that day and which letters they decide to guess first. That random element is part of the fun, but there are some skills and strategies you can use to master the puzzle.

According to the *Guardian*'s David Shariatmadari, author of *Don't Believe a Word: The Surprising Truth About Language*, a bit of linguistics knowledge goes a long way when playing Wordle. Once you've guessed a couple of letters correctly, your challenge becomes determining what other letters fit around them and in what order. *m* and *p* go together, for example, but most of the time only when the *m* is in front of the *p*, and never at the beginning of a word. When pairing *t* and *r*, it's always *tr* at the start of a syllable and *rt* at the end.

These linguistic rules are called *phonotactics*. Like all languages, English follows some restrictions regarding which consonants pair together and where they belong in a word. In general, "hard" sounds like *p* and *c*, which are less sonorous, appear before more sonorous "soft" sounds like *l* and *r* at the beginning of a syllable. At the end of a syllable, the more sonorous sound appears first. This rule is called the *sonority sequencing principle*, and it's on display in words like *blurt*, *crust*, and *trawl*.

Unlike some quirks of English, this rule isn't arbitrary. Words that smoothly transition in and out of their more sonorous sounds are easier for speakers to say and for listeners to understand. If words break this rule, they sound awkward and unnatural. (Try starting a syllable with *rt* or *lb* to hear what we mean.) This is why languages other than English also follow the sonority sequencing principle.

Keeping this principle in mind can help you take your Wordle game to the next level. If you know the word of the day contains a hard consonant like *b* but you don't know where to put it, the first and last spots in the word are your best guesses. Just remember that how sonorous a word sounds isn't a fixed value. A *c* might become soft when it's placed in front of an *h*, and a *g* is totally silent before an *n* in the same syllable.

STRATEGIC OPENING WORDS *to* USE IN WORDLE

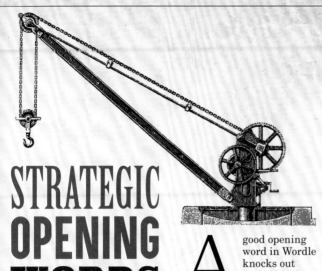

A good opening word in Wordle knocks out several of the most common letters in the alphabet in one go. Packing your first word with as many different vowels as possible is a winning approach. No matter what the word of the day is, it has to include vowels, and knowing which ones to use and where (or where not) to put them is crucial information. For this reason, vowel-heavy, five-letter words like *adieu*, *audio*, and *ouija* are solid choices for your first guess of the game.

Another strategy is to pick an opener that will set you up for success in subsequent guesses. Not many words look like *adieu* or *ouija*, so even if these guesses help you figure out the correct letters (which are highlighted in yellow when they're in the wrong place), they're less likely to show you the correct placement (highlighted in green). Words like *trace* and *crate* feature both common letters and word construction, which makes them effective guesses according to information theory.

To take your Wordle gameplay to the next level, consider using this list of winning word openers, presented in alphabetical order.

About
Adieu
Aisle
Audio
Canoe
Crane
Crate
Equal
Irate
Later
Ouija
Pious
Queue
Raise
Ratio
Roate
Samey
Slice
Stare
Trace

WORDS BROUGHT TO YOU BY

HOLLY

Over the years, Hollywood has brought some unforgettable spectacles to the big screen, from the parting of the Red Sea in *The Ten Commandments* (1956) to recreating the sinking of the RMS *Titanic* in James Cameron's 1997 hit film and beyond. Tinseltown is also responsible for introducing many words and idioms we use every day into the lexicon. In the spirit of cutting to the chase, below are some of our favorite Hollywood slang terms, many of which have origins that might seem like the ultimate plot twist.

Blockbuster

Although Steven Spielberg's *Jaws* (1975) is widely considered the first summer blockbuster, the term *blockbuster* is much older than that. It first appeared in the mid-twentieth century and was used in two ways: first, in reference to World War II–era bombs that were powerful enough to obliterate a whole city block, and subsequently, as a metaphor in the U.S. to describe something explosively shocking. By the 1950s, Hollywood had co-opted it as a label for flicks that were a major success at the box office, which is how it's still used to this day. (It may also refer to Blockbuster, the video-rental chain that's all but nonexistent these days—unless you want to make a trip to Bend, Oregon, where, as of 2022, the last remaining store was still open seven days a week.)

Boob Tube

Depending on whom you ask, we're still living in the Golden Age of Television—a period marked by an exceptional number of high-quality shows—but the *boob tube*, as it has come to be known, wasn't always so celebrated. According to *Green's Dictionary of Slang*, the moniker was first used in the U.S. back in the early 1960s as another word for *television*, but with a derogatory bite: The term *boob* was commonly used then to describe a "fool [or] idiot," but could also suggest something "stupid [or] foolish," (and in the U.K., *boob* is synonymous with "an error, a blunder"). Ipso facto, *boob tube* was often evoked by detractors of seemingly low-quality television shows to cast shade on the entire medium.

Cut to the Chase

It should come as no surprise that this turn of phrase originated in showbiz. We'll get to the point, though (which, incidentally, is what it actually means): *Cut to the chase* is a throwback to the silent films of the early twentieth century, when directors who couldn't rely on dialogue to move a plot forward would simply . . . well, you know. It crossed over to casual usage circa the mid-1950s when a journalist used it in his memoir, and to this day, *cut to the chase* is commonly used whenever someone wants to speed things along.

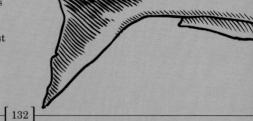

WOOD

Embiggen

From *d'oh!* to *dorkus malorkus*, the English language owes a lot to *The Simpsons*, particularly when it comes to made-up neologisms—like the Springfield-originated verb *embiggen*, which was added to Merriam-Webster's online dictionary in 2018.

The word dates back more than twenty years, to a seventh-season episode of *The Simpsons* titled "Lisa the Iconoclast." In it, the students of Springfield Elementary School are treated to *Young Jebediah Springfield*, an educational film that depicts the early days of the founder of their great town. His secret? "A noble spirit embiggens the smallest man." The rarity of the word led Edna Krabappel to question its authenticity, but fellow teacher Ms. Hoover assures her that "it's a perfectly cromulent word," a reference to yet another piece of *The Simpsons* lexicon. Writer Dan Greaney actually coined *embiggen* for the episode.

Amazingly, it turns out that Jebediah Springfield may have been very hip to the times when he used the phrase after all; the word was also used by author C. A. Ward in *Notes and Queries: A Medium of Intercommunication for Literary Men, General Readers, Etc.*, which was published in 1884.

Gaslight

Under modern usage, to *gaslight* someone means to psychologically manipulate them over an extended period of time until they begin to distrust their own thoughts, feelings, and perceptions of reality. The term owes its roots to the 1938 play *Gas Light* (and to subsequent adaptations, including the 1944 film *Gaslight*, which starred Ingrid Bergman), wherein a woman is slowly deceived by her husband into believing she's going insane, with the flickering gaslights around their home used to symbolize her declining mental state. By at least 1956, it had entered American parlance as a verb, meaning "to trick an otherwise perfectly healthy person into psychosis."

Jump the Shark

Audiences were none too pleased in 1977 when legendary cool guy Arthur Fonzarelli (aka The Fonz) legit jumped over a shark while rocking a leather jacket and water skis on the hit ABC sitcom *Happy Days* (1974–1984). For some, it signaled the beginning of the end for the critically acclaimed show, which is how the idiom—officially coined in the 1980s by writer–radio personality Jon Hein and his college roommate Sean Connolly—is used in modern times. It's since spilled over from Hollywood, and can be applied to any attention-grabbing stunt that doesn't quite land the way its architects thought it would. (Except fortunately for The Fonz, his did.)

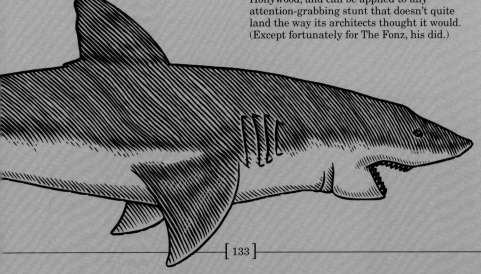

A *Brief History* OF THE PHRASE
Wa Wa Wee Wa

THE ORIGIN OF BORAT'S FAVORITE CATCHPHRASE

When *Borat: Cultural Learnings of America for Make Benefit Glorious Nation of Kazakhstan* was released in 2006, a new audience was exposed to Borat Sagdiyev, a "journalist" portrayed by Sacha Baron Cohen who had made frequent appearances on the comedian's *Da Ali G Show*. People began mimicking Borat's catchphrases, *very nice* and *wa wa wee wa*, incessantly. The latter phrase was used to connote surprise or happiness on Borat's part, and while some may have assumed it was made up, it turns out that it actually means something.

Wa wa wee wa is Hebrew, which Cohen speaks throughout the film and which helped make *Borat* a hit in Israel. (Cohen is Jewish.) It was taken from an Israeli comedy show and is the equivalent of the word *wow*. Reportedly, the expression was popular among Israelis, and they appreciated Cohen's use of it. The original *Borat* also sees Cohen singing a popular Hebrew folk song, "Koom Bachur Atzel," or "get up, lazy boy," among other Hebrew mentions.

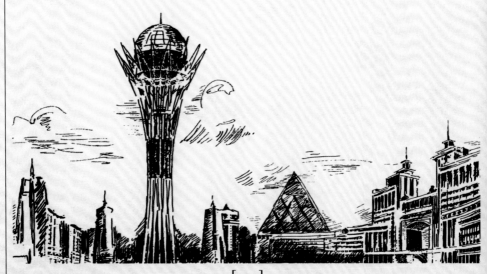

MUSICIAN *and* BAND NAMES

YOU'VE PROBABLY

BEEN
MISPRONOUNCING
ALL ALONG

Billie Eilish may have sold millions of records before she turned twenty-one, but that hasn't stopped a number of news outlets from butchering the pronunciation of her last name. (It's "EYE-lish," not "EE-lish" or "EL-ish.") Indeed, if you know your favorite musical act only by what comes up on their Spotify tracks, you may be surprised to find you've been mispronouncing their name all along.

Bjork

The Icelandic singer has likely given up correcting people who say "Bee-york" a long time ago, but you probably stand a better chance of an autograph if you say it properly: "Bee-YERK."

David Bowie

Proving you can be as famous as any person who has ever lived and people will still mess up your name, rocker David Bowie wasn't "Bow-ee" where the "bow" rhymes with *bow* as in "take a bow." It's "BOH-wee," like *doughy*.

Ray Davies

The lead singer of the Kinks didn't pronounce it "Day-veez" but "DAY-viz."

Haim

The trio of sisters get "Haim" as in Corey Haim, but it's actually pronounced "HI-uhm."

Hozier

Irish singer Hozier has heard it all, from "Hose-ee-air" to "Hozzer." According to the musician himself, it rhymes with *cozier*—"HOH-zee-ur."

Macklemore

The "Thrift Shop" and "Can't Hold Us" singer gets "Mackle-more" a lot, but it's actually "MACK-la-more."

Ric Ocasek

The Cars member is "Oh-CASS-ick," not "Oh-CASE-ick."

Rihanna

If you've been saying the "Umbrella" singer's name as "Ree-AH-na," you're all wet. Her name is pronounced "Ree-ANN-uh." Writing a song titled "What's My Name" may not have been a coincidence.

Sade

Born Helen Adu, this graceful singer is often labeled "Sadie" or even "Shar-day." It's actually "Shah-DAY." That's also the name of her band, but most people consider Sade a solo act.

Adam Yauch

The Beastie Boys co-founder might have gotten "Yuck," but it's "Yowk."

The ORIGINS

(AND MEANINGS) OF

HOLIDAY PHRASES

From Valentine's Day to New Year's Eve and
everything in between, the holidays are full of words
and phrases we use without a thought.

Why Is It Called *Valentine's Day?*

There are a few theories as to the origins of Valentine's Day. According to some, it originated after the Roman fertility festival, Lupercalia, was banned by Pope Gelasius I; per this version of the tale, Gelasius took the day's moniker from two men—one a priest, one a bishop—named Valentine who were executed by the Romans during the rule of Claudius II. (Those two Valentines might actually have been the same person, though.) In some versions of the story, the future saint was illegally performing marriages, but this is possibly a medieval legend rather than Roman fact. Indeed, the entire Gelasius story is unlikely; while he did suppress Lupercalia, there's no evidence he replaced it with a day for Valentine.

One thing we know is that love wasn't a part of Valentine's Day until the 1300s, when Chaucer mentioned it in his poem "The Parliament of Fowls": "For this was on Seynt Valentyne's day / Whan every foul cometh ther to choose his mate." At the time, King Richard II was finalizing a marriage contract with Anne of Bohemia, and it's been proposed that Chaucer—who may have been attempting to curry favor with the king—decided on the saint with the feast day most convenient to the conclusion of marriage negotiations: the obscure St. Valentine of Genoa. But without any clues as to the month, people naturally assumed that Chaucer meant the more famous Valentine's Day in February—according to this theory, anyway. Not all historians are convinced this is the case.

Is It *President's Day*, or *Presidents' Day*, or *Presidents Day*?

The short answer is: It depends on whom you ask. According to the *Associated Press Stylebook*, it's *Presidents*, but *The Chicago Manual of Style* and Merriam-Webster prefer *Presidents'*. The latter formatting acknowledges Presidents Washington and Lincoln, whose birthdays (February 22 and 12, respectively) the long weekend is usually taken to honor. Some states don't even use the *p*-word, opting for the names of particular presidents and other political figures instead. If you want to skirt the whole issue, just call the third Monday in February *Washington's Birthday*—the federal name of the holiday.

Is It *St. Patty's Day* or *St. Paddy's Day*?

Since *Paddy* and *Patty* are usually pronounced the same way, it hardly matters whether you're wishing someone a "Happy St. Paddy's Day!" or a "Happy St. Patty's Day!" aloud. If you're writing it out, however, only one is technically correct.

Patrick is the anglicized version of the Gaelic name *Pádraig*. Because St. Patrick's Day is originally an Irish holiday—and Gaelic is a traditional Irish language—the right nickname is *Paddy*, rather than *Patty*.

St. Patty's Day probably became popular in America because people heard "St. Paddy's Day" and assumed it was spelled with a *t*, like *St. Patrick*.

The word *Paddy* has a bit of a contentious history. According to Merriam-Webster, it's also sometimes used as a derogatory term for an Irish person—so if you'd rather forgo the nicknames altogether and just stick with *St. Patrick's Day*, that's fine, too.

Why Do Ghosts Say "Boo"?

People have screamed "boo," or at least some version of it, to startle others since the mid-sixteenth century. But ghosts? They've only been yowling "boo" for less than two centuries.

The etymology of the word is uncertain (the *Oxford English Dictionary* compares it with the Latin *boare* or the Greek *βοᾶν*, meaning "to shout," while older dictionaries suggest it could be an onomatopoeia mimicking the lowing of a cow), but *boo* (or, in the olden days, *bo* or *bu*) was initially used not to frighten others but to assert your presence. By 1738, Gilbert Crokatt was writing in *Presbyterian Eloquence Display'd* that "Boo is a Word that's used in the North of Scotland to frighten crying children." *Bo*, *boo*, and *bu* latched onto plenty of words describing things that went bump in the night, like *bu-kow*, which was applied to anything scary, from hobgoblins to scarecrows. It was only a matter of time until ghosts got lumped into this creepy crowd.

Boo's popularity rose in the mid-nineteenth century during the age of spiritualism, a widespread cultural obsession with paranormal phenomena that sent scores of people flocking to mediums and clairvoyants in hopes of communicating with the dead. It's probably no coincidence that ghosts began to develop their own vocabulary—limited as it may be—during a period when everybody was curious about the goings-on within the spirit realm.

It may also help that *boo* was Scottish. Many of our Halloween traditions, such as the carving of jack-o'-lanterns, were carried overseas by Celtic immigrants. Scotland was a great exporter of people in the middle of the 1800s, and perhaps it's thanks to the Scots-Irish diaspora that *boo* became every ghost's go-to greeting.

[137]

Why Do We Say "Trick or Treat" on Halloween?

Halloween wasn't always about cosplay and chocolate bars. During the nineteenth century, Irish and Scottish children celebrated the holiday by wreaking (mostly harmless) havoc on their neighbors—blowing cabbage smoke through a keyhole to stink up someone's house, frightening passersby with turnips carved to look ghoulish, etc. Kids didn't give up that annual mischief when they immigrated to the U.S., and Americans happily co-opted the tradition. Toppled outhouses and trampled vegetable gardens soon gave way to more violent hijinks, and these pranks escalated during the Great Depression.

In short, tricks were a huge part of Halloween throughout the early twentieth century. So, too, were treats. For All Souls' Day in the Middle Ages, people went door to door offering prayers for the dead in exchange for food or money, a tradition known as *souling*. A similar custom from nineteenth-century Scotland, called *guising*, entailed exchanging jokes or songs for goodies. While it's not proven that modern treat-begging is directly derived from either souling or guising, the practice of visiting your neighbors for an edible handout around Halloween has existed in some form or another for centuries.

With tricks and treats on everyone's minds come October, it was only a matter of time before someone combined them into a single catchphrase. Based on the earliest known written references to *trick or treat*, this may have happened in Canada during the 1910s or 1920s: According to Merriam-Webster, a Saskatchewan newspaper mentioned the words together in an article from 1923, and by 1927, young trick-or-treaters had adopted the phrase themselves. The phrase appeared in Michigan's *Bay City Times* the following year, describing how children uttered "the fatal ultimatum 'Tricks or treats!'" to blackmail their neighbors into handing out sweets.

What Does *Talk Turkey* Mean?

Around Thanksgiving, you may use the phrase *talk turkey* literally to discuss the bird you're having for dinner—but originally, it meant "to discuss something pleasantly." Then, *talking turkey* came to mean having an honest and frank discussion (in the U.S. and Canada, anyway). Legend has it the phrase originated in a joke where a white man and Native American were hunting together; after nabbing birds both tasty (turkey) and not (buzzards), the white man tried to persuade the Native American to take the buzzards, not the turkey—to which the Native American allegedly responded, "You're not talking turkey to me."

What Does *Bah, Humbug!* Actually Mean?

In Charles Dickens's 1843 story *A Christmas Carol*, Ebenezer Scrooge exclaims "Bah! Humbug!" in reference to Christmas. He famously hates the holiday, so it's easy to assume that *humbug* is just an expression used to convey dislike for something popular. In fact, thanks to the cultural impact of the Victorian Christmas classic, that's often how *humbug* is used today. But Scrooge didn't originate the term—and he meant something more specific than "I hate Christmas!" when he uttered it.

Humbug first appeared in writing in a 1750 issue of *The Student, or the Oxford and Cambridge Monthly Miscellany*, where it was described as "a word very much in vogue with the people of *taste* and *fashion* . . . though it has not even the *penumbra* of a meaning." In short, it seemed to have been trendy slang coined by the cool kids of the era, and its etymology remains unclear. That said, *humbug* was used widely enough that its definition, at least, is clear. According to the *Oxford English Dictionary*, it referred to a trick or something that isn't what it appears to be, like a sham or fraud. Eventually, people started using it to mean "nonsense" in general.

When Scrooge repeatedly calls Christmas *humbug*, it's because he believes the holiday fits the bill in more ways than one. He thinks Christmas tricks people into feeling cheerful and thankful when they have nothing to feel cheerful about or thankful for: Dickens's curmudgeonly character considers Christmas a financial and emotional scam on a global scale—a humbug any way you slice it. The only way Scrooge doesn't use the word *humbug* is in reference to the striped, peppermint-flavored hard candies of the same name. (Those humbugs date at least as far back as the 1820s in the U.K., so it's possible Scrooge would have been familiar with them, too.)

Why Do We Call It *Eggnog*?

The *egg* in the word *eggnog* needs no explanation, but the path to *eggnog*'s second syllable isn't quite so linear. There are a few old-fashioned words that may have played a part in its provenance, however. Before the word *noggin* became slang for *head*, it described a small drinking container like a cup or mug. According to the *Oxford English Dictionary*, the term dates at least as far back as the late sixteenth century.

By the mid-seventeenth century, people had started using *noggin* to describe what you might find in a noggin itself: a modest quantity of liquor. Robert Louis Stevenson even mentioned the word in *Treasure Island*, first published in the early 1880s: "Jim, you'll bring me one noggin of rum, now, won't you, matey?" Billy Bones says to Jim Hawkins.

At that point, the term *eggnog* had already entered the lexicon, first written in an 1825 novel by John Neal. It's possible that it came straight from *noggin*, but it's also possible that the word *nog* itself factored into the coinage of *eggnog*. Beginning in the late seventeenth century, *nog* showed up as a word of its own, referring to a potent type of beer that usually hailed from Norfolk, England. While today's eggnog traditionally contains liquor—be it rum, bourbon, or whiskey—the medieval milk drink that inspired it, posset, could also contain ale or wine.

That said, it's not exactly clear where the word *nog* originated: It very well may have stemmed from *noggin*. So even if *eggnog* was inspired by *nog*, there's a good chance that *noggin* is still part of its origin story.

Another theory posits that grog is actually the key to solving the mystery. In 1740, British admiral Edward Vernon ordered his sailors to start diluting their rum with water so they wouldn't guzzle their whole ration in one sitting. The sailors had taken to calling the admiral "Old Grog" because he often wore grogram—a rough silken fabric—and they co-opted the word *grog* for the watered-down drink. (*Treasure Island* mentions grog several times, too.) The term caught on, and it's been suggested that *eggnog* is actually a truncation of *egg-and-grog*.

Where Does the Word *Yule* Come From, Anyway?

Ah, Christmas. That time for caroling, hot chocolate, and yuletide cheer. Wait, what on Earth is a *yule*? And what do the tides have to do with Christmas?

Yule's origins are far from clear, and even world-class scholars are only able to agree on the basics, which are: *Yule* is an incredibly old word (for English, anyway) that may trace back to celebrations of the new year and may or may not involve a lot of drinking and eating, sacrifices, and making oaths. According to Old Norse expert Jackson Crawford, *jól* was a three-night festival starting on Midwinter (the winter solstice). *Yule* is thought to be from the same mysterious Germanic origin as *jól*—one name didn't descend from the other.

Wherever the word came from, by around 900, *Yule* was being used as a word for *Christmas* (and it still is, in some areas of the world). This was a time when the two holidays began blending together. According to the saga of King Hakon the Good (who reigned circa 920–961, and whose saga was written down in the thirteenth century), Hakon, a Christian, demanded that people had to celebrate either Christmas or *jól*, both of which were to happen in late December. They were able to celebrate whichever one they chose, but each free man had to have ale for the entire celebration. According to Crawford, this amounted to four gallons of ale in three nights. The party also featured sacrifices (especially of horses) and oaths (especially on boars).

The exact origins of *Yule* still leave many open questions—though at least modern Christmas celebrations don't tend to feature over a gallon of beer a day.

Now, on to tides and yuletides. A popular folk-etymological origin for the word *jolly* relates to the Old Norse *jól*, either directly or via some cognate German word. If that's true, wishing someone a "jolly yuletide" would be a little redundant. However, according to the *Oxford English Dictionary*, this origin is unlikely. The word comes to English from French, but beyond that, it's unclear; it doesn't seem to be Old Norse in origin, either. Instead, the *OED* suggests that it's ultimately from the Latin *gaudium*, meaning "joy."

And as for what the tides have to do with a midwinter celebration, *tide* originally meant "a span of time or a season"—the meaning of the word as it appears in *Beowulf* and other Old English texts (and would give rise to similar constructions like *New Year's tide* or *eventide*). Etymologically, ocean tides might come from Middle Low German *getide*, meaning "fixed time," or from Middle Dutch—or, perhaps, it developed naturally in English. No matter what, it's thought that *tide* was originally "the time of high water," and came about from that.

Why Do We *Ring In* the New Year?

These days, you can say you're *ringing in* the New Year with plenty of things that don't ring: a toast, a kiss, an ambitious New Year's resolution, an entire sheet cake to yourself, and so forth. When the phrase originated, however, it involved something that actually rang: bells.

Communities used to bid adieu to the old year and welcome the new one by ringing bells, often in churches. The tradition may have grown out of other occasions where bells marked an end (as in tolling bells when someone died) or celebrated a beginning (like wedding bells).

Decades before hordes of revelers started flocking to Times Square to watch the ball drop (an event that first occurred in 1907), they congregated farther downtown at Wall Street's Trinity Church, where they rang in the New Year with a veritable concert put on by the church's official bell ringer, James E. Ayliffe. As the *New York Herald* reported in 1860, "There floated from the high church tower the stirring music of eight bells chiming in changes and making the air redolent with harmony."

According to Trinity Church's archives, the earliest mention of the tradition is from the minutes of an 1801 meeting where parishioners allotted eight pounds "to the Persons who rang the Bells in New Years day." It might have been going on long before that, considering the church got its first bell back in 1698.

In short, ringing bells was once a central part of the holiday. The fact that it's faded from memory—and *ring in the New Year* makes little sense if you don't know the phrase's history—may help explain why so many people now say "bring in the New Year" instead.

11
OLD-FASHIONED
TERMS
TO BRING BACK
For
VALENTINE'S
DAY

Valentine's Day is the opportune holiday to express all the lovey-dovey feelings you may not usually take the time to put into words—simply calling your partner *pretty* on the most romantic day of the year, however, might not exactly make the sparks fly. To help you get creative, here are eleven old-fashioned romance terms from the days of yore.

1. Bughouse
Decades before Beyoncé created a chart-topping melody to describe the feeling of being "crazy in love," early-twentieth-century Americans simply called it *bughouse*.

2. Buss
Buss is an old-fashioned synonym of *kiss* that originated around 1570, possibly from the Middle English verb *bassen*, meaning "to kiss." It also sounds fairly similar to a few *kiss* terms from Romance languages, like the French *baiser*, the Spanish *beso*, and Italian's *bacio*.

3. Dainty Duck
In the play within Shakespeare's *A Midsummer Night's Dream*, Pyramus refers to his lover, Thisbe, as a "dainty duck." They didn't exactly live happily ever after, but that's no reason not to bring back *dainty duck* as an adorable (and alliterative) term of endearment.

4. Dimber
From *stunning* to *hunky*, there are plenty of satisfactory ways to call someone attractive. None, however, have quite as much old-timey appeal as *dimber*, a gender-neutral term for "pretty" from the seventeenth century. *Dimber cove* refers to a handsome man, while *dimber mort* is used for a pretty girl or woman.

5. Dulcinea
In Miguel de Cervantes's *Don Quixote*, the titular character nicknames a lovely peasant girl *Dulcinea*, derived from *dulce*, the Spanish word for "sweet." Over time, people started using it as a general term for *sweetheart*.

6. Face Made of a Fiddle
If you find your partner irresistibly charming, you can tell them that they have a "face made of a fiddle"—a face so welcoming and attractive that it seems to mirror the smile-like curves of a fiddle. Just be careful not to confuse it with *face as long as a fiddle*, which describes a dismal, unhappy demeanor.

7. Jam Tart
Because Valentine's Day is filled with sweet treats already, it's only fitting that you'd replace the word *heart* with *jam tart*—a classic bit of Cockney rhyming slang for your ticker.

8. Prigster
If you're fighting for the heart of a fair maiden, you can call your competitor a *prigster*, a word dating back to the 1670s that means "a rival in love."

9. RILY
Lovers were expressing their feelings in shorthand long before the invention of texting—starting in the mid-1940s, telegrams sometimes contained the acronym RILY, for "Remember, I love you."

10. Spoon
Engaging in a little foolish flirtation on Valentine's Day? Your nineteenth-century ancestors might call that *spooning*.

11. Sugar Report
Sugar report caught on during World War II as a slang term for the letters that soldiers received from their wives and girlfriends back home. If you're sending a lengthy email to your partner detailing your romantic itinerary for Valentine's Day, feel free to type *Sugar Report* as the subject line.

Addle Pate

According to English lexicographer Francis Grose's *A Classical Dictionary of the Vulgar Tongue*, first published in 1785, this term refers to "an inconsiderate foolish fellow."

Blatherskite

To *blather* is to talk a lot of nonsense; a *blatherskite* (or *bletherskate*), therefore, is a person who talks a bunch of nonsense loudly. The term dates back to around the mid-seventeenth century.

Gollumpus

This insult is meant to be aimed at exactly what it sounds like: "a large, [clumsy] fellow." (A *gundiguts*, meanwhile, was a "fat, pursy fellow.")

Loathly

This alternate form of *loathsome*, meaning "repulsive," could be found as early as 900; it eventually fell out of favor before being revived in literary works in the nineteenth century.

Mooncalf

This obscure term for a foolish person could also once be used to refer to someone who was unstable or had a tendency to flip-flop. Shakespeare used the term in *The Tempest* in another one of its meanings: "a deformed creature or monster."

Poltroon

The next time you encounter an utter coward, you can call them a *poltroon*. They're probably too much of a poltroon to ask you what *poltroon* means.

STICKS *and* STONES: OLD-FASHIONED INSULTS WE SHOULD BRING BACK

For history buffs and word nerds, "you jerk" just doesn't have the same ring as "you unlicked cub," an insult from Georgian England—and history has plenty more where that came from. Here are a few of our favorite old-fashioned insults that deserve a comeback.

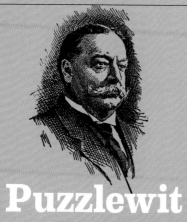

Puzzlewit

This nineteenth-century insult for a foolish or silly person was used with great effect by former president Theodore Roosevelt in reference to his successor and former friend, William Howard Taft, during the 1912 presidential campaign. (TR was running as a Progressive against both Taft, a Republican, and Woodrow Wilson, a Democrat.) He also called Taft a "fathead" as well as "a flubdub with a streak of the second-rate and the common in him," and declared him to have "brains less than a guinea pig."

The twenty-sixth president was truly gifted in the art of the insult: He declared novelist Henry James a "little emasculated mass of inanity," called Secretary of State William Jennings Bryan "a professional yodeler, a human trombone," and derided a nameless Supreme Court justice as "an amiable old fuzzy-wuzzy with sweetbread brains."

Quidnunc

From the Latin phrase *quid nunc*, or "What now?," a *quidnunc* is a nosy, bossy person who's constantly sniffing around for the next juicy morsel of gossip. Bring it back for that friend who unabashedly reads your text messages over your shoulder.

Rapscallion
and # Scapegrace

Rapscallion and *scapegrace* are both wonderful ways to offend a mischievous person (if such a person would even be offended). While *scapegrace* refers to an incorrigible character who literally escaped God's grace, *rapscallion* is an embellished version of the identically defined (but rather less fun to say) word *rascal*.

Scaramouch

In Italy's *commedia dell'arte*—a type of theater production with ensemble casts, improvisation, and masks—Scaramouch was a stock character easily identified by his boastful-yet-cowardly manner. Much like *scrooge* is now synonymous with *miser*, the word *scaramouch* was used from the 1600s through the 1800s to describe any boastful coward. Wondering why the obsolete expression sounds so familiar? The band Queen borrowed it for their operatic masterpiece "Bohemian Rhapsody," though scaramouches aren't necessarily known for doing the fandango.

Sciolist

A *sciolist* is someone who pretends to have a lot of knowledge. Though they might fool a mooncalf or two, any expert would see through their facade.

Shabaroon

This two-for-one insult (also spelled *shabbaroon*) could refer to "an ill-dressed shabby fellow" or "a mean-spirited person," per Grose, and dates back as far as 1699.

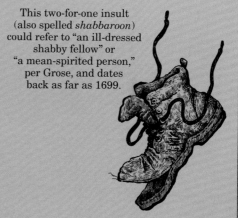

Shag-Bag

A term for "a poor sneaking fellow, a man of no spirit," according to Grose, and also a way to refer to something that's shabby in general.

Slugabed

Though this term for "a person who stays in bed late" hasn't been used much since the early twentieth century, it's the perfect insult for your roommate who perpetually hits the snooze button.

Charming
OLD-FASHIONED
COMPLIMENTS

The only thing more rewarding than receiving a fine compliment is doling one out. Here are a few charming, cute, and kooky kudos from the days of yore, all sure to land you in good favor with those on the receiving end.

Bawcock

As far as compliments go, this term for a gentleman of character and integrity, coined by William Shakespeare, is pretty hard to beat.

Bellbone

Even four hundred years ago there were instances of delicacy: Romantic knights, well-read royals, and love-struck troubadours all knew their way around some fancy words. For instance, we have this delightful term for a lady rich in personality as well as physical beauty.

Bricky

Bricky was a nineteenth-century adjective used to laud a friend for being reliable, likening the tough and unyielding nature of the party in question to—what else?—a brick.

Bully

This is a bit of a confusing one, considering the word's modern, negative connotation—but originally, *bully* was a sixteenth-century term of endearment. (According to the *Oxford English Dictionary*, it may be derived from the Dutch word *boel*, which was used for friends and companions.) You'll probably want to explain to your friend that you're intending to point out their good nature and strong moral fiber before calling them a *bully*.

Elephant's Adenoids

All of these words and phrases are great, but what need have you for any other compliment when you can tap into the wide variety of zoological possessive couplets that earned popularity in the 1920s? You've got your choice of *caterpillar's kimono*, *bullfrog's beard*, *clam's garter*, *eel's ankle*, *sardine's whiskers*, and *butterfly's book*—and our favorite, *elephant's adenoids*.

Fairhead

Say you just caught a glimpse of an attractive stranger across the room—this assessment of them as a person brimming with physical allure should win you due favor.

Pippin

When *pippin* popped up in the seventeenth century, it was a term for a young, naïve person; later, it came to be used as a term for a person of high esteem and admiration. Granted, it's also a type of apple, but context clues should clear things up in conversational use.

Snuggery

It's always appropriate to pay notice to a friend's living quarters when stopping by. If a warm, cozy, or otherwise pleasant little abode wins your notice, make sure to remark on what a fine *snuggery* your chum has managed to land.

Jammiest Bits of Jam

Granted, it sounds a bit like a compliment you'd pay to a nice piece of toast, but this Victorian Cockney slang superlative actually signifies absolutely perfect young ladies.

Liquorous Rolling Eyes

In the mid-seventeenth century, someone—possibly English author John "J. G." Gough—made a living off the art of niceties by publishing *The Academy of Complements*, in which he offers a wide variety of options for laying some charm on a romantic partner. Along with the above line, Gough included things like "Her breath doth [scent] of Amber."

Truepenny and Straight-Up

During the sixteenth century, honesty became a characteristic of newfound acclaim in the English language. If you happen upon someone whose trustworthiness cannot go without commendation, try one of these.

Lummy

Charles Dickens coined this term in 1838's *Oliver Twist* to refer to someone who is smart and attractive.

Peerless Paramour

If you're looking for a bit of Middle Ages jargon that feels a little romantic, this phrase denoting unbeatable affection is the way to go.

Wag

If you spend your time among particularly humorous company, this diminutive designation will come in handy. After your funniest friend earns a particularly big laugh, champion them as the group's beloved wag.

What's the Longest Word in the World?

If you can find a way to work *pneumonoultramicroscopicsilicovolcanoconiosis* into a conversation, congratulations! You've just managed to use the longest defined word you'll find in any dictionary in everyday chatter. But also: We hope you're feeling okay, as the forty-five-letter word is a disease that causes an inflammation of the lungs due to the inhalation of very fine silicate or quartz dust.

There *are* longer words out there: Guinness World Records champions *Nirantarāndhakāritā . . . lokān*, "a compound 'word' of 195 Sanskrit characters (transliterating to 428 letters in the Roman alphabet) describing the region near Kanci, Tamil Nadu, India," as the longest word, while chemical words, like naming a single molecule of DNA, could eventually translate to well over one billion letters. But you won't find those in the dictionary.

pneu- mo- noul- tramicro- scopic- silico- volcano- coniosis

A WORLD of WORDS

The world's languages contain words that are beautiful, thrilling, and evocative—and often, they convey feelings or concepts that English can't condense into a single term. Here are just a few of our favorite words from around the globe.

Bananenbieger // GERMAN

In Germany, someone who's engaged in a pointless task, who can't concentrate, or has no direction in life can be called a *bananenbieger*, or "banana bender." (One more delightful German insult for you: *Teletubbyzurückwinker*, which means "someone who waves back at Teletubbies," describes someone who isn't too bright.)

Ch'arachchi // ARMENIAN

If you're looking for a way to tell a kid in your life that they're naughty without actually *saying* they're naughty, use the Armenian word *ch'arachchi*.

Commuovere // ITALIAN

Have you ever seen something so beautiful it made you cry? That's *commuovere* in action. The Italian word describes the feeling of being moved, touched, or stirred by something you witness or experience.

Còsagach // SCOTTISH GAELIC

Còsagach, like *hygge*—a Danish concept related to the warm, contented feeling of being indoors during wintertime is the sensation you get when you're snug, sheltered, and cozy. The comforting feeling can be found almost anywhere (at a restaurant, a ski resort, or, in true Scottish tradition, a pub). Or at least that's what Scotland's tourism agency claimed. According to the BBC, one Gaelic expert said most Gaelic speakers think of it as "a wee hidey hole or nook that a creepy crawly might live in." Which is a useful phrase in its way, if a bit less relaxing.

Cwtch // WELSH

A very Welsh term for a hug that makes you feel warm inside. (It rhymes with *butch*.)

Esprit de L'Escalier // FRENCH

Did you think of the perfect retort, but only well after the opportunity to deliver it? The French have a phrase for that: *esprit de l'escalier*, or "wit of the staircase." (In German, the word is *treppenwitz*.)

Fjaka // CROATIAN

If you can manage to surrender your whole mind and body to not doing anything at all, it can feel almost euphoric. Croatians call this all-encompassing relaxation *fjaka*.

Gigil // TAGALOG

Ever get that feeling where you see something that's so cute you have the nearly irresistible urge to smoosh it? Tagalog, one of the languages spoken in the Philippines, has a word for that strong emotion: *gigil*. It can also be used in a less positive way—*nakakagigil ka* is basically what you'd say when you're super mad or frustrated with a person or situation.

Gluggaveður // ICELANDIC

This word gets a lot of traction in Iceland: It means "window-weather." As in, the kind of weather that's nice to look at, but not experience. Icelandic also has *sólarfrí*, or "sun holiday"—when people are given time off to enjoy good weather.

Hanyauku // KWANGALI

Taken from Kwangali, a language spoken in Namibia, *hanyauku* is the act of tiptoeing across hot sand.

Jakoś to Będzie // POLISH

The Polish have a saying for the universal experience of using hope to get through tough times: *jakoś to będzie*, which literally translates to "things will work out in the end." It's not an excuse to be passive in the face of obstacles. Rather, it's a way to let go of the things you can't control and act on the things you can without overthinking the consequences.

Jompikumpi // FINNISH

This word, meaning "one or the other," is pronounced a bit like "yompi-koompi," and was once voted one of Finland's happiest words.

Kabab Mein Haddi // HINDI/URDU

This phrase literally means "bone in kebab," something that no doubt would disrupt your eating experience. In Urdu and Hindi, *kabab mein haddi* is what you'd call a person who's always tagging along on dates—in other words, a third wheel.

Kalsarikänni // FINNISH

Kalsarikänni is the Finnish concept of taking off your pants and getting sloshed on your couch. The term roughly translates to "pants drunk" and means drinking at home, often alone, in your underwear.

Kummerspeck // GERMAN

Literally, *kummerspeck* translates to "grief bacon." But what it really refers to is the weight you gain after eating your feelings.

Lagom // SWEDISH

In Sweden, people focus on *lagom*, an idea that roughly translates to "not too much, not too little, just the right amount." *Lagom* can be found everywhere in Swedish culture. Swedes might use it to describe the strength of their coffee or slip it into conversation with sayings like *lagom är bäst* ("*lagom* is best"). But you don't need to speak Swedish to embrace the concept.

Nunch'i // KOREAN

Nunch'i translates to "eye measure," and essentially describes being able to ascertain the moods of the people around you (and how to best respond). Korean culture stresses harmony, and thus it's important to avoid doing or saying anything that could hurt another person's pride.

Qué Pedo? // SPANISH

Pedo means "fart," so this term literally translates to "what a fart"—but in Mexico, it's slang for "what's up?"

Qué Piña! // QUECHUA/SPANISH

This phrase—which means "what a pineapple!" or "such a pineapple!" in Spanish, but might derive from different history in Quechua—is said in Peru when someone is experiencing a spate of bad luck.

Ramé // BALINESE

This Balinese word refers to something that is crowded and bustling with activity.

Rosh Gadol
// HEBREW

Are you a problem solver, a person willing to go beyond your duties or your job description to get things done? There's a Hebrew word for that: *rosh gadol*, which translates to "big head"—and unlike in the U.S., it's meant as a compliment.

Sentak Bangun // INDONESIAN

The next time you dream that you're falling and wake up suddenly, use this Indonesian verb, which means "to wake up with a start."

Shinrin-Yoku // JAPANESE

This Japanese word means "forest bathing," and it's considered a form of natural medicine and stress reliever. There are now forest bathing clubs around the world, but you can try it out for yourself on your next camping trip. Take deep breaths, close your eyes, and bask in the smells and sounds of the forest. Simple.

Skitterend // AFRIKAANS

Afrikaans, one of the official languages of South Africa, is derived from Dutch (the Netherlands colonized the country beginning in 1652), but is also a distinct language all its own. *Skitterend*, meaning "luminous, dazzling," first appeared in Afrikaans in 1902; it was developed from the Dutch *schitteren,* which itself came from an earlier word with a less delightful meaning: *schetteren*, "to blare"—as in a blaring noise.

Tartle // SCOTS

A Scots verb meaning "to make out after some difficulty"; you can use it when you hesitate in recognizing or introducing a person or thing.

Uitwaaien // DUTCH

Uitwaaien, which translates to "outblowing," involves doing physical activity, like going for a brisk jog, in chilly, windy weather. It may lack the warmth and fuzziness of *hygge*, but many Dutch people swear by its energizing effects. The practice has roots in the Netherlands going back at least a century, and the name comes from the concept of replacing "bad air" with "good air." While there may not be a lot of science to support that idea, exercise does have scientifically proven benefits, such as boosting energy and lowering stress.

Ya'aburnee // ARABIC

This Arabic phrase means "you bury me"—the idea being that the speaker would prefer to die before their loved one so they don't have to live without them.

Yalla // ARABIC

This super common Arabic word—which translates to "let's go" or "come on"—is used across the Middle East to let people know they need to get a move on.

What Does *Mea Culpa* Actually Mean?

Even if you didn't study a lick of Latin in school, you might have guessed the phrase *mea culpa* came from the language. After all, English has borrowed quite a few Latin phrases over the years. This one is used as an apology. But while *I'm sorry* doesn't necessarily convey that whatever happened is your fault, *mea culpa* does.

The term hails from an old Roman Catholic prayer of confession known as the Confiteor. (The first word of the prayer is *Confiteor*, which literally means "I confess.") Though there are a number of versions of the Confiteor across multiple Christian religions, you'll typically see this line in the more traditional iterations: *meā culpā, meā culpā, meā maximā culpā.*

Without accent marks or context, this could simply be translated as "my fault, my fault, my greatest fault." But with both those components, it's a more nuanced phrase—often translated as "Through my fault, through my fault, through my most grievous fault." (Some translations drive the point home by using "through my *own* fault.")

According to the *Oxford English Dictionary*, people were exclaiming "Mea culpa!" outside of the prayer as far back as the early thirteenth century. Geoffrey Chaucer even mentioned it in his epic poem "Troilus & Criseyde," written sometime around 1385: "Now, *mea culpa*, lord! I me repente." For the next several centuries, *mea culpa* continued to be used as an interjection; much like you'd say "My bad!" or even just "My fault!"

Then, in the twentieth century, English speakers began using *mea culpa* as a noun that could describe any personal acknowledgment of guilt, fault, or error. This sense often pops up in relatively formal scenarios—if, for example, a politician admits wrongdoing in a public statement, the media might say they "issued a mea culpa." If your partner utters an offhand "I'm sorry" after forgetting to buy lemons, on the other hand, you may not feel like such a casual apology counts as a mea culpa. Though maybe if they said "Now, mea culpa, lord! I me repente" instead, you'd feel differently.

A *Brief History* OF THE WORD

Née

For especially common French loan words, you probably use them without thinking too much (or at all) about their literal meaning. Some you may use without even realizing they're French—like *RSVP*, which is an initialism for *répondez s'il vous plaît*, meaning "Reply, if it pleases you."

Unless you speak French, the word *née* probably falls in one of those two categories. Its literal translation is simply "born," from the verb *naître* ("to born"). The *-ée* ending indicates that it's modifying a feminine noun, which helps explain why English speakers have historically used it when mentioning a woman's maiden name.

If you're referring to a man who's changed his name, you should technically use *né*—the masculine ending—the same way that you'd use *fiancé* for a man engaged to be married (whereas *fiancée* is the feminine form). But *né* hasn't quite caught on in the same way, most likely because when the term entered the English language, people were only really using it to talk about women's maiden names.

According to the *Oxford English Dictionary*, the first written instance of that appeared in a 1758 letter sent by Lady Mary Wortley Montagu. "The advantage of being casually admitted in the train of Madame de *B*., *née O*," she wrote. Other notable authors adopted the tradition throughout the nineteenth century; William Makepeace Thackeray, for example, mentioned "Rebecca Crawley, née Sharp," in his 1848 classic *Vanity Fair*.

During the latter half of the twentieth century, writers started getting more creative with their usage of *née*. In 1970, a book called *Molecular Approaches to Learning and Memory* had modified the phrase *behavioral modification* with "née transfer of training" to let readers know that the terminology had changed. In short, no longer is *née* just for someone (again, usually a woman) born with some other name, but for anything or anyone formerly known as anything or anyone else.

Beyond
WANDERLUST:
WORDS
EVERY
TRAVELER
SHOULD
KNOW

For those who travel, wanderlust is a familiar feeling. It's that nagging voice in your head that says, "Yes, you do need to book that flight," even if your bank account says otherwise. Regardless of how many passport covers this word may adorn, it doesn't begin to cover the spectrum of emotions and experiences that can be revealed through the act of travel. Here are travel words from around the world to keep in your back pocket as you're exploring.

Dépaysement

Anyone who has traveled abroad will recognize this feeling. The French word refers to the sense of disorientation that often sets in when you step outside your comfort zone, such as when you leave your home country.

Dérive

Another gift from the French, this word literally translates to "drift," but thanks to some mid-twentieth-century French philosophers, it can also refer to a spontaneous trip, completely free of plans, in which you let your surroundings guide you.

Dustsceawung

This Old English word describes what might happen when you visit a place like Pompeii or a ghost town. While reflecting on past civilizations, you realize that everything will eventually turn to dust. A cheery thought.

Fernweh

Who hasn't felt a strong desire to be somewhere—anywhere—other than where you currently are? That's *fernweh*, or "farsickness," and this German word has been described as a cousin of *wanderlust*, another German loan word.

Flâneur

Taken from the French *flâner*, meaning "to stroll or saunter," this word describes someone who has no particular plans or place they need to be. They merely stroll around the city at a leisurely pace, taking in the sights and enjoying the day as it unfolds.

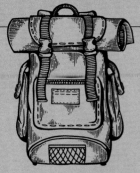

Gadabout

This could be construed as the traditional English equivalent of *flâneur*. Likely stemming from the Middle English verb *gadden*, meaning "to wander without a specific aim or purpose," a *gadabout* is one who frequently travels from place to place for the sheer fun of it. In other words: a modern-day backpacker.

Hiraeth

Sometimes, no matter how amazing your vacation may be, you just want to come home to your bed and cats. This Welsh word (pronounced "HERE-eyeth") sums up the deep yearning for home that can strike without warning.

Komorebi

This beautiful Japanese word is a good one to save for a sunny day spent in the woods. *Komorebi* translates to "sunshine filtering through the leaves." Does it get any lovelier than that?

Lehitkalev

Backpackers and budget travelers, this one is for you: The Hebrew word *lehitkalev* translates to "dog it" and means "to deal with uncomfortable living or travel arrangements."

Numinous

This English word could appropriately be used to describe the Grand Canyon or the Northern Lights. Something *numinous* is awe-inspiring and mysterious. It's difficult to understand from a rational perspective, which gives it a spiritual or unearthly quality.

Perambulate

This word essentially means to travel over or through an area by foot. So instead of saying that you'll be walking around London, you can say you'll be *perambulating* the city's streets—much more sophisticated.

Peregrinate

To *peregrinate* is to travel from place to place, like *perambulate*, especially on foot. Its Latin root, *peregrinus* (meaning "foreign"), is also where the peregrine falcon (literally "pilgrim falcon") gets its name.

Peripatetic

The young and the restless will want to incorporate this word into their lexicon. The adjective refers to those who are constantly moving from place to place—in other words, people living a nomadic existence. It stems from the Greek word *peripatein* ("to walk up and down"), which was originally associated with Aristotle and the shaded walkways near his school (or, according to legend, his habit of pacing back and forth during lectures).

Resfeber

You just booked your flight. Your heart starts racing. You're a little nervous about your journey, but mostly you just can't wait to get going. The anticipation, anxiety, and excitement you get before a big trip is all rolled into one word—*resfeber*—and you can thank the Swedes for it.

Schwellenangst

Translating to "threshold anxiety," this German word sums up the fears that are present before you enter somewhere new—like a theater or an intimidating café—and by extension going anywhere unfamiliar. The fear of crossing a threshold is normal, even among the most adventurous of travelers—but it often leads to the most unforgettable experiences.

Selcouth

An Old English word that refers to something that's both strange and marvelous. It's a great way to sum up those seemingly indescribable moments spent in an unfamiliar land.

Smultronställe

This Swedish word translates to something along the lines of "place of wild strawberries," but its metaphorical meaning is something along the lines of a "happy place." Whether it's a hidden overlook of the city or your favorite vacation spot that hasn't been "discovered" yet, *smultronställe* refers to those semi-secret places you return to time and time again because they're special and personal to you.

Solivagant

In those moments when you just want to run away from your responsibilities, you may consider becoming a *solivagant*: a solo wanderer.

Trouvaille

Translating to a "lucky find," this French word can be applied to that cool café, flower-lined street, or quirky craft store that you stumbled upon by chance. Indeed, these are the moments that make travel worthwhile.

Ullassa

Just in case you needed another reason to plan that trip to Yosemite, here's one more term for nature lovers. The Sanskrit word *ullassa* refers to the feelings of pleasantness that come from observing natural beauty in all its glory.

Vacilando

In some Spanish dialects, the word *vacilando* describes someone who travels with a vague destination in mind but has no real incentive to get there. In other words, the journey is more important than the destination.

Vagary

From the Latin *vagari*, meaning "to wander," this sixteenth-century word originally meant "a wandering journey." Nowadays, *vagary* refers to an unpredictable or erratic situation, but that doesn't mean the old sense of the word can't be invoked from time to time.

Waldeinsamkeit

You're alone in a forest. It's peaceful. The sun is filtering through the trees and there's a light breeze. That's *waldeinsamkeit*. (Literally "forest solitude.") Use it on your next hike.

Yoko Meshi

This Japanese phrase literally translates to "a meal eaten sideways," which is an apt way to describe the awkwardness of speaking in a foreign language that you haven't quite mastered, especially over dinner.

Yūgen

This Japanese word can be taken to mean "graceful elegance" or "subtle mystery," but it's much more than that. It's when the beauty of the universe is felt most profoundly, awakening an emotional response that goes beyond words.

THIS IS
WHY
IT'S SO **HARD** TO **LEARN** A SECOND LANGUAGE **AS AN ADULT**

If learning a foreign language seems to get harder and harder with age, it isn't just your imagination. A 2018 study by Massachusetts-based researchers found that language-learning ability starts to decline around age eighteen.

And if you want to sound like a native speaker, your chances are better if you started learning before the ripe old age of ten.

Using the results of an online grammar test that was circulated on Facebook, researchers determined that children have the best capacity for learning complex grammar rules, while those of us who started learning a language in adulthood "are often saddled with an accent and conspicuous grammatical errors." Their findings were published in the journal *Cognition*.

The online test was taken by nearly 670,000 people of all ages from around the world—one of the largest linguistic studies ever conducted, according to *Scientific American*. Test takers were asked their age, how long they had been learning English, and the countries they had lived in for at least six months. The study found that people who learned a language by immersion were more fluent than those who learned in a classroom. Based on these test results and demographics, researchers developed models to predict how long it takes to achieve fluency in a language.

Researchers aren't sure what causes the drastic decline after age eighteen, but they believe it has something to do with the fact that the brain becomes less adaptable in adulthood.

But that's no reason to sell your Rosetta Stone software just yet. Researchers say dedicated language learners can still become proficient—even fluent—well into adulthood. A study from 2014 revealed that learning a new language as an adult can help slow brain decline, and other studies point to the benefits of being bilingual, including a later onset of dementia. But the Boston researchers also found that it takes thirty years to fully master a language, so it's best to get started right away.

Why Is Latin a Dead Language?

Calling a language dead seems more like an insult than a simple categorical designation—as though it's less important than its living counterparts. And if we're talking about a language specifically as a way to have a conversation, a dead one is less important.

A dead language is any language that's no longer in use by a group of people. That definition may vary slightly depending on your source: According to the *Cambridge Dictionary*, a language is also sometimes considered dead if it's no longer anyone's *main* language or just not used for ordinary communicating.

Latin checks all these boxes. It used to be spoken in ancient Rome, and eventually evolved into the Romance languages after the fall of the Roman Empire. It's not necessarily that nobody *can* speak Latin today, or even that they don't—it's more that nobody needs to use Latin to say something like "Where's the bathroom?" for lack of another option.

But just because Latin is technically dead doesn't mean it's gone. For one thing, plenty of people study it, from high schoolers with an interest in etymology to classics scholars who prefer to read Virgil's *Aeneid* in its purest form. Because Latin is still studied and spoken in some contexts, it's not considered an extinct language, or one that has no remaining speakers at all.

Even people who don't study or speak Latin still use parts of the language. Scientists, for example, give Latin names to newly discovered species—though some Latinized terms, like the Taylor Swift–inspired *swiftae* in *Nannaria swiftae*, definitely weren't around in Julius Caesar's day. Vatican City actually still counts Latin as one of its two official languages (along with Italian). And that's not to mention all the Latin terms that regularly crop up in English: legal jargon like *habeas corpus*, journalistic customs like *sic* (see page 100), and general expressions like *mea culpa* (see page 150) and *quid pro quo*.

FREQUENTLY *Mispronounced* COUNTRY NAMES

While it's always good to respect the cultures and traditions of countries around the world, we can sometimes make an innocent error in completely butchering their pronunciation. If you plan on traveling or talking foreign policy—or just want a refresher—take a look at nine of the most frequently mispronounced country names in the world.

Antigua

Many people mistakenly add a "gwah" to make "Ann-TEE-gwah." The companion of Barbuda is actually pronounced "An-TEE-guh."

Iran

Iran isn't "I ran." It's "Eee-RAHN." However you say it, bring water. In 2017, the city of Ahvaz in Iran recorded a temperature of nearly 129°F.

Belarus

Do you say "Bel-air-us"? It's "Bel-uh-ROOZ."

Iraq

If you're saying "Eye-RACK," you've got it messed up. It's "Ee-ROCK." A lost Bronze Age city named Mardaman was identified ("eye-den-tee-fied") there in 2018.

Nepal

You'll hear this country name often, as it's the home of Mount Everest. But many say "Neh-paal" when they should say "Ni-PAUL."

Kyrgyzstan

Don't say "Cry-gee-stan." Opt for "KEER-gihs-tahn" instead—the *z* is silent.

Pakistan

Do you say "Pack-iss-stan"? Forget *pack*. It's pronounced "POCK-kee-stahn." And if you're wondering why so many country names end in *-stan*, it's because the word means "settlement," "state," or "place" in various languages. Pakistan was formed from the country's constituent units of the 1930s: Punjab, Afghan, Kashmir, Sind, and Balochistan. (They did have to add an *i*.) It's also likely from the Urdu *pak*, meaning "pure."

Samoa

This island—and Girl Scout Cookie flavor—is often said as "Sam-OH-uh." It's "Saah-MOH-uh." And no, no one is quite sure about the cookie connection, though it might have something to do with coconuts.

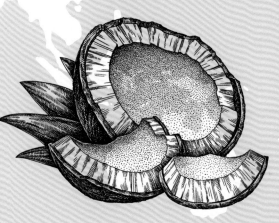

Qatar

This Middle Eastern country's name is often cited as "Kah-TAHR," but it's more like "KUT-uhr."

The SURPRISINGLY DARK ORIGINS OF POPULAR PHRASES

Many English speakers don't give much thought to the idioms they use on a regular basis. Some common sayings have silly backstories, while others are more disturbing than they seem out of context. From poisoning to warfare to racism, here are the dark origins behind common phrases that may be part of your vocabulary.

Bite the Bullet

Someone is usually told to *bite the bullet* before pushing through something unpleasant. Centuries ago, that something unpleasant was considerably more painful than a bothersome chore or inconvenient meeting. According to one theory, the phrase originated with wounded soldiers undergoing surgery on the battlefield without anesthesia; they were given something solid but malleable to bite down on, like a bullet, which prevented them from crying out in pain or biting their tongues. But some have cast doubt on this theory, pointing to a lack of evidence and the fact that surgeons had leather straps in their kits for patients to bite down on.

An alternate origin story applies the same idea to victims of whipping. In the definition of the slang term *nightingale* in his 1796 book *A Classical Dictionary of the Vulgar Tongue*, English lexicographer Francis Grose mentions soldiers who would "chew a bullet" while being flogged: "A soldier who, as the term is, sings out at the halberts. It is a point of honour in some regiments, among the grenadiers, never to cry out, or become nightingales, whilst under the discipline of the cat of nine tails; to avoid which, they chew a bullet."

Punishments by flogging and surgeries without anesthesia are, thankfully, less common today, but the saying has stuck around.

Cakewalk

In the antebellum South, some enslaved people spent Sundays dressing up and performing dances in the spirit of mocking the white upper classes. The enslavers didn't know they were the butt of the joke, and even encouraged these performances and rewarded the best dancers with cake, hence the name.

Possibly because this was viewed as a leisurely weekend activity, the phrase *cakewalk* became associated with easy tasks. Cakewalks didn't end with slavery: For decades, they remained (with cake prizes) a part of Black life, but at the same time white actors in blackface incorporated the act into minstrel shows, turning what began as a satire of white elites into a racist caricature of Black people.

Drinking the Kool-Aid

The origin of this saying, meaning "following the crowd," comes from the Jonestown massacre. On November 18, 1978, more than nine hundred members of the Peoples Temple movement died in a mass murder-suicide event that involved a fruit-flavored beverage laced with cyanide and other drugs. The murder-suicide orchestrated by cult leader Jim Jones is considered one of the deadliest non-natural catastrophes in U.S. history. (Though the tragedy took place in Guyana, the majority of the victims were American citizens.)

Today, *drinking the Kool-Aid* can be applied to anyone who blindly embraces a group or trend, especially if it's to their detriment, but there are a couple of reasons you should rethink using the phrase. In addition to being in poor taste, it's not accurate: The victims at Jonestown actually drank an off-brand powdered drink called Flavor Aid, leading to one of the more unfortunate cases of brand-name generalization of all time.

Indian Giver

Merriam-Webster defines an *Indian giver* as someone who gives something to another person before taking it back. One of the first appearances was in Thomas Hutchinson's *History of the Colony of Massachusets-Bay in the mid 18th century*. In a note, it says "An Indian gift is a proverbial expression, signifying a present for which an equivalent return is expected." In the nineteenth century, the stereotype was transferred from the gift to the giver, the idea of an "equivalent return" was abandoned, and it became used as an insult. An 1838 *New-York Mirror* article mentions the "distinct species of crimes and virtues of schoolchildren," elaborating, "I have seen the finger pointed at the Indian giver. (One who gives a present and demands it back again.)"

Even as this stereotype about Indigenous people faded, the phrase *Indian giver* has persisted into the twenty-first century. The word *Indian* in *Indian giver* also denotes something false, as it does in the antiquated phrase *Indian summer*.

Long Time, No See

The saying *long time, no see* can be traced back to the nineteenth century. In a *Boston Sunday Globe* article from 1894, the words are applied to a Native American speaker. The broken English phrase was also used to evoke white people's stereotypical ideas of Native American speech in William F. Drannan's 1899 book *Thirty-One Years on the Plains and in the Mountains, Or, the Last Voice from the Plains, an Authentic Record of a Life Time of Hunting, Trapping, Scouting and Indian Fighting in the Far West.*

It's unlikely actual Native Americans were saying *long time, no see* during this era. According to the *Oxford English Dictionary*, this type of isolating construction would have been unusual for the Indigenous languages of North America. Rather, it originated as a way for white writers to mock Native American speech, and that of non-native English speakers from other places like China. By the 1920s, it had become an ordinary part of the American vernacular.

Mad as a Hatter

The phrase *mad as a hatter* may sound whimsical, but it likely refers to a serious medical condition that once plagued the hat-making industry. In the eighteenth and nineteenth centuries, fur felt (which is more durable and lightweight than wool felt) for hats was made by treating animal pelts with mercury nitrate. Workers exposed to this toxic substance over time developed symptoms such as tremors, speech problems, hallucinations, and mental and emotional instability. The popularity of the phrase *mad as a hatter* shows how widespread the ailments were, but mercury continued to be used in hat making into the twentieth century. The U.S. officially banned it from felt production in the 1940s.

Meet a Deadline

The word *deadline* was meant to be taken literally in the nineteenth century. During the Civil War, a dead line marked the boundary surrounding a prison—sometimes in the form of a ditch or line in the dirt. Captive soldiers who crossed it risked getting shot. Decades after the war, the term took on less serious implications. Coming up against a deadline isn't exactly a desirable situation today, but you won't be killed for handing in your term paper late.

Mumbo Jumbo

Before it was synonymous with jargon or other confusing language, the phrase *mumbo jumbo* originated with religious ceremonies in West Africa. In the Mandinka language, the word *maamajomboo* described a masked dancer who participated in ceremonies. Former Royal African Company clerk Francis Moore transcribed the name as *mumbo jumbo* in his 1738 book *Travels into the Inland Parts of Africa*. In the early 1800s, English speakers started to divorce the phrase from its African origins and apply it to anything that confused them.

No Can Do

Similar to *long time, no see*, *no can do* originated as a jab at non-native speakers of English. According to the *OED*, this example was likely directed at Chinese immigrants in the early twentieth century. Today, many people who use the phrase as general slang for "I can't do that" are unaware of its cruel origins.

Riding Shotgun

Today, *riding shotgun* simply means sitting in the passenger seat of a vehicle, but that spot came with big responsibilities on stagecoaches in the Wild West. If a coach was transporting something valuable, the person who sat beside the driver might be tasked with fending off potential thieves and wild animals with a literal shotgun.

Although the concept originated in the Old West, the phrase *riding shotgun* itself wasn't used widely until the twentieth century—after occasionally popping up in newspapers, then often in Hollywood Westerns, until it got its less violent interpretation that applies to car travel.

Show Your True Colors

The phrase *show your true colors* is thought to have originated on the high seas. To gain the trust of an enemy vessel, warships used to take down their flag and fly the colors of a different country—also known as *false colors*—and once they came within firing range, the disguised ship would switch flags, thus showing its true colors. Pirate ships were known to use the same trick to get close to the vessels they targeted. Now the same expression is applied to people who act in deceitful ways to get what they want before revealing their true nature.

Sold Down the River

Before the phrase *sold down the river* meant "betrayal," it originated as a literal slave-trading practice. Enslaved people from more northerly regions were sold to cotton plantations in the Deep South via the Mississippi and Ohio rivers. For enslaved people, the threat of being sold down the river implied separation from family and the guarantee of a life of hard labor and brutal conditions. A journal entry from April 1835 mentions a person who, "having been sold to go down the river, attempted first to cut off both of his legs, failing to do that, cut his throat, did not entirely take his life, went a short distance and drowned himself."

Tipping Point

This common phrase describes the critical point when a change that had been a possibility becomes inevitable. When it was popularized, according to Merriam-Webster, it was applied to one phenomenon in particular: white flight. In the 1950s, as white people abandoned urban areas for the suburbs in huge numbers, journalists began using the phrase *tipping point* in relation to the percentage of non-white neighbors it took to trigger this reaction in white city residents. *Tipping point* wasn't coined in the 1950s (it first appeared in print in the nineteenth century), but it did enter everyday speech during the decade thanks to this topic.

WORDS
THAT
CAME
From
SPORTS

Sports slang has escaped the confines of the field and seeped into our everyday lives, most notably when it comes to workplace culture. It's not uncommon for a PowerPoint presentation by a CEO or conference call with marketing to include terms like *slam dunk* for an easy assignment or *hail Mary* when a company is looking to pull off a last-ditch effort for success. But the colorful language of baseball, football, and the like has gifted us with far more than just office platitudes. Here are some fun words and phrases that come to us from sports.

Bush League

Whenever anyone's behavior isn't quite up to professional standards, you might hear them described as *bush league*. The *bush* in question used to refer to the rural area that a minor-league sports team operated in.

Can of Corn

When a fielder settles under a lazy fly ball for an easy out during a baseball game, it's known as a *can of corn*. It's said that this term comes from the supermarkets of the nineteenth century, when a clerk would use a long stick to nudge a can off the highest shelf and catch it in their outstretched apron. Now it can be used for anything—from an easy work assignment to a simple household fix—that can be done effortlessly. For the basketball equivalent, opt for *layup*.

Deke

Allegedly a shortened form of *decoy*, a *deke* is a quick move specifically designed to fool an opponent. It was popularized in the world of hockey and generally refers to an offensive player doing some fancy footwork (rather, skate work) to get around a defender.

Goat

Muhammad Ali used to refer to himself as the greatest of all time—so when it came time to name his company in 1992, he went with G.O.A.T.; a few years later, LL Cool J worked the acronym into a song. These days—whether we're talking sports or pop culture—when someone is excellent in what they do, we say they're "the goat."

Hat Trick

This term for scoring three goals in the course of a game originated with cricket circa 1868; it came from the fact that players who achieved the feat would be given the gift of a new hat. By the 1890s, it had transcended cricket for use in sports in general. (Except for bowling, where getting three strikes in a row is known as *bowling a turkey*.)

Lettuce and Flow

Next time you're watching lacrosse and spot some wonderful hair sticking out of the back of a player's helmet, call it by its proper name: *lettuce*. This fun term is designated for those luscious locks that drape down to a player's shoulder.

In hockey (and sometimes in lacrosse as well), *flow* is the preferred slang and often refers to a hairstyle that is similar to a mullet but with a bit more panache. And if a player lets their hair grow a bit too long, that's known as *overflow*.

Mendoza Line

This phrase is in reference to Mario Mendoza, a light-hitting shortstop in the late 1970s. He was known for a paltry batting average that hovered around .200, leading his teammates at the Seattle Mariners to declare the number the *Mendoza line*. Anything lower and you likely weren't big-league material.

The term has since been used outside of baseball to describe any threshold that you don't want to be under—financial analysts, for example, use a 2-percent yield on ten-year U.S. Treasury Bonds as their own Mendoza Line separating a healthy economy from a recession.

Palooka

Today, *palooka* is a put-down referring to anyone with oafish or clumsy qualities, but it originally referred specifically to mediocre boxers. The exact origins are unknown, but the term was popularized in the 1930s comic strip *Joe Palooka*, about a middling fighter with a heart of gold. *Palooka* has since transcended the ring and packs a far more negative punch.

Slobberknocker

A hard-nosed football player infamous for making big hits used to be known as a *slobberknocker*. In recent years, that bit of salivary slang has evolved past the individual player and is now used to describe any hard-fought game, fight, or match. It's common to use the term for big championship showdowns or heavyweight title bouts, but don't be surprised if your boss uses it to describe a tough financial quarter.

WHY DO QUARTERBACKS SAY "HUT" AND "HIKE"?

At the start of their 2009–2010 season, the National Football League (NFL) wondered why a quarterback screams *hut* just before a play is initiated—so they asked linguist Ben Zimmer to provide some context. According to Zimmer, a quarterback yelling "hut" or variations like "hut one," "hut two," or "hut three" is taking a cue from military cadence.

In the service, *hut* often replaces a syllable in a word to make it sharper and more distinctive. Think of a drill sergeant yelling "atten-hut!" ("attention!") at cadets. The wordplay seems to galvanize the listener's focus, which is particularly helpful when you're about to undergo a rigorous military march or are in imminent danger of being obliterated by a three-hundred-pound lineman.

Hut likely originated during World War II at the latest, and it wasn't until the 1950s that football players began adopting it for their simulated war game on the field. (Many players and coaches were former soldiers, making the evolution of the word easy to chart.) Zimmer added that *hut* is a clean, concise word that can be barked over distances, which is beneficial to quarterbacks who need to be heard.

The military got *hut* from animal herders. Words like *hip*, *hup*, and *hep* date back centuries, with *hup* in use beginning in the eighteenth century and *hut* in the nineteenth century. The military adopted variations early in the twentieth century before settling on *hut*.

That other football staple, *hike*, has a much more linear origin. It came from football legend John Heisman, who started shouting it while playing for the University of Pennsylvania during the 1890–1891 season. He did it to avoid being tricked.

As a center responsible for snapping the ball to the quarterback to begin the play, he usually got scratched on his leg as a signal. When an opposing player deviously touched his leg and made him flip the ball, it screwed up the play. Saying *hike*—which means "to pull or raise with a sudden motion"—eliminated the leg-rubbing deception. (It should be noted that other sources put Heisman's *hike* epiphany later in his career, after he became a coach.)

A *Brief History* OF THE PHRASE
The Whole Nine Yards

In 1982, *New York Times* language columnist William Safire appeared on Larry King's radio show and asked the general public to help him solve what he'd later describe as "one of the great etymological mysteries of our time": What were the yards in the phrase *the whole nine yards* originally measuring?

A Texas seamstress speculated that it could have been fabric. A Connecticut man wrote in to claim that it was actually cement, as some cement trucks carry a maximum of nine cubic yards. Fred Cassidy, founder of the *Dictionary of American Regional English*, had another idea. *Yard* was an old nautical term for a wooden rod connected to a sailing ship's masts to support its sails. Square-rigged, three-masted ships had three yards each, said Cassidy, "so the 'whole nine yards' would mean the sails were fully set."

Four years after Safire's 1982 plea, the *Oxford English Dictionary* printed a supplement dating *the whole nine yards* back to 1970. Jonathan E. Lighter's *Historical Dictionary of American Slang*, published in the mid-1990s, unearthed a slightly earlier citation: Elaine Shepard's 1967 Vietnam War novel, *The Doom Pussy*.

As Yale Law librarian Fred R. Shapiro wrote in a 2009 article for the *Yale Alumni Magazine*, it seemed likely at the time that the phrase had originated in the Air Force. *The Doom Pussy* followed Air Force pilots, and other mentions of

SAY WHAT? Why Do Golfers Yell "**Fore!**" When Teeing Off?

If you hear someone shout "Fore!" while you're on or near a golf course, you may want to quickly scan the skies to make sure a golf ball isn't careening toward your head—or better yet, just duck and cover: Golfers use the interjection when an airborne shot runs the risk of hitting a fellow player or spectator.

Why they yell "Fore!" rather than "Look out!," "Incoming!," or some other slightly more self-evident warning boils down to tradition's sake. And while people generally agree that the tradition began in Scotland—the birthplace of modern golf—how it began is a matter of some debate.

the whole nine yards from the era also involved that particular military branch. One theory held that the nine yards first referred to certain twenty-seven-foot-long ammunition belts used by Air Force pilots in World War II.

Then, in 2007, a recreational lexical investigator named Sam Clements discovered the phrase in a 1964 syndicated newspaper article on NASA jargon. "'Give 'em the whole nine yards' means an item-by-item report on any project," Stephen Trumbull wrote.

Linguist Ben Zimmer pointed out in 2009 that this didn't necessarily debunk the military origin story: After all, NASA and the Air Force had close ties. But it didn't prove it, either—so the sleuths soldiered on. American Dialect Society member (and neuroscience researcher) Bonnie Taylor-Blake found citations in a 1962 Car Life article about "all nine yards of goodies" in the Chevrolet Impala sedan, and in the July 1956 and January 1957 issues of a magazine published by the Kentucky Department of Fish and Wildlife. Taylor-Blake's most notable contribution to the case occurred in September 2012, when she uncovered a 1921 newspaper headline that read "The Whole Six Yards of It." The article below it was an inning-by-inning account of a baseball game, which didn't mention anything about actual yards. A subsequent hunt for this older variant of the phrase turned up three mentions in Kentucky's Mount Vernon Signal newspaper: two from 1912, found by Shapiro, and a third from 1916, which Taylor-Blake spotted.

Since then, even earlier citations have shown up for both versions of the expression.

The OED now dates the whole nine yards back to 1855 in a humorous story and 1907 in the modern meaning. Never mind that the evidence has ruled out any relation to the Air Force or cement trucks.

The switch from six yards to nine propagated a whole new theory: If the number could change, maybe it never actually was measuring anything. As Shapiro told the New York Times, this type of "numerical phrase inflation" isn't unheard of; before cloud nine, for instance, there was cloud seven. Moreover, yards aren't the only thing we combine with the word whole to convey all the way, everything, or pulling out all the stops. There's also the whole enchilada, the whole ball of wax, and the whole shebang, among others.

The specificity of the phrase has given rise to countless explanations involving just about any kind of yard: yards in a football down (which is really ten yards), yards of cloth used for a Scottish kilt, and so forth. On his linguistics blog World Wide Words, etymologist Michael Quinion lists some of the more colorful theories that he's come across, including "the size of a nun's habit," "the volume of a rich man's grave," and "how far you would have to sprint during a jail break to get from the cellblock to the outer wall."

The creativity of these ideas—and the commitment to finding the phrase's definitive backstory—suggests that we tend to have a tough time admitting that some questions might just not have an answer. So maybe the real mystery behind the whole nine yards is more of a psychological one than an etymological one.

According to a theory endorsed by the United States Golf Association, fore is short for before or afore; and soldiers originally shouted it to alert their comrades on the front lines that they'd soon be firing from behind them. Another (albeit unlikely) possibility is that fore derives from Faugh a Ballach!—a nineteenth-century Irish battle cry meaning "Clear the way!," which is now sometimes used in Irish road bowling.

But the most common origin story involves forecaddies.

Basically, before a golfer took a swing, their forecaddie would run along to the general vicinity where the ball was expected to end up and watch it come down. That way, the golfers themselves wouldn't have to waste time hunting for their balls and waste money replacing ones they never found. In this case, fore is short for forecaddie, and golfers shouted it so their forecaddies would know that the balls were headed their way.

The timing of fore's appearance in the lexicon seems to support this theory, too. Its earliest known written instance in reference to golf, per the Oxford English Dictionary (which supports the before hypothesis), is from 1878—a good eighty-six years after forecaddie (or rather fore-cadie) was first mentioned in print. That said, it is technically possible that people had been bellowing "Fore!" for decades before it made its way into writing—perhaps having borrowed it from the military—and forecaddie got its name from that practice.

Why Do We Call the NCAA Basketball Tournament **March Madness**?

E very year in March, the nation's sixty-eight best college basketball teams battle for the chance to take home the NCAA championship trophy after a high-energy, single-elimination tournament aptly nicknamed "March Madness." The nickname came from a surprising place.

Back in March 1939, an Illinois High School Association (IHSA) administrator and basketball coach named Henry V. Porter penned an article titled "March Madness" for the association's magazine. In it, he discussed the excitement surrounding the annual statewide basketball tournament, suggesting that a "little March madness may complement and contribute to sanity and help keep society on an even keel." As *TIME* points out, 1939 also happened to be the first year that the NCAA held a championship game, which the University of Oregon won against the Ohio State University.

Porter's enthusiasm for youth basketball was so great that he followed up his article with a 1942 poem called "Basketball Ides of March," which included the line "A sharp-shooting mite is king tonight / The Madness of March is running." The alliterative nickname caught on throughout the state, and Illinoisans continued to use it without interference for the next forty years.

According to Slate, it was CBS broadcaster Brent Musburger (a former sports writer in Chicago) who first co-opted the moniker for college basketball while covering the NCAA tournament in 1982. By the end of the decade, IHSA had submitted a trademark application for "March Madness," and the organization butted heads with an NCAA partner over its use of the name on a computer game in 1996. To prevent further legal conflicts, they formed

the March Madness Athletic Association and decided the IHSA could use *March Madness* for high school sports, and the NCAA could use it on the collegiate level—though according to some trademark lawyers, the NCAA got full rights in 2012.

While Porter is usually credited with coining the phrase, Dictionary.com reports the idea of "March Madness" had been around for centuries before he made it all about hoops. The earliest known record of the aphorism *mad as a March hare*, which refers to hares' noticeable aggression during breeding season, is from the early sixteenth century. The phrase and its derivatives, including *March mad* and *March madness*, appeared intermittently through the next several centuries; perhaps the most memorable of these mentions was Lewis Carroll's character, the March Hare, in his 1865 book, *Alice's Adventures in Wonderland*. (The Hatter was also mad, but for a different reason—see page 160.) The phrase *March Madness* was even being applied to basketball at least eight years pre-Porter: in reference to a championship in Indiana. That early history has all but disappeared, possibly because Musburger just didn't happen to work in Indianapolis.

EVERYDAY PHRASES YOU DIDN'T KNOW CAME *From* HORSE RACING

The English language is full of common phrases coined so long ago that their original—often literal—meanings have long been forgotten, like these everyday utterances that came straight from the horse races.

Across the Board

Before *across the board* referred to everything in a given category, it was used to describe a bet in which you chose one horse and put equal sums of money into all three possible lucrative outcomes: winning (first place), placing (first or second place), and showing (first, second, or third place). Since bookies kept track of odds on blackboards back in the early twentieth century, this type of wager meant you were literally selecting all the options across the board.

Fast Track

In the mid-nineteenth century, per the *Oxford English Dictionary*, a *fast track* was a hard track with a dry surface that allowed horses to run quickly; a *slow track*, meanwhile, was the exact opposite. Though *slow track* did catch on as a metaphorical phrase, *fast track* is the more popular of the two. Today, a fast track can be any accelerated path, literal or figurative; it's even been turned into a verb. Fast-track that report of most hated business jargon, please (see page 189).

Give-and-Take

As far back as the late 1760s, a *give and take plate* was the prize for a race in which the playing field was evened out by having taller horses carry extra weight. By the late 1770s, people had already started using it to describe other situations that called for compromise and fair exchange. The first known mention of this broader sense comes from Frances Burney's 1778 novel *Evelina*: "Give and take is fair in all nations."

Hands Down

These days, *hands down* usually means "indisputably" or "effortlessly." When it originated in the nineteenth century, the phrase specifically described a horse race that was won indisputably or effortlessly—so much so that the jockey would slacken the reins and cross the finish line with hands down.

Home Stretch and Home Straight

If you assumed this entry began as baseball slang, you're probably not alone—it makes sense that the last segment of the diamond, from third base to home plate, would be called the *home stretch* or *home straight*. But it was originally used in horse racing: It's the last (straight) leg of the track between the final corner and the finish line. These days, the final push before the end of anything—a trip, project, etc.—can be a home stretch.

Jockey for Position

Jockeying for position just means you're trying to move into a better position—maybe for a better view at a concert, or for a clearer path to the finish line in an actual race. The origins of the phrase may seem obvious, since jockeys angle for better positioning during today's horse races. But its history is a little more complicated than that, because the word *jockey* didn't always just refer to racehorse riders. It also described horse dealers, who had a reputation for cheating, making crooked deals, and generally being untrustworthy.

So people started using *jockey* as a verb that basically meant "to gain an advantage over someone by tricking them" or "to get something by cheating or outwitting someone." According to the *OED*, it was this sense that gave rise to the phrase *jockey for position*. In other words, if you nabbed a better position, the implication was once that you got there on the backs of those less cunning or more moralistic than you.

Neck and Neck

Neck and neck originally described well-matched horses who didn't pull ahead of each other during a race: Their necks stayed even. The earliest known written instance of the phrase with regard to horses is from 1799, and it almost immediately got co-opted for other types of races—specifically political ones. "The contest for Kent is the keenest that has yet been run. The three candidates are neck and neck," the *Morning Post* reported in July 1802.

Run for Your Money

If you were a nineteenth-century race-goer backing a certain horse, you wanted to get a *run for your money*—preferably a profitable one, but any run was better than no run. After all, there's always a chance that a horse might be withdrawn from the lineup (or "scratched") at the last minute because of injury, illness, subpar racing conditions, or any number of other reasons. Before long, people started using *a run for one's money* outside the racetrack in scenarios where someone or something proved to be a worthy competitor.

Under the Wire and Down to the Wire

Because a wire was sometimes hung above the finish line so judges could more easily identify the winning horses, people started calling the finish line *the wire* around the 1870s. If you said a horse came in *under the wire*, you just meant that they crossed the finish line; and if you said two horses raced *down to the wire*, you meant that they ended the race in close competition. Probably owing to the dramatic and last-minute nature of horse racing in general, *under the wire* and *down to the wire* both came to describe something finished or accomplished at the last possible minute.

Win by a Nose

Thanks to those aforementioned necks, horses' noses often cross the finish line before their legs. If the first-place finisher in a nineteenth-century horse race eked out a win by a tiny margin, they quite literally only won by a nose. Today, any kind of close victory can be described as being *won by a nose*.

Who Created the Crossword Puzzle?

Will Shortz may be the biggest name in word puzzles today, but you probably wouldn't have the *New York Times*'s Sunday edition to struggle over if it weren't for Arthur Wynne.

Originally from England, Wynne was an itinerant newspaperman who eventually got a job at Joseph Pulitzer's *New York World*. He edited the paper's "Fun" section, which included everything from comics to riddles to a rotating cast of word games. For the December 21, 1913, supplement, Wynne gave the world a lasting Christmas present: a diamond-shaped puzzle that Shortz himself has called the world's first true crossword.

Wynne's invention had precursors—chief among them the word square. Like crosswords, those puzzles provided a series of clues to be solved with particular words. They often (but not always) resulted in a solved grid that had the same set of words across and down, a sort of linguistic variation on "magic squares," the mathematical game in which each line of a grid adds up to the same sum. Frederick Planche's Guess Me, from 1872, may be the first published word square puzzle. A few decades later, Giuseppe Airoldi provided players with a printed grid of boxes to write their answers in, removing the need to play in one's head or scribble in the margins.

Wynne's creation combined Airoldi's printed boxes with negative space, opening up endless possibilities for future puzzle makers. In time, he also began the convention of coloring the unused spaces black. Wynne initially called his game a "Word-Cross Puzzle," but a typesetter's error on the third installment inadvertently renamed the feature a "Cross-Word." The rest, as they say, is H☐S☐O☐Y.

CRAZY ABOUT CROSSWORDS

How a Crossword Puzzle Helped Break the Enigma Code

Some people complete crossword puzzles to relax on Sunday morning; others test their wits with a daily puzzle to stay sharp as they age. But for a group of British volunteers in January 1942, the *Telegraph*'s crossword puzzle number 5062 was the first step in a journey to crack secret Nazi codes that had vexed the Allied powers.

The amateur cruciverbalists assembled at the paper's Fleet Street newsroom that day thought they were just responding to a friendly challenge—the *Telegraph*'s editor, Arthur Watson, invited twenty-five people to see who could complete the provided puzzle in less than twelve minutes. Unbeknownst to the word game enthusiasts, the four successful participants would soon receive invitations to join British codebreakers at Bletchley Park.

There, they became part of a team that included mathematician Alan Turing, and their primary goal was to decode encrypted communications being sent by German forces and their allies. The messages were created using German engineer Arthur Scherbius's Enigma Machine, a cipher device so effective that the Nazis considered it practically uncrackable.

In fact, Polish cryptanalysts had broken the code in the early 1930s—but at the onset of World War II, German experts improved its security, necessitating new efforts from the British. The team at Bletchley Park eventually succeeded, helping the Allied war effort with critical intelligence and, perhaps inadvertently, providing crossword lovers one more reason to cherish their beloved hobby.

8 HELPFUL TIPS

for ## SOLVING CROSSWORD PUZZLES

For some people, the crossword puzzle is a relaxing way to start the day.
For others, it's an obsession. If you want to raise your crossword game
to the next level, follow these tips for success.

1. Pay attention to the day of the week.
When it comes to conquering the crossword, timing matters. Many newspapers vary the type of puzzles they publish throughout the week. Thursday's edition, for example, tends to have a theme linking all the answers together. The difficulty of the clues changes as well, with the challenges getting harder as the week progresses. If you only do the crossword on Saturdays, you may be setting yourself up for a headache. Start with Monday's puzzle and ease yourself into the trickier brainteasers that come later in the week.

2. Punctuation can tip you off.
Crossword prompts follow certain formulas, and learning to recognize them will give you an edge in the game. Clues that end in a question mark are almost always hinting at some kind of wordplay. Seeing "cabinetmaker?" on its own may leave you stumped, but if you know the question has a double meaning and the answer has nine letters, your deductions may lead you to the word *president*.

3. Jump around.
There's no rule stating you have to start a crossword puzzle at 1-across. Instead, scan the page and find the easiest words to fill in first. Some clue formats tend to be more forgiving than others. Fill-in-the-blank prompts, such as "The Good, The Bad, and The ___," are what crossword editors call *gimmes*. Shorter words are usually easy to solve as well. Compass directions (NNE, SSW, etc.) are a standard three-letter answer in crossword puzzles, so if you see a prompt like "Chicago-to-Boston direction," you know the solution is one of eight possibilities.

4. Grammar matters.
Keeping basic grammar conventions in mind is an easy way to boost your crossword skills. If you're at a total loss for an answer, take a closer look at how the clue is phrased. If it's written in past tense, that means the solution is past tense as well—and you can begin brainstorming words that end in -ed. This also applies to clues that are plural. Knowing that a word ends in s isn't enough to solve a puzzle, but it's a good place to start.

5. Crossings are your allies.
If a crossword clue leaves you baffled, don't lose hope. Solving the words that intersect with it could give you enough letters to make an educated guess. You can also use the crossings to check your work as you go. If your down words spell out gibberish in one of your across answers, you likely made a mistake somewhere along the way.

6. Mistakes are part of the game.
The boxes in a crossword puzzle are meant to be filled in, cleared out, and filled in again. In a game where the solutions become clearer the more you play it, changing your guesses as you go is expected. That's why most crossword apps give users a *delete* option. And if you're filling out the print crossword puzzle longhand, you don't get extra points for using ink instead of pencil.

7. Stick with the same source.
The previous tips can be applied to most popular crossword puzzles, but the only way to know the quirks of your preferred outlet is through practice. Different editors may have specific clue formats—or even subject matter—they return to often. By picking one publication to commit to at the start of your crossword career, you can learn to recognize these patterns when they arise.

8. Keep common words in mind.
When you're totally stuck, try plugging some common crossword terms into the blank squares of your puzzle. Short (three- to four-letter) words packed with vowels are often used to string longer answers together. So if you can't decipher a clue, words like *era*, *area*, and *emu* make pretty good guesses. If you suspect the word is a proper noun, *Soho*, *Ohio*, and *Yoko Ono* are all popular crossword answers.

Think Outside the Box

The figurative meanings of some phrases—like *close, but no cigar* (see page 29) and *cut to the chase* (see page 132)—seem different enough from the words themselves that you might assume they were once meant literally. And in both those cases, you'd be right. But *thinking outside the box*, meaning "to think unconventionally or creatively," doesn't fully fall into this category. Even if a literal box had never been involved, the phrase would still make sense: Conventional practices and thought processes all fit nicely into a box, and you have to venture outside of that in order to come up with innovative ideas and solutions.

When the phrase first arose in the 1970s, however, an actual box of sorts *was* involved. What's known as the nine dots puzzle entails drawing a box of nine evenly spaced dots and then connecting them all with just four lines, without lifting your pencil. In trying to do so, people tend to assume that they're not allowed to extend their lines beyond the boundaries of the grid. But, of course, the only way to solve the puzzle is to do just that. In other words, you need to think outside the box.

It's unclear exactly how old the nine dots puzzle is. One variation is featured in *Sam Loyd's Cyclopedia of 5000 Puzzles, Tricks, and Conundrums with Answers*, published in 1914; some even credit British mathematician Henry Dudeney with having developed today's version.

Whatever the case, the puzzle gained popularity in the 1970s as a way for academics to illustrate how people think and work. As *Forbes* reports, psychologist J. P. Guilford used it in experiments in the early 1970s; leadership expert John Eric Adair claims to have introduced it in 1969.

The phrase *think outside the box* soon followed. The earliest known written reference, per the *Oxford English Dictionary*, comes from a 1971 piece in the journal *Data Management*.

But before *think outside the box*, we briefly had *think outside the dots*, which showed up in a June 1970 article in Alberta, Canada's *Lethbridge Herald*. And in a 1959 newspaper column, Hal Humphrey mentioned a method of thinking that "gets outside the nine-dot square."

While encouraging people to think outside the dots might earn you some quizzical looks, it might leave more of an impression than the now overused cliché of thinking outside the box.

OLD-TIMEY WORD GAMES YOU CAN PLAY TODAY

The crossword puzzle, that pinnacle of all word games, seems like it's been around forever. In fact, it was introduced relatively recently (1913), making it something of a newcomer for games that use language as fodder for both hints and solutions. Take a look at some very vintage word games that can still give you a verbose victory today.

Crambo

Crambo is a rhyming game dating back to at least 1660. The first player announces they have a word that rhymes with *sea*. The other player can then ask, "Is it a vegetable?" The first player then says, "No, it's not a pea." The guess must allude to a rhyme that the first player then utters. After a few rounds of this, both players sit down and wait for television to be invented.

Doublets

The brainchild of author Lewis Carroll (*Alice's Adventures in Wonderland*), this game tasks players with taking one word and transforming it into an entirely different one by changing just one letter at a time—all while making sure the transitional steps are actual words, too. The bookended words are usually related. One could, for example, try to turn *fire* into *hose* by opting for *tire*, *tore*, *pore*, *pose*, and then *hose*.

Fictionary

Victorians amused themselves with this game in which one player produces a dictionary and finds a very obscure word that's read aloud to other players. Those players then jot down a made-up definition. The first player then reads all definitions out loud, including the real one, and invites the others to guess which is legitimate. Participants get points when their fake definition is guessed or when someone guesses correctly.

Jotto

First devised by real estate developer and word lover Morton Rosenfeld in 1955, Jotto might sound familiar to Wordle enthusiasts. Using pen and paper, players try to guess the other's five-letter word by seeing how many letters they got right and where. Mental Jotto, in which one player tries to guess another player's word without writing anything down, tells you how many correct letters you got—but not *which* letters, making it a good deal harder than Wordle enthusiasts have it today.

Minister's Cat

This group game tasks players with declaring that "the minister's cat is a ____ cat," with the blank being an adjective beginning with *a*, then *b*, then *c*. Each round begins with a new letter. If a player misses, repeats a word, or otherwise makes a mistake, they're eliminated and a new round—with a new letter—begins. (Some versions of the game increase the difficulty by having players repeat the previous answers before adding their own.)

À la King

À la is a phrase that appears a lot on French restaurant menus. It literally means "in the style of." Food that's served *à la king* comes in cream sauce with mushrooms and pepper, and despite its royal name, chicken à la king didn't originate within the walls of a palace. It likely didn't even originate in Europe. Most plausible origin stories attribute the name to an American with the last name King.

According to one legend, the head chef of the Brighton Beach Hotel first served the dish to the hotel's proprietor, E. Clark King II, in the early 1900s. He liked it so much that he requested seconds, and the dish appeared on the menu as *chicken à la King* the next day.

Like many culinary legends, this may be more fun fiction than food fact. According to an early-twentieth-century account, the King in question was Philadelphia, Pennsylvania, chef William King, who was asked to invent a recipe for an annoying customer. When the customer asked who invented the dish, the waiter responded "Bill King, he works in the kitchen" to which the customer replied "chicken à la King."

À la Nage

The phrase *à la nage* is French for "in the swim." Chefs use it to describe food, usually seafood, that's been simmered lightly in a flavorful broth.

À la Boulangère

When meat, potatoes, and onions are baked together in an oven, they're prepared *à la boulangère*. The name means "in the style of the baker" or perhaps "the baker's wife." Being on good terms with the local baker used to be the only way to make the dish: For most of French history, people in rural parts of the country didn't have access to ovens at home. To make something *à la boulangère*, they had to take a dish of ingredients to their neighborhood bakery and pick it up when it was done cooking.

The UNEXPECTED ORIGINS OF CULINARY TERMS

The etymologies of the words and phrases we use when cooking and eating are so delicious they might just make your mouth water.

Al Dente

Pasta that's cooked *al dente* still has some bite to it—some resistance you wouldn't get from a gummy, overcooked noodle—hence the Italian phrase's literal meaning, "to the tooth."

Amuse-Bouche

Amuse-bouche is fun to say, and if the food lives up to its name, it should be fun to eat. The French term for small, complimentary appetizers served at the beginning of a meal translates to "entertains the mouth," though it remains unclear if the phrase comes from France or is just an English phrase using French words.

Bellini

Venetian restaurateur Giuseppe Cipriani sometimes took inspiration from Renaissance-era artists when coining culinary terms—according to legend, at least. He's said to have once mixed prosecco and peach together into a cocktail whose colors he likened to the work of Giovanni Bellini.

Baker's Dozen

The phrase *baker's dozen* can be traced to England in the thirteenth century, appropriately enough. But why is a baker's dozen thirteen?

In medieval England, bread was a basic staple of the populace, and in the 1260s, King Henry III enacted a law that controlled the size and cost of a loaf. One popular story to explain the baker's dozen says that bakers would add an extra loaf to a lot of twelve in order to avoid the stiff penalties for selling underweight bread to customers. But scrupulous food historians point out that there's little evidence for this explanation. Besides, buying twelve loaves of bread at a time would have been an awful lot for a medieval peasant.

Instead, the phrase seems more likely to come from transactions with bread middlemen, known as *hucksters*, who would buy bread from bakeries and then roam the streets hawking their carb-heavy wares. Since the law controlled how much the baker charged a retailer *and* how much the retailer could charge the customer, there wasn't a way for the retailer to make a profit, so a thirteenth loaf—sometimes called the *in-bread* or the *vantage loaf*—was thrown in as a freebie so the retailer could make some money. It made sense for bakers to incentivize street peddlers with this free loaf; they could move a lot more product through roaming retailers than if they had to sell all the bread themselves.

Barbecue

When Spaniards landed in the New World, they observed Indigenous people using raised, wooden frames to cook their meat and fish. The apparatuses could be placed directly on a heat source, the way Americans grill hamburgers and hot dogs today, or they could be propped near a fire and heated indirectly, similarly to how barbecue pitmasters slow-cook their meat. The word for these tools was *barbacoa*, according to a Spanish account recorded in 1526. This became *barbecue* in English, and at some point, a q got thrown into the mix. Some sources suggest the q comes to us from the French phrase *barbe à queue*, or "beard to tail," a nod to a whole animal being cooked, but this explanation is probably more folklore than fact.

Brunoise

If you want to develop some impressive knife skills, learn to *brunoise*. The standard brunoise cut in France gives you vegetable cubes that are just one-eighth of an inch in size, while a fine brunoise produces pieces half that size on each side. The name for this technique comes from Brunoy, a commune located twelve miles from the center of Paris. The chefs of Brunoy popularized the method of dicing veggies as finely as possible, and the name stuck.

Carpaccio

The origins of some Italian culinary terms are easy to identify. Beef or fish that's prepared carpaccio style—that is, raw and thinly sliced—is named after Italian Renaissance painter Vittore Carpaccio. He wasn't the person who invented it, however. Cipriani — the restaurateur who also reportedly coined *bellini*—first served the dish to Countess Amalia Nani Mocenigo after she had been instructed by her doctor to abstain from eating cooked meat. Raw meat isn't for everyone, but the sight of it inspired romantic feelings in Cipriani. Upon noticing the red color of the dish, he named it after Carpaccio, who used similar shades in his artwork.

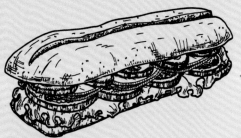

Hoagie

Try ordering a hero, grinder, or submarine sandwich in the Philadelphia area and prepare to get dirty looks. There's only one word for a sandwich served on a split Italian roll in this part of the country, and that's *hoagie*. Numerous theories purport to explain the term's origins; according to one story, the word can be traced to Hog Island in the Delaware River, which was used as a shipyard during the First World War. The sandwiches Italian immigrant workers ate for lunch there were dubbed *hoggies*, and thanks to the Philly accent, the word *hoagie* was born.

Hoku-Hoku, Shuwa-Shuwa, Zuru-Zuru, and Churu-Churu

The Japanese language employs some evocative culinary onomatopoeia. *Hoku-hoku*, for example, describes the experience of biting into something hot, such as a sweet potato or winter squash, with a dense texture that fills your mouth with "a starchy steaminess." *Shuwa-shuwa* is a descriptor for carbonated beverages, and *zuru-zuru* is the sound you make when you slurp ramen. That's unless, of course, you want your slurping to be on the quieter side, in which case you would use the more discreet *churu-churu*.

The Holy Trinity

The Holy Trinity is the mirepoix (see next column) of Creole and Cajun cuisine. Instead of carrots, it uses green bell peppers, along with onions and celery, as the base for various recipes. It originated with the Acadians, who immigrated to Louisiana in the eighteenth century. Carrots didn't grow in the region's swampy soil, but bell peppers flourished. With one simple ingredient swap, the Holy Trinity, and the flavor profile of a new cuisine, was born. The biblical name, meanwhile, is a reflection of Cajun country's Catholic roots, though it may date back only to the late 1970s.

Hors D'Oeuvre

Don't confuse *amuse-bouche* with hors d'oeuvres, which aren't necessarily complimentary and can be shared between guests. The term *hors d'oeuvre* is French for "outside of work," as in outside the work of the main meal, either figuratively or in terms of its literal, physical placement on the edge of the table, depending on the source you consult.

Mirepoix

Mirepoix is a mixture of sautéed carrots, onions, and celery used as the foundation for many French dishes. The name likely comes from the eighteenth-century French aristocrat Duke Charles-Pierre-Gaston François de Lévis, duc de Lévis-Mirepoix. It's believed that the duke's chef de cuisine named a flavor base after him, though what that base originally consisted of is unclear. Fortunately for future generations of chefs, he didn't use Mirepoix's full title when naming the recipe.

Pasta alla Carbonara

The names of some Italian pasta dishes tell you more about the dishes' origin stories than their ingredients. *Pasta alla carbonara*, for example, translates to something like pasta "in the manner of charcoal makers." According to legend, workers first made the dish over campfires to fuel their long days. Consisting of eggs, cured pork, and pasta, carbonara makes sense as a low-maintenance, high-energy, working-class lunch.

But there's no way to confirm the validity of this explanation. The name *carbonara* could be a reference to the charcoal fire the dish was prepared over rather than the people who made it, or to the generous grating of pepper placed on top, which might have looked like coal dust. Some believe that pasta carbonara originated with the Carbonari, a nineteenth-century secret society of Italian revolutionaries.

Tandoori

Tandoori chicken is named after the cylindrical, charcoal-fired clay oven it's cooked in. It's also one of the oldest dishes on this list. In modern-day Pakistan, archaeologists unearthed five-thousand-year-old clay vessels similar to tandoors along with charred chicken bones. This may technically be the scraps of an early tandoori chicken dinner, but it would take thousands of years before the dish became what people know today.

The details are somewhat disputed, but the most popular story goes that in the 1930s, a restaurant called Moti Mahal opened up in Peshawar, modern Pakistan. After the Partition of India, a new version of the restaurant opened up in India, bringing the dish to widespread popularity. In the early 1960s, First Lady Jackie Kennedy was served tandoori chicken on a flight from Rome to New Delhi, and today you can order tandoori chicken in restaurants around the world. The success of the dish spurred many variations, including chicken tikka masala.

Umami

Umami means something like "deliciousness" in Japanese, but the true meaning of the word is hard to capture in English. In the early twentieth century, a Japanese chemist named Kikunae Ikeda boiled down umami to its pure essence—literally. He was enjoying a bowl of dashi, a savory broth made from kelp called *kombu*, when he realized there must be a fifth taste beyond salty, sweet, sour, and bitter.

Determined to get to the root of dashi's indefinable flavor, he conducted some experiments. Chemically treating the seaweed used to make dashi caused small crystals to form on the outside of it. These crystals were concentrated glutamic acid, a nonessential amino acid, and after some tinkering, when Ikeda added them to food or liquid he was hit with that same full, savory flavor he noticed in his soup.

He dubbed this fifth taste *umami*, which has been described as a sort of meatiness, or earthiness. It's responsible for the savory depth of flavor in a number of beloved items, from Bloody Marys to Parmesan cheese.

Zatsumi

Umami isn't the only hard-to-translate food term used in Japan. The word *zatsumi* is used to describe an undesirable flavor, usually in sake. It doesn't refer to any bad flavor in particular—the word even translates to "miscellaneous taste" in English. So next time you taste something funky in the leftovers that have been sitting in your fridge for weeks, just call it *zatsumi* and don't think about it too hard.

Where Did the Word (and Color) **Orange** Come From?

*O*range comes from, well . . . oranges. Its predecessors include the Middle French *orange* and the Sanskrit *naranga-s*, but English didn't really have a word for this color for centuries. Geoffrey Chaucer, describing a fox in "The Nun's Priest's Tale," went with the phrase "bitwixe yelow and reed." *Giolureade*, or yellow-red, was a somewhat clumsy Old English construction that basically served the linguistic function of today's *orange* for almost a millennium. Only once the fruit became widely available in Europe did the color start to infiltrate the continent's languages.

And by the way, despite what you might have heard, there are words that rhyme with *orange*: There are several words that at least partially rhyme, including *hinge*. The *Blorenge*, the name of a Welsh mountain, will also do the trick. But if you're looking for the closest rhyme, it's the word *sporange*—a sac where spores are made.

Avalanche

In pizza parlor parlance, an *avalanche* is what occurs when all the toppings slide right off your slice as soon as you pick it up. This tends to happen when a pizza is still piping hot from the oven, so be smart and give it a minute to cool down.

What's the **Scratch** in **Made from Scratch**?

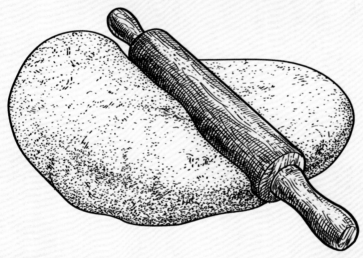

This phrase didn't actually originate in the kitchen. As far back as the late eighteenth century, *scratch* referred to the starting line in sports like running and cricket, where that line might literally have been scratched into the ground. It was also the name of the line in a boxing ring where participants faced off before a round commenced. That definition of *scratch* soon propagated a wave of related phrases—*toe the scratch*, *bring to the scratch*, and *come up to (the) scratch*—which basically meant "meet the standard." These days, we use *up to snuff* (see page 42) in a similar way.

Though the phrase *start from scratch* arose from sports, too, it didn't just mean you were starting at the beginning with everyone else. According to Merriam-Webster, it meant that if you were a runner you lacked a head start or some other advantage given to less skilled athletes in order to level the playing field. This definition of *scratch* still exists today, in sports like golf and bowling. By the early twentieth century, people were using *scratch* and its phrasal derivatives figuratively, to describe anyone doing anything without a leg up.

Exactly when *from scratch* was first applied to food remains unclear. But the earliest written mention that Grammarphobia unearthed came from a 1946 article in the *New York Times* claiming that "the old-fashioned style of cooking—from scratch, as it were, without frozen or canned products—is on the wane." When TV dinners took off in the early 1950s, the author of that article probably said "I told you so" to at least a few people.

Why Do We Tell People to Take Something "With a Grain of Salt"?

If an unverified gossip account on Instagram posts that your favorite celebrity couple just broke up, you might take that rumor with a grain of salt—that is, exercise a healthy bit of skepticism and wait for more evidence.

Though no literal salt is involved now, it was when the phrase was first mentioned (that we know of) in ancient Rome. In his *Natural History*, written around 77 CE, Pliny the Elder recounted the story of how Pompey—best known for warring with Julius Caesar—found directions for the concoction that Mithridates VI used to inoculate himself against certain poisons. Mithridates VI famously ingested small doses of poison to build up his immunity, but according to Pliny, the recipe called for other ingredients, too: dried nuts, figs, and rue leaves. Everything should be minced together and taken after having added a grain of salt: *addito salis grano*.

It's not totally clear how the phrase ended up with its modern meaning after that. Some people who read Pliny's *Natural History* later on may have mistaken his mention of salt as a figurative warning. As in: "Be skeptical

about this recipe, since I'm not sold on its efficacy and you might accidentally poison yourself to death," or something to that effect. But without any evidence that other ancient Romans used *grain of salt* as an idiom, it seems more likely that salt was part of the actual recipe. It's also possible that the idea of using salt to make poison easier to swallow just seemed like an apt description for adding a little skepticism when consuming questionable information.

In any case, *grain of salt* showed up again in John Trapp's 1647 *A Commentary or exposition upon all the Epistles and the Revelation of John the Divine*, but didn't really catch on until the twentieth century, when the literary journal *The Athenaeum* mentioned it in a 1908 issue that read, "Our reasons for not accepting the author's pictures of early Ireland without many grains of salt . . ." By that point, the idiom was presumably common enough for readers to understand its meaning.

But considering the large gaps in the history of the phrase, this rundown can't exactly be called a comprehensive origin story. In other words: Take it with a grain of salt.

WHAT'S *the* DIFFERENCE?

Doughnut vs. Donut

While it's clear where the first half of the term *doughnut* comes from, the *nut* in *doughnut* is more mysterious. Some etymologists think it's a reference to the original shape of the snacks, which were small and round—like nuts—before they gained their distinctive hole.

Another theory posits that the *nut* comes from literal nuts. Or at least culinary nuts, like almonds and pecans. To solve the problem of under-cooked dough in the middle of their *olykoeks*, or "oil cakes"—one possible forerunner to the modern doughnut—Dutch cooks sometimes stuffed them with ingredients like nuts. The rise of the ring-shaped donut made this unnecessary, but the trick may have had a lasting impact on the dessert's name.

The language we use to describe fried rings of dough underwent another transformation over the next century. By the early 1900s, many doughnut purveyors had shortened the name to *donut*. Today this alternate spelling is nearly as common as the original, but it didn't get to be that way overnight. The version starting with *dough* maintained its domination until around 1950, when the simplified word began to steadily increase in popularity. The first Dunkin' Donuts opened in Quincy, Massachusetts, that same year, and the business went with the snappier spelling of *donut* for its name. The growth of the chain in the latter half of the twentieth century correlates with the shorter word's upswing—though now that Dunkin' has dropped the *Donuts* from its title, the older spelling may be poised for a comeback.

FOOD
NAMES
YOU MIGHT BE
MISPRONOUNCING

When ordering a meal at a restaurant, taste should be the main concern. Whether you can pronounce the name of the dish shouldn't factor into your decision, but that's not always the case. If you've ever ordered a salad to avoid saying *vichyssoise* to your server, it's time to brush up on your culinary vocabulary. Here are some common food names you may be mispronouncing.

Açai

Since this super fruit became a trendy ingredient, people have struggled to pronounce it. Instead of "ah-KAI," say "ah-sah-EE."

Beignet

When in New Orleans, earn respect from the locals and say "ben-YAY" when ordering this pastry from a coffee shop.

Cacao

Distinct from the processed chocolate called *cocoa*, raw cacao beans are pronounced "kah-COW."

Camembert

This French cheese is pronounced "kah-mum-BEHR" with a silent *t*.

Cassoulet

"Kah-soo-LAY" is the right way to say
the name of this famous French dish.

Champagne

Champagne makes any occasion feel fancier, especially
when you pronounce it the right way: "sham-PAYN."

Crudités

Asking for "CROO-dites" at an upscale event may get you funny looks.
"Kroo-de-TAY" is the correct pronunciation.

Elote

The name of this Mexican street corn is pronounced "eh-LOH-tay."

Filet Mignon

Don't try to say the name of this famous beef cut in phonetic English.
Follow the French pronunciation and say "fuh-LAY muhn-YAWN" instead.

Foie Gras

Even if you know *foie gras* is pronounced "fwah-grah," the name
can still trip up non-native French speakers.

General Tso's

The name is spelled differently at various
Chinese American restaurants, but the *Tso* in
General Tso's chicken is always pronounced "tsahow."

Macaron

This French sandwich cookie shouldn't be confused
with American macaroons. Say "mah-kuh-RAHN"
if you want to sound like you know what you're talking about.

Mole

The name of this famous Mexican sauce has two syllables, as in "MOH-lay."

Niçoise

Say "nee-SWAHZ" when ordering this French salad to impress your server.

Pho

Pho is pronounced "fuh," as in, "this soup is pho-nomenal."

Quinoa

"KEEN-wah" is the correct way to say the name of this nutritious South American staple.

Sriracha

Years after it became the trendiest condiment on the planet, people are still saying *sriracha* wrong. "See-ROTCH-ah" is the correct pronunciation.

Tzatziki

Don't let the *z*s in the name scare you.
You can order this Mediterranean yogurt dip by saying "zaht-siki."

Vichyssoise

Saying the name of this potato soup out loud doesn't have to be nerve-racking. *Vichyssoise*—pronounced "vih-shee-SWAHZ"—is actually pretty fun to say.

Worcestershire

The name of this condiment is pronounced "WOO-stuh-sher."
(Now try saying that three times fast.)

When
McDONALD'S
WENT TO WAR
WITH THE
DICTIONARY

Fast food giant McDonald's has sold billions of hamburgers, but that success hasn't come without getting into a few pickles. In the 2000s, the company butted heads with both the *Oxford English Dictionary* and *Merriam-Webster's Collegiate Dictionary* over an entry they felt was disparaging to the brand: the word *McJob*, a term that gained widespread popularity after being featured in *Generation X*, the influential 1991 novel by Douglas Coupland about disenfranchised young adults.

The *OED* began including the word in its 2001 edition, defining it as "an unstimulating, low-paid job with few prospects, esp. one created by the expansion of the service sector." *Merriam-Webster's Collegiate Dictionary* followed suit in 2003, using harsher language to describe a McJob as "low-paying and dead-end work."

McDonald's was not amused. Company CEO Jim Cantalupo wrote an open letter to Merriam-Webster objecting to the characterization. McDonald's employees, he wrote, were undeserving of such condescension.

In the U.K., McDonald's reportedly considered legal action and suggested the definition of *McJob* be changed to reflect a "rewarding" occupation. The *OED* offered a rebuttal by saying their definitions reflect popular usage, not how a particular group wished a word to be used.

When it became clear the word was staying put, the company launched an advertising campaign in 2006 to highlight new buzzwords like *McFlexible*, *McDiscount*, and *McProspects* to reflect the opportunities for employees with the tagline, "Not bad for a McJob."

McDonald's wasn't alone in challenging perceived dictionary offenses. In 2005, Britain's Potato Council made a similar complaint against the *OED* for associating *couch potato* and thus potatoes with unhealthy living. The council's preferred phrase, *couch slouch*, failed to catch on.

1. **Billy Boys**

If you've ever had an internship and been asked to fetch coffee for the boss, you were doing the job of a *billy boy*. Billy boys made tea for trade workers during their breaks; many used the entry-level positions as a form of apprenticeship.

2. **Cereologist**

The word may look like it's related to *cereal* (and tangentially, it is—both words derive from *Ceres,* the Roman goddess of agriculture), but don't expect to find a cereologist studiously eating a bowl of Cheerios each morning. You may, however, find them surveying an unusual corn or wheat field. Cereologists study crop circles.

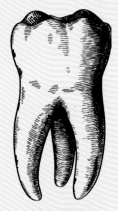

4. **Fang-Faker**

This Victorian slang term for a dentist combines *fang*—a sharp, elongated tooth—with the common verb *to fake*, meaning "to forge, make, or fabricate." *Fang-farrier* is another term for a dentist—more on that second word below.

5. **Farrier**

About every six weeks, many horses will receive a routine visit from a farrier. The name sounds fantastical, but it's a practical job: A farrier shoes and trims horses' hooves. The word is rooted in the Latin word *ferrum,* which means "iron" and, in medieval Latin, "horseshoe."

FARM MARKET

3. **Costermonger**

Next time you pass a fruit stand by the side of the road, be sure to say hello to the local costermonger. Originally, costermongers sold apples (*costard* is an old word for a large apple or an apple tree; *monger* refers to a merchant), but the term has expanded to include vendors of other produce or fish.

The
ORIGINS OF
13
BIZARRE
PROFESSION
NAMES

It's easy to tell what a mail carrier or bartender does based on the job name alone. Some professions, however, have more unusual titles. Here are thirteen jobs, past and present, with odd names.

6. Haberdasher

Here's a fun one to say out loud. Haberdashers sell items related to men's fashion, such as hats and thread. (A woman haberdasher is a haberdasheress.) The word's etymology is unclear, though it's been linked to the Anglo-French word *hapertas*, which was thought to be a kind of fabric.

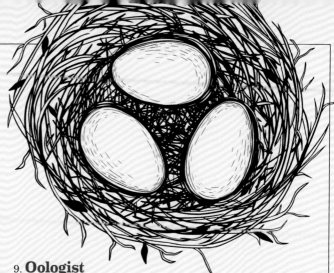

7. Hayward

Surprisingly, this isn't directly related to hay. In the past, haywards were in charge of overseeing fences to keep cattle from roaming freely. A wayward hayward could complicate a community's grazing practices.

8. Knocker Upper

Before alarm clocks, industrial workers in the U.K. were roused by the sound of a few quick raps on their doors. The job title is pretty self-explanatory: The knocker uppers would wake people up by knocking on their houses with a stick. (The phrase could also be used as a verb; to be *knocked up* was to get a knock on the door to wake you up.)

9. Oologist

If you're super into looking at bird eggs, you may be an oologist. Oologists are professionals (and in the past, hobbyists) who study bird egg shells. The *oo-* in *oology* comes from the Greek word *ōon*, which means "egg." Someone who sells eggs, on the other hand, is an eggler.

10. Perukier

If you're in the market for a wig, swing by your local perukier. This bygone word for a wigmaker comes from *parrucca*, an Old Italian word for "wig."

11. Slop-Seller

Slop-seller sounds like a job for someone who hawks mushy, soupy food for pigs. But it actually refers to a person who sells cheap, ready-to-wear clothing. Slop-sellers originally sold uniforms before the trade expanded to include other mass-market items. *Slop* is a fourteenth-century word for a loose outer garment.

12. Snake Milker

No, snake milk won't be the next buzzy product lining the shelves of health food stores—there's no actual milk involved in this job. Snake milkers extract venom from the reptiles, which is then used for research and in various pharmaceuticals, including antivenin.

13. Vulcan

In *Star Trek*, a Vulcan is a humanoid from the planet of the same name; here on Earth, it's another term for a blacksmith. The profession gets its name from the Roman god of metalworking.

WHAT'S *the* DIFFERENCE?

Blue Collar vs. White Collar Jobs

In the early twentieth century, American industrialization gave rise to a new sartorial distinction between classes. Managers, administrators, and anyone else who worked in an office favored crisp white shirts on the job. Manual laborers, meanwhile, donned dark, durable attire better suited to factory and farm work.

Before long, the white collar became both an emblem of aspirational prosperity for urban newcomers and a loathsome reminder of pencil-pushers' privilege. "If the boy raised in jeans and gingham and permitted a white collar only on Sundays and holidays comes subconsciously to associate the white collar with ease, enjoyment and respectability, is it not natural?" a Louisiana newspaper editorial argued in 1910. "And if he follows the lure of the white collar to the city and gets a job in which he can wear a white collar all the week, and though he spends all his extra pay in keeping his collar and cuffs and shirt white, what does it matter, so long as he is satisfied?"

People had begun using *blue collar* by the 1920s, which etymologist Barry Popik suggests may have just been the most natural way to distinguish the working class from their white-collar counterparts. Blue wasn't the only color worn by laborers, but it was popular—American demand for denim predated the Gold Rush, and its lightweight cousin, chambray, was worn by everyone from farmhands to military members.

Though white-collar workers were purportedly better educated, better paid, and all around better off than blue-collar workers, it was something of an open secret that only the upper echelons of businesspeople experienced such success.

"It is a fact with which every union workingman is familiar, that his most bitter despisers are the petty underlings of the business world, the poor office-clerks, who are often the worst exploited of proletarians, but who, because they are allowed to wear a white collar and to work in the office with the boss, regard themselves as members of the capitalist class," Upton Sinclair wrote in 1919.

Despite the fact that new machinery helped ease the physical strain on blue-collar workers—and they could even earn more than desk dwellers—the social prestige that came with an office job often outweighed those considerations. As one New York banker told the *New York Times* in 1924, "It is quite possible that to this white-collar host money means less than a respected place in the community—one which, according to common belief, cannot be attained if overalls are worn to work."

A century later, society is still struggling to shake off that mentality. While construction workers, electricians, mechanics, and many other blue-collar laborers are highly skilled and highly compensated, a stiff white collar continues to carry a certain air of importance (though today's white-collar workers are just as likely to be wearing T-shirts).

The MOST HATED BUSINESS BUZZWORDS AND JARGON

If you've ever tried to give 110 percent to a task, chances are you've worked in an office. In the workplace, employees and supervisors tend to speak a distinctive kind of corporate jargon that can sound like a lot while meaning very little. These buzzwords can appear in emails, in meetings, and in conversations.

In 2022, language learning site Preply surveyed more than 1,500 Americans who worked in an office setting either in-person or remotely to find out which words and phrases most rankled them. See if you agree.

New Normal
This phrase, which typically tasks the listener with coming to grips with an unpleasant new reality, topped the list. Forty-three percent of respondents declared it their least-liked term in a business setting. And though it might be most associated with the chaos wrought by the COVID-19 pandemic, the term *new normal* actually dates back to the 1920s.

Culture
Specifically, *company culture*, which usually denotes a company M.O. or motto employees are expected to adhere to. This sense of the word *culture* didn't rise with startups, but originated in the 1940s, with *corporate culture* debuting in 1961.

Circle Back
Revisiting a topic you probably didn't want to address in the first place makes this phrase unwelcome in the workspace.

Boots on the Ground
This 1980s term—military lingo for putting people on a task—is an eye-roller for many.

Give 110 Percent
It's mathematically impossible. Everyone knows it. People use it anyway.

Low-Hanging Fruit
Aspire to achieve an easy objective? You're reaching far below your capabilities. This phrase dates back to 1968, when it appeared in the *Guardian*.

Win-Win
When something has no obvious downside, it's a win all the way around. According to the *Oxford English Dictionary*, this phrase first appeared in the 1962 book *Deterrence, Arms Control, & Disarmament*.

Move the Needle
When you want to make progress or create enthusiasm, you probably don't need to be using this tired phrase in the process.

Growth Hacking
Setting new goals doesn't necessarily need to involve invoking any kind of "hacking" reference.

Think Outside the Box
Thinking outside the box would require you not to use the phrase *think outside the box* (for more, see page 172). Preply found that respondents didn't particularly mind *at the end of the day*, *table this*, or *game changer* when it came to tired clichés.

THE REASON SOME BUSINESSES REFER TO CUSTOMERS AS GUESTS

For decades, retailers and other businesses referred to customers as *customers*. (If they were rude, possibly as *jerks*.) Increasingly, some proprietors like to call patrons *guests*. It happens at Target, Walgreens, and other locations. It's exceedingly polite and slightly strange. How and why did it start?

You can probably blame Disney.

In 1955, when Disneyland opened in Anaheim, California, employees occupying the Happiest Place on Earth were instructed to refer to park attendees as *guests*. It was part of the company's devotion to going the extra mile to create a welcoming fantasy atmosphere.

Where Disney goes, others follow. Executives at other businesses took lessons on their approach from the Mouse in the hope of emulating their success. In 2015, a Target spokesperson confirmed to the *New York Times* that Target employees began using *guest* to refer to customers in 1993 as a direct result of Disney's policy.

It may be comforting, but it is grammatically correct? Not really. *Guest* means "someone being entertained at the house or table of another." It's more appropriate to use in the context of patronizing a hotel or restaurant, not a retail business. *Customer*, a noun meaning "someone who visits a place to make a purchase," is far more fitting.

COLORFUL PIECES of TRUCK DRIVER SLANG

There's a lot the average driver doesn't know about the trucks they pass on the highway. For instance, the spikes on truck wheels are often made of plastic, and the word *semi* doesn't indicate half a vehicle (see page 192). But one of the most inscrutable aspects of big-rig culture is trucker slang.

If you've ever eavesdropped on a CB radio frequency, you know that truck drivers communicate in their own language, discussing everything from hazards on the road to the best spots for coffee. Even if you only drive vehicles with four wheels, you can still have fun using these pieces of truck driver slang on your next road trip.

Alligator
A piece of tire on the road, usually from a tire blowout.

Backdoor and Front Door
What truck drivers say when there is something behind and in front of them, respectively.

Bear, Bear Bite, and Bear in the Bushes
In truck driver lingo, *bear* is a slang word for "police," including state troopers and highway patrol—making a *bear bite* a speeding ticket and a *bear in the bushes* a police officer hidden from view, usually with a radar gun waiting for speeders. (An *Evel Knievel*, meanwhile, is a police officer riding a motorcycle.)

Black Eye
A headlight that's out.

Bobtail
A tractor without the trailer attached to it.

Bumper Sticker
A *bumper sticker* is a tailgating vehicle.

Cash Register
A tollbooth.

Chicken Coop
A weigh station. When a weigh station is closed, truck drivers say it's *all locked up.*

Hundred Mile Coffee and Go-Go Juice
Very strong coffee. Not to be confused with *go-go juice,* which is diesel fuel.

Pay the Water Bill
Stop for a bathroom break.

Reading the Mail
Listening to CB radio without talking on it.

Sesame Street
Channel 19 on CB radio (because everyone lives there).

10-4
Message received.

Why Is It Called a *Semi Truck*?

Semi trucks are known by many other monikers, from *tractor-trailer* and *eighteen-wheeler* to the more informal *big rig*. Some people even drop the *truck* and just call them *semis*. Considering how much larger these vehicles are than most other trucks on the road, a title that essentially means "half truck" or "partial truck" may seem a little misleading.

But as International Used Truck Centers explains, *semi truck* is actually a shortened version of *semi-trailer truck* (or sometimes *semi-tractor-trailer*). Basically, a regular trailer can typically bear its own weight and gets attached to the vehicle in front of it with a drawbar or something comparable. A semi-trailer, on the other hand, is a type of trailer that only has rear wheels; its wheel-less front is hitched atop the back wheels of a tractor, which then bears some of its weight.

There's a lot of variation when it comes to describing and defining these vehicles. Sometimes, people call the tractor itself a *semi-truck* or *semi-tractor*, presumably because it's one of two parts needed to make a full semi-tractor-trailer. It could also just be for clarity's sake, since *truck* could mean a pickup truck (or some other type of truck), and *tractor* could refer to a farm tractor (or some other type of tractor).

In casual conversation, if someone mentions a *semi* or a *semi truck*, there's a good chance they're talking about the whole big rig, rather than just the front or back. But if the conversation includes truck drivers (who'd probably be familiar with the technical differences between all the terms), you might want to ask for clarification.

Why Are Road Partitions Called *Jersey Barriers*?

Concrete road barriers were first used in California in 1946; they replaced the standard (but weak) wood beam guardrails on the treacherous Grapevine section of the state's Ridge Route highway—the home of the original "Dead Man's Curve"—where the roads had a 6-percent downgrade that led to many head-on collisions. Then, in 1949, the state of New Jersey adopted comparable concrete structures and installed preventative parabolic median barriers on the Jugtown Mountain section of U.S. Route 22 in Hunterdon County, which had a similarly hazardous downgrade to the one on the Ridge Route highway.

Though the initial barriers were somewhat successful in reducing the impact of collisions, New Jersey state highway engineers continued to tinker with the design, creating progressively larger prototypes based on numbers of observed accidents (as opposed to performing controlled crash testing). Eventually, in 1959, they settled on a standard barrier height of thirty-two full inches above the pavement with a twenty-four-inch-wide base. The base is three inches high and is followed by a thirteen-inch side slope before the barrier becomes vertical. These barriers were implemented in various states (and underwent some design changes), but continued to bear the name of the state in which they were developed.

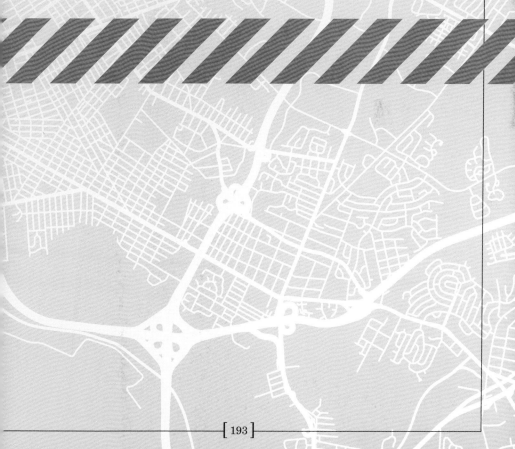

EGGCORNS
THAT MAKE A LOT OF *Sense*

Verbal mix-ups slip into our language often, and it can sometimes seem like the wrong word or phrase makes just as much sense as the right one does. Those are *eggcorns*, a term coined by linguist Geoff Pullum in 2003 as a nod to people's long-running habit of mistaking the word *acorn* for *eggcorn*—you can kind of see how eggcorn seemed like a suitable description for a small, egg-shaped nut.

Eggcorns are about as bountiful in the English language as acorns are in autumn. Take, for example, *free rein* and *free reign*. The correct version is *rein*, as in: You're a horse, and your rider is holding the reins so loosely that you can do whatever you want. In fact, horseback riders used it when talking about actual horses and reins. That said, *reign* seems logical, too. If you're a monarch who reigns over a whole kingdom, you have at least as much autonomy as your average independent equine.

Right now, we know that *free rein* is technically the correct phrase and *free reign* is the eggcorn. But it's possible that in another hundred years or so, people will have lost track of which is which, and they'll be equally acceptable—we've already reached that point with plenty of other everyday expressions. These phrasal gaffes, for example, make just as much (if not more) sense than their correct counterparts.

THE EGGCORN: Bad Rep
THE CORRECT TERM: Bad Rap

When the word *rap* arrived on the scene in the fourteenth century, it described a physical blow—as in *a rap across the knuckles*, a later phrase that sheds light on how *rap* became associated with punishment and then a prison sentence (think *rap sheet*). But *rap* came to accommodate verbal blows, too. And if people are constantly talking negatively about you (especially unfairly), you're said to have a bad rap. You also probably have a bad reputation, so it's understandable how *bad rap* gets mistaken as *bad rep*.

THE EGGCORN: Bold-Faced Lie
THE CORRECT TERM: Bald-Faced Lie

The *bald-faced* in *bald-faced lie* is a variant of *barefaced*. In other words, the lie is as apparent and uncovered as a clean-shaven and maskless face. But *bold-faced* has existed since the 1600s—Shakespeare used it in *Henry VI, Part 1*—and if you're telling an obvious lie, chances are good that you're doing it with a pretty bold face. It's also possible that people these days assume the bold face in question is a typeface: A lie printed in bold would be especially obvious.

THE EGGCORN: Cold slaw
THE CORRECT TERM: Coleslaw

The term *coleslaw* derives from the Dutch *koolsla*, a truncated version of *kool-salade*—in English, "cabbage salad." Since coleslaw, like most salads, is traditionally served cold, the eggcorn *cold slaw* is a little redundant. But it's not inaccurate (and considering the existence of hot slaw recipes, it may occasionally help to clarify). It's not new, either: The first known written mention of *cold slaw* is from 1794.

THE EGGCORN: Coming Down the Pipe
THE CORRECT TERM: Coming Down the Pike

Something that's *coming down the pike* is going to arrive (or happen) soon, just like something that's literally coming down the turnpike—i.e., a central road or expressway, which is what *pike* in the phrase refers to—is going to arrive soon. But isn't something that's coming down the pipe going to arrive soon, too? Probably so, making *down the pipe* an effective, albeit technically incorrect, expression. As Merriam-Webster points out, the *pipe*-or-*pike* confusion is likely compounded by the existence of the phrase *in the pipeline*, which also alludes to things happening soon.

THE EGGCORN: Deep-Seeded
THE CORRECT TERM: Deep-Seated

Calling something *deep-seeded* implies that its seeds were planted far into the ground; so by the time it breaks the surface, it's likely established a vast network of strong roots that aren't easy to yank out. A deep-seeded fear or prejudice, for example, isn't easy to get rid of. But the proper phrase is *deep-seated*, meaning the subject's seat—as in its center or central power—is situated deep below the surface. This paints a much less literal picture than *deep-seeded*, which helps explain why *deep-seeded* versus *deep-seated* is one of many word usage mistakes that even smart people make.

THE EGGCORN: Extract Revenge
THE CORRECT TERM: Exact Revenge

Back in the sixteenth century, *exact* was used as a verb that meant "to forcefully require or demand something" (payment, labor, etc.). By the nineteenth century, people had started using it to mean *inflict*—as in *exact revenge*. You don't often hear *exact* used as a verb these days. *Extract*, meaning "to take out with force or effort," is much more common. And because revenge usually involves force and effort—the same type of painful process that you might associate with extracting a tooth—it's no surprise that some people think the phrase is *extract revenge*.

THE EGGCORN: Happy as a Clown
THE CORRECT TERM: Happy as a Clam

The phrase *happy as a clam* is generally believed to have begun as *happy as a clam at high tide*. At low tide, the mollusks are much more likely to get plucked from the sand by clam harvesters. But the shortened version of the phrase makes little sense without that context, and plenty of people have unwittingly (or wittingly) replaced *clam* with *clown*. After all, clowns are known for being jolly, even if their antics have a tendency to terrify us.

THE EGGCORN: Last-Stitch Effort
THE CORRECT TERM: Last-Ditch Effort

A *last-ditch effort* or attempt is one final, no-holds-barred, possibly desperate push to accomplish (or prevent) something. It's a reference to the military tradition of defending your territory to the death, even when invaders have reached your very last trenches; the phrase *die in the last ditch* has been around since the early eighteenth century. *Last-stitch effort*, though technically incorrect, evokes a similar sense of eleventh-hour determination and futility: If there's only a single stitch holding your pant legs together, it's probably working quite hard to keep them from separating.

THE EGGCORN: Old-Timers' Disease
THE CORRECT TERM: Alzheimer's Disease

Alzheimer's disease is named for Dr. Alois Alzheimer, the German psychiatrist and neuropathologist credited with identifying the affliction in 1906. Alzheimer's surname is often misheard as *old-timers'*—an apt eggcorn, as most people diagnosed with the disease are older than sixty-five. In fact, if you're diagnosed with it before you turn sixty-five, it's considered younger-onset or early-onset Alzheimer's.

THE EGGCORN: Take for Granite
THE CORRECT TERM: Take for Granted

If you take something for granted, you're failing to appreciate it because you assume it will always be there, or failing to question it because you assume it's true. The phrase dates all the way back to the early 1600s. Though it's unclear when its eggcorn, *take for granite*, first appeared, it's pretty clear why some people think it makes sense. Granite is a relatively hard rock—sturdy enough to last at least a good century as a countertop (and much, much longer in nature). Taking something for granite, therefore, could mean you're assuming it will be around for at least as long as you are.

THE EGGCORN: Wet Your Appetite
THE CORRECT TERM: Whet Your Appetite

You can't wet something abstract, and an appetite falls into that category. The verb you want is *whet*, meaning "sharpen." That said, wetting your appetite could insinuate that you're salivating at the sight, smell, or thought of food, which would probably whet your appetite.

DELIGHTFULLY UNUSUAL WORDS *for* EVERYDAY THINGS

Many things we experience regularly go by some pretty uncommon names. The following terms for everyday things are ones you'll want to add to your lexicon ASAP.

Asportation
This fancy word for theft dates back to the sixteenth century.

Back-Berend
Taken from the Old English *bæc-berende*, this law term refers to a person who is caught while carrying off stolen goods. The *Oxford English Dictionary* traces its first use to 1292. Later came *backbear*, which specifically referred to carrying off illegally poached deer.

Baragouin
A word meaning "gibberish" that dates back to the early 1600s.

Bumfodder
Why yes, this *is* a seventeenth-century word for toilet paper. According to the *OED*, a second use that popped up not long after this one referred to writing or literature deemed worthless or unnecessary— in other words, pages you could probably use as toilet paper. Ouch.

Blattnerphone
Journalists, you'll make your interview subjects take notice if you refer to your tape recorder as a *blattnerphone* instead. The word derives from the name of the early recorder's inventor, Ludwig Blattner.

Breedbate
This term for someone looking to start trouble or an argument dates back to the late sixteenth century, but would be right at home in today's social media landscape.

Clinchpoop

If you get into a confrontation with a jerk, consider calling them a *clinchpoop*. The word originated in the mid-sixteenth century and is now obsolete, but is definitely ready to make a comeback.

Companage

This word for food consumed alongside bread dates back to 1350.

Emption

A mid-sixteenth-century word for buying something.

Enchiridion

Don't call your copy of *Wine for Dummies* a *manual*—call it an *enchiridion*.

Eructation

A fancy word for belching.

Faffle

"To be inconsistent in speech," according to one 1781 text, but according to some sources, it can also refer to mumbling or stuttering.

Feriation

An obsolete term for not working or for going on a holiday. It's not a vacation, it's a *feriation*!

Fimblefamble

A nineteenth-century British slang term for a really lousy excuse—think "I can't go out because I have to, uh . . . wash my hair!"

Forel

From the Old French *forrel*, meaning "case" or "sheath," this word dates back to 1393 and refers to a book jacket or other covering for a tome.

Galligaskins

Initially a term for a particular type of wide pants worn in the 1500s and 1600s, *galligaskins* later came to be used as a silly term for all kinds of loose pants, according to the *OED*.

Gallinipper

When the mosquito you're looking at is huge, call it a *gallinipper* instead.

Hogo

An obsolete term from the 1600s for a strong flavor. As the author of 1653's *The Compleat Angler*—a book devoted to fishing that apparently also included cooking tips—advised, "To give the sawce a hogoe, let the dish (into which you let the Pike fall) be rubed with [garlick]."

Icker

A Scottish word for an ear of corn.

Jigamaree

It's time to retire *trifle* and use this word instead.

Join-Hand

Another word for cursive handwriting.

Kindergraph

A kindergraph is what you get back after school picture day: a photograph of a kid.

Lallation

Basically baby talk.

Lentiginous

If you have a lot of freckles, you're *lentiginous*.

Lilly-Low

This British dialect phrase, often used with kids, is derived from *lowe*, meaning "a fire" or "bright flame."

Loof

Use this delightful Scottish word to refer to the palm of your hand or your cat's toe beans.

Makebate

A word from the 1500s for a troublemaker.

Matutolypea

Another way to say you've gotten up on the wrong side of the bed, this word comes from the name of the Roman goddess of Dawn, Matuta Mater, as well as the Greek word *lype*, which translates to "grief."

Meldrop

A *meldrop* is a much more pleasant way to refer to a bit of snot or mucus coming out of your nose.

Mixty-Maxty

A Scottish word that the *OED* traces back to a 1786 poem by Robert Burns, *mixty-maxty* refers to something that is weirdly muddled together or confused.

Necrologist

Another word for a person who pens obituaries.

Nicknackatory

Why call it a *toy shop* when you can call it a *nicknackatory*?

Nid-Nod
To *nid-nod* is to nod repeatedly when you're sleepy.

Nixie
A *nixie* is a letter addressed in handwriting so terrible that it can't actually be deciphered—or delivered. (This is such an issue that the U.S. Postal Service has a whole plant dedicated to decoding bad handwriting.)

Obeliscolychny
A seventeenth-century word for a lighthouse or lamp bearer.

Ombibulous
Ombibulous refers to a person who will drink anything. It was coined by H. L. Mencken, who used it to describe himself.

Oneirodynia
According to one book, published in 1800, an *oneirodynia* is "inflamed or disturbed imagination during sleep"—in other words, a nightmare.

Pozzy-Wallah
British slang for a guy who really, really loves jam, according to *The Long Trail: What the British Soldier Sang and Said in the Great War of 1914–18*.

Quakebuttock
The next time you encounter a coward, call them by another name: *quakebuttock*.

Recubation
A mid-seventeenth-century word for lying down.

Rummer
According to the *OED*, this seventeenth-century word for a large glass for wine or boozy beverage probably has its roots in Dutch, Middle Low German, and German. Used until the first half of the nineteenth century, *rummers* were usually round and short with a thick stem.

Scarebabe
Pretty much exactly what it sounds like: something that scares a baby.

Shilly-Shallying
Who among us hasn't suffered from a little *shilly-shallying*, aka indecision?

Slobber-Chops
There are multiple definitions for this phrase, which dates to 1670: It refers to someone— human or animal— that slobbers or drools a lot, but it can also be used to discuss a person who eats noisily, as well as a messy, wet kisser . . . or a foolish person.

Spizzerinctum
There are two possible definitions of this word: One is gimcrackery (a word coined by Ben Franklin, by the way), a fantastic way to refer to tacky decorations; the other is ambition or the will to succeed.

Tapster
Another word for a bartender.

Ventoseness
This word, which derives from the Latin *ventōse*, essentially means "being gassy."

Whisterpoop
If you would like to deliver a hard blow but call it by a much more pleasant name, consider *whisterpoop*, or *whister-clister*, or *whister-sniff*, or *whister-twister*.

10

WAYS *to* SAY YOU'RE TIRED

If you're so exhausted that saying "I'm tired" just doesn't cut it, don't worry—we have you covered. Whip out these terms the next time you're feeling wiped out.

1. Bog-Eyed

Bog-eyed was slang in the 1920s for tired eyes, either from lack of *z*s or too much booze.

2. Choofed

To be choofed is to be wiped out from doing *way* too much.

3. Comfoozled

This delightful word, meaning "exhausted, overcome," was probably coined by Charles Dickens, who wrote in *The Pickwick Papers*, "He's in a horrid state o' love; reg'larly comfoozled, and done over with it."

4. Crawling on One's Eyebrows

According to *A Dictionary of Slang and Unconventional English, crawling on (one's) eyebrows* dates back to World War I and was an army way of saying you're tired.

5. Cream-Crackered

This is a term from the eighties meaning "exhausted, tired out" (in fact, it's rhyming slang for *knackered*). According to *Cassell's Dictionary of Slang*, the term apparently originates from a brand of biscuits called Jacob's Cream Crackers (which is why you can also say you're *Jacob's crackers* when you're tired).

6. Forjesket

"Forjesket sair, with weary legs," Scottish poet Robert Burns wrote in 1785's "Second Epistle to J. Lapraik." Burns was using another way to describe being exhausted or broken down.

7. Kerry-Packered

Aussie slang from the 1970s, this term—which was based on Australian media tycoon Kerry Packer—is also rhyming slang for *knackered*.

8. Mondayish

Here's one we can all relate to: According to 1897's *A Dictionary of Slang, Jargon & Cant, mondayish* meant "used up, tired," and apparently originated "in the clergyman's supposed state of fatigue on Monday, after the work of Sunday."

9. Off Your Saucer

"Tired, not in the humour, out of sorts" is what this turn of phrase means, according to the 1897 book *A Dictionary of Slang, Jargon & Cant.*

10. Wall-Falling

If you ever find yourself tuckered out in Ireland, make sure to tell people that you're *wall-falling*.

SAY WHAT?

What Do A.M. and P.M. Stand For?

If you know how to tell time, you probably know how to understand and use *A.M.* and *P.M.*, and you might even know the terms come from Latin phrases. But do you know what exactly those phrases are, or what they mean in English?

A.M. stands for the Latin phrase *ante merīdiem*, which translates to "before midday." *P.M.*, on the other hand, is an abbreviation of *post merīdiem*, or "after midday." Have you ever noticed somebody write "12 m." or "12:00 m."? Though uncommon, it's technically a correct way to express "noon."

As with many modern-day practices with Latin roots, the idea of splitting the day into two twelve-hour chunks is very, very old. So old, in fact, that we don't know exactly how it became a worldwide habit; its history dates back to ancient Egypt at the very least.

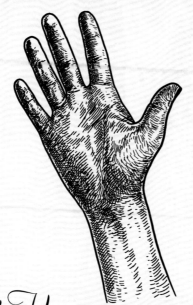

A *Brief History* OF THE WORD
Goodbye

When you tell someone "Good night," you're basically saying "I hope you have a good night" or something to that effect. The same goes for most other greeting and parting expressions that begin with *good*: *Good day*, *good morning*, *good evening*, *good afternoon*, etc. Following that trend, it seems like *goodbye* must be short for "I hope you have a good bye" and *bye* must be some obsolete term for a certain time of day.

But neither of those assumptions is true. In fact, *bye* started out as an abbreviation—and *good* wasn't originally *good* at all.

As far back as the fourteenth century, English speakers were saying "God be with you" and "God be with ye" when they parted ways. It took a little while for them to land on a suitable shortening of the phrase, but they got there by the mid-sixteenth century. In 1575, per the *Oxford English Dictionary*, *godbwye* appeared in print for the first time, in a letter from English scholar Gabriel Harvey. "And then to requite your gallonde of godbwyes, I regive you a pottle of howedyes," he wrote.

In today's English, Harvey's poetic sentiment loosely translates to this one: "And then to reciprocate your gallon of good-byes, I give you back a half-gallon of howdies."

But the evolution of *God be with you* to *godbwye* and then to *goodbye* wasn't linear—people seemingly spelled the expression however they wanted to. Examples include *God be wy you*, *God buoye*, *good bwi't'ye*, *good b' w' y*, and so on. Shakespeare alone wrote it at least three different ways in three different plays.

As for how *God* became *good*, it's generally believed that people were influenced by all those other *good* phrases: *Good day* and *good night* had already been around since the thirteenth century. While *God be with you* remains a relatively common utterance in religious circles, *goodbye*—which started cropping up in the early 1700s—eventually supplanted it as a secular farewell. In other languages' versions of *goodbye*, however, the religious connection is still crystal-clear: Both the French *adieu* and the Spanish *adiós* literally translate to "to God."

10 WAYS *to* SAY "GOODBYE"

Why say "Bye!" when you can say "Tinkerty-tonk!" instead? Here are ten forgotten farewells to punctuate future conversations.

1. Audi 5000

When LL Cool J used the word *Audi* at the end of his 1989 song "Droppin' Em," he wasn't talking about the car (though he did feature his own Audi 5000 on the cover of his 1987 album *Bigger and Deffer*). *Audi*, or *Audi 5000*, is a play on *outie*—as in: "I'm outta here."

2. Catch You on the Flip Side

Back in the 1970s, anyone listening to the hit song on a 45 record would need to flip the vinyl to listen to whatever song was on the B-side. Eventually, *catch you on the flip side* became a way to bid someone adieu.

3. Cheerioski

Cheerioski is one of several colorful alternatives to *cheerio* that cropped up around the 1920s and beyond. There's also *cheeribye* and *cheery-pip*, if either of those is more your speed.

4. E Ya Later

The dawn of the internet practically birthed a whole new language—including, thanks to nineties teens, *e ya later*, a version of *see ya later* meant for electronic adieus.

5. Got to Get Back to My Rat Killing

The origins of this evocative phrase are unclear, but it and similar rat-killing-related utterances were once popular in the American South as a way to close a conversation. You can also tell someone to "go on about their rat killing" if you want them to leave you alone.

6. Hist

Before peacing out, eighties college kids might say "Hist"— short for "I'm history"—to convey that their presence was about to become part of the past. By the following decade, the saying *I'm archives* had also arrived on the campus scene.

7. Olive Oil

Funny folks in the late nineteenth and early twentieth centuries might wave goodbye with a cheerful *Olive oil!*—an intentional mispronunciation of the French *au revoir*. Other variants have included *over the river*, *o revolver*, and even *Paul Revere*.

8. Plant You Now, Dig You Later

In the mid-1900s, Black Americans sometimes used *dig* as a synonym for "meet up." *Plant you now, dig you later* was a punny riff off that term, essentially meaning "Bye for now, see you later." The expression was also used as the title of a song in the 1940 Broadway musical *Pal Joey*.

9. Tinkerty-Tonk

While P. G. Wodehouse did invent certain nonsensical terms for his humor novels, *tinkerty-tonk*—a *farewell* alternative that shows up in his 1934 book *Right Ho, Jeeves*—wasn't one of them. As the author wrote in a letter, it came from "knut slang of about 1912." A knut, per the *Oxford English Dictionary*, was a "fashionable or showy young man."

10. Vale

In Latin, *vale* means "goodbye"—or, more literally, "be well." People started saying it outside the language at least as far back as the sixteenth century; Miguel de Cervantes even used it in *Don Quixote*. If you want to impress Latin scholars, pronounce it "wah-lay." But "vay-lee" works, too.

MENTAL FLOSS's
FAVORITE WORDS

A random and unscientific list of the Mental Floss team's
most beloved terms. (Spoiler alert: Some of us couldn't pick just one!)

Bamboozle

Aside from being generally fun to say,
I feel like *bamboozle* is one of those
words that sounds exactly like its meaning.
Also, if you've ever been bamboozled, just
saying the word makes light of the situation
and will make you feel a little better.
Hoodwinked is a really close runner-up.
— **ANGELA TROTTI**, SOCIAL MEDIA MANAGER

Blizzard

I'm really into typography and the way words
look, and the word *blizzard* is like . . .
perfectly symmetrical to me. I love it.
Phonetically? Terrible. Visually? Amazing.
— **JUSTIN DODD**, VIDEO PRODUCER

Borborygm

Yes, those stomach rumbles you experience
when hungry have an official medical name.
The fact that this term exists is enough to
make me love it, but its appropriately
delightful origin story pushes it to the top
of my word ranking: *Borborygm* derives from
the Greek word *borborygmos*, which is
likely onomatopoeic.
— **MICHELE DEBCZAK**, SENIOR STAFF WRITER

Comeuppance

Imagine karma catches up to the worst
person you know. *Punishment* doesn't
capture the satisfaction, and *retribution*
is too serious. *Comeuppance* is victorious,
celebratory, and perfectly encapsulates
the feeling of pointing and laughing at
someone who deserves it.
— **BETHEL AFFUL**, VIDEO PRODUCER

Divisibility

No, I haven't taken a math class since high
school. I just like that this word is spelled
d I v I s I b I l I t y.
— **JON MAYER**, HEAD OF VIDEO

Emblematic

I love words that do the work of many words,
because I aim to use as few words as possible
in my writing. *Emblematic* encapsulates
"this thing is like that thing in multiple,
specific ways" without having to name them
all and gum up my paragraph.
— **KAT LONG**, SCIENCE EDITOR

Fustigate

I came across *fustigate* the same way I came
across most things I've learned over
the years: on an episode of *The Simpsons*.
The original seventeenth-century definition
of the word was pretty rough—it basically
meant "to beat someone with a short, heavy
stick." But that definition has changed over
time, and *fustigate* is now a wonderfully
obscure term meaning "harsh criticism."
However you use it, *fustigate* is an old-timey
gem that should always be in your rotation.
— **JAY SERAFINO**, SPECIAL PROJECTS EDITOR

Halcyon

Ogden Nash's poem "Pretty Halcyon Days"—
about the lazy bliss of lying on the beach—
illustrates the meaning of *halcyon* better than
any definition ever could. But if you must
have one: *Halcyon* basically describes an
idyllic (and often bygone) time. It's also a
genus of colorful kingfishers and a beautiful
song by the Paper Kites.
— **ELLEN GUTOSKEY**, STAFF WRITER

Horrigust

Roald Dahl always had a way with words—even if he made lots of them up. (For *The BFG*, Dahl invented 238 never-before-heard terms and phrases, which he dubbed *Gobblefunk*.) While he struggled in school because of his penchant for using nonexistent words, today there's an entire dictionary dedicated to them. What's so wonderful about Dahl-speak is that you don't even need a reference source to understand it. Case in point: *horrigust*, an adjective describing something that is not just horrible or disgusting—it's *horrigust!*
— **JENNIFER M. WOOD**, MANAGING EDITOR

Kerfuffle

Kerfuffle is one of those words that sounds exactly like what it means—"commotion" or "fuss"—and tracing its etymology is just as wonderful: It came into English in the 1940s from the sixteenth-century Scottish verb *curfuffle*, which was derived from the verb *fuffle* (also Scottish). Everything about it screams delight. I would make a kerfuffle about *kerfuffle*.
— **ERIN McCARTHY**, EDITOR-IN-CHIEF

Omnibus

Once used to refer to a horse-drawn mode of public transportation in Paris, *omnibus* has since come to mean a stacked, comprehensive collection of a creative work. It's a completist's dream.
— **JAKE ROSSEN**, SENIOR STAFF WRITER

Rue and Earnest

Sometimes it's not enough to simply say that you regret something—to *rue* puts those remorseful feelings on an almost epic scale, inviting the kinds of formal (and dramatic) declarations that feel like they belong to another time, place, and century, especially when used for comedic effect. "I rue the day I bought that car," you might say in earnest, reflecting back on all the myriad repair bills you've had to deal with over the years. But on the flip side, you could evoke it just for fun: "You'll rue the day you ate the rest of my ham sandwich," you might declare to a leftover-stealing family member when you want to spread a little panache onto your statement.

Speaking of earnest . . . Oscar Wilde's *The Importance of Being Earnest* was one of the first plays I ever saw performed live, and right from the jump, I adored the wordplay, even just within the title. *Earnest*, in this context, has two meanings: It refers quite literally to a character (Jack, also known as Ernest in the play), but also, it speaks to the importance of being sincere in one's words and actions (a big problem for the characters within said story). Ever since, I've loved the word for the seriousness and tacit sweetness it conveys; if someone calls you "earnest," it might be because they're an Oscar Wilde fan who's playing at puns, but more than likely, it's because you come across as heartfelt and genuine, which is never really a bad thing.
— **SHAYNA MURPHY**, ASSOCIATE EDITOR

Snuggery

I'm a fan of all things quaint and homey, and this British term is no exception. It's a delightfully cute way to describe a small, cozy room. Sure, sipping tea while wrapped in a soft blanket by a fire in the living room sounds nice, but doing it in a *snuggery*? That just adds a whole extra layer of hygge.
— **KERRY WOLFE**, STAFF EDITOR

Acknowledgments

Thank, derived from the Old English *þanc* for "thinking" or "thought," is an old word: According to the *Oxford English Dictionary*, as a noun it first popped up around 735, and as a verb for giving thanks around 950. Between then and now, we've gotten fresh spins on the phrase—from *thanks loads* (coined by F. Scott Fitzgerald) to *thenks aw'fully* (apparently from Cockney English) to *ta* (how a child might have tried to say "thank you"). While not all languages have words that express the sentiment, English has lots—and thanks be for that, because we have a lot of people to thank.

Putting together *The Mental Floss Curious Compendium of Wonderful Words* was a logophile's dream. Ta muchly to our agent, Dinah Dunn, and our designer, Carol Bobolts, at Indelible Editions, as well as our publisher, Weldon Owen, Inc., especially Roger Shaw and Karyn Gerhard.

This book would not have been possible if not for the Mental Floss team, who brings their endless enthusiasm for words, language, and beyond to work every day. There is no dictionary they won't dig into, no weird phrase they won't track down. I am endlessly grateful to Jennifer M. Wood, Jake Rossen, Jason Serafino, Jon Mayer, Ellen Gutoskey, Michele Debczak, Kat Long, Kerry Wolfe, Shayna Murphy, Angela Trotti, Justin Dodd, and Bethel Afful, as well as the former Mental Floss staffers whose work appears in this book: Lucas Reilly, Caitlin Schneider, Jason English, Erika Berlin, Hannah Keyser, Kirstin Fawcett, Shaunacy Ferro, and Emily Petsko. Thankee to Minute Media's Jack Gallagher and Davy Diamond for contributing entries and to Matan Har, Chad Payne, and Kimberly Holland for their help and support.

Thanx a million to our fact checker Austin Thompson, who would *never* mistake a factoid for a fact; to Rebecca Maines for copyediting; and to the writers whose work appears in this book: Keith Johnston (Nineties Slang, research for entries in sports words), Stacy Conradt (Edgar Allan Poe and Scrabble, research for Presidents' Day), Austin Thompson (Yule, entries in Words Coined by Authors), Mica Arbeiter (Old-Timey Compliments), and Sean Hutchinson (Jersey Barriers).

Finally, we are indebted to the work done by the linguists and lexicographers behind the *Oxford English Dictionary* and Merriam-Webster; Jonathon Green of *Green's Dictionary of Slang*; the legendary Eric Partridge; and the many word nerds across history and the internet who are just as curious about etymology as we are.

Image Credits